Touching the Future

Touching the Future

My Odyssey from Print to Online Publishing

ROGER FIDLER

Published Independently
ISBN: 978-1-6925-9539-5

This book also is available as a Kindle e-book from Amazon.com.
.

To Ada, my best friend, muse, and loving wife,

and

To all of the newspaper journalists and designers who
endured the transition from print to online publishing.

Contents

Acknowledgments

I will be forever grateful to four Knight-Ridder executives who recognized my talents and provided me with the freedom to pursue new media technologies and concepts no matter how crazy they might have seemed at the time: Bill Baker, who hired me in 1974 when he was the features editor at the *Detroit Free Press* and continued to endorse me when he moved to corporate headquarters as a vice president for news; Larry Jinks, the senior vice president for news, who always supported my digital initiatives even though he honestly admitted to not understanding all of them; Frank Hawkins, the vice president for corporate relations, who became one of my most ardent corporate champions; and above all James K. Batten, who mentored me and whose trust in me never wavered throughout his rise from a vice president for news to president, chief executive, and chairman.

Batten was one of the rare executives who valued independent thinkers, innovators, and risk takers, even when their views conflicted with his own. His caring, inclusive management style inspired confidence and trust in the company's ability to confront difficult challenges without sacrificing its core values of quality journalism and public service. Under his leadership, these qualities and values made it possible for Knight-Ridder newspapers to attract many of the brightest and most talented young people in the industry. In those years, the company was widely recognized for its commitment to journalistic excellence and regularly ranked as one of the best to work for among all industries.

Additionally, I am sincerely grateful to Barrie Hartman, David Smith, Tom Priddy, Peggy Bair, Yukari Miyamae, and Mort Goldstrom for taking time to critique my chapter drafts and offer thoughtful suggestions. I would be remiss if I also didn't acknowledge the valuable contributions and encouragement provided by my wife and best friend, Ada.

Prologue

We all touch the future more frequently than we realize. Most future occurrences we sense are within the realms of proximate anticipations and premonitions. Sometimes, we are accorded gauzy glimpses of possible distant future events or developments that arouse our interest, but usually we soon relegate them to remote sectors of our memory. If versions should become real in the future, we might recall the glimpses we once touched, but in the interim they have little or no influence on our daily lives.

On rare occasions, however, an experience or thought will trigger synapses in the brain to conceptualize something novel that inspires entrepreneurially inclined individuals to not just touch the future, but to devote themselves to realizing their envisioned futures. For those individuals, there are, of course, no guarantees that their visions will become real. Few actually do, even after expending a great deal of time, energy, and money. And those that do usually will have taken much longer to be realized than the visionaries assumed.

In major and minor ways, all of our lives are influenced by motivated visionaries who, through their dogged pursuit of new concepts, processes, techniques, and products, have helped to shape the present that once was the future they touched.

Those we know about tend to be the ones who became famous billionaires in this digital age, such as Steve Jobs with Apple, Jeff Bezos with Amazon, and Mark Zuckerberg with Facebook, but they are the exceptions.

While other visionaries have achieved a measure of fame within their respective endeavors and may even be well rewarded, most are unknown to us. Typically, they have been employed by companies, institutions, or governments that funded their efforts.

My modicum of fame came from conceiving and pursuing a vision of digital newspapers delivered online and displayed on mobile devices, beginning in 1980, that anticipated today's tablets and smartphones. I was employed by Knight-Ridder, one of the largest and most distinguished American newspaper chains of its time. For more than two decades, my life and career were tightly intertwined with the computerization of the company's papers, and its pioneering efforts to develop electronic alternatives to ink printed on paper in the years preceding and immediately following the debut of the commercial internet.

This book is about the world-changing transition from Gutenberg-age print to digital-age online publishing and more specifically about touching the future of newspapers and print journalism during my lifetime. I recognize that another book about newspapers might not have a wide appeal in this internet-connected era of mobile displays and social media. However, given the consequential role of newspapers in launching the digital publishing revolution, I felt compelled to narrate some of Knight-Ridder's trailblazing digital and online initiatives before they are forgotten. I have drawn the stories from my memory banks and those of former colleagues, as well as from my collection of reports, correspondences, articles, and books.

While most stories about the digital publishing revolution narrowly focus on electronic books, established book publishers actually were reluctant, relatively late adopters of digital technologies. What generally is overlooked is that newspaper publishers were among the first to recognize that the future of print emanated from the power of computers and to make major investments in the development of digital publishing and online systems.

There can be little doubt today that the interconnection between computers and text that commenced in the 1960s has beget a third great revolution in the methods for storing and communicating information. As with the two previous great revolutions in human communication systems engendered by the development of writing and mechanized printing, the computerization of print is having a complex, profound influence upon enterprises and institutions as well as the ways in which humans think and interact.

Five hundred years ago, Europeans were coping with the equally profound and disruptive consequences of the publishing revolution wrought by mechanized printing and the explosion of printed books and documents. In the first fifty years after Johann Gutenberg invented the essential components and processes in Germany, the technology rapidly displaced established monastic *scriptoria* and manual copying as it spread out across Europe.

Nascent print shops produced millions of copies of books between 1450 and 1500, a period that historians refer to as the *incunabula* (first stage) of mechanized printing and print media. Many of the books and documents printed during that period have been well preserved in libraries and private collections. However, much about Gutenberg's life and efforts to develop the tools and methods that made mechanized printing practical sadly remains a mystery. Most of what is known about his "Work of the Books" came from a small number of documents relating to his loans and bankruptcy.

When future historians study the waning decades of the twentieth century — the *incunabula* of digital printing and online media — they also are likely to find a dearth of source material. Much has already been lost. Ironically, almost all that remains of the early digital and online initiatives are the stories about them that were printed on paper.

My Google searches, for example, have found scant information about the Knight-Ridder chain and its development of Viewtron, one of the first commercial online services. I found even less about the Knight-Ridder Graphics Network, PressLink, Vu/Text, Information Design Lab, and Mercury Center.

If this book survives long enough in print or in some other form for future historians to use in their research, perhaps it will contribute in some small way to their understanding of how a great newspaper company that was among the first to touch the future of print and lead the digital publishing revolution failed to negotiate the global disruptions fermented by the internet and its progeny at the turn of the twenty-first century.

Introduction

A Media Pioneer's Quest: Portable Electronic Newspapers

The New York Times, June 28, 1992

Meet tablet man: He dreamt the future (and the iPad)

The Washington Post, March 11, 2012

These are just two of the headlines from the hundreds of articles about my quixotic vision of reading digital newspapers on tablet screens published worldwide over the course of three decades. During those years, I often was portrayed as either the savior of newspapers or the killer of newspapers; a visionary or a contrarian; a genius or a nutcase.

After Steve Jobs unveiled the Apple iPad in 2010, a digital copy of *The Tablet Newspaper* video that I produced 16 years earlier at the Knight-Ridder Information Design Lab went viral on the internet. The striking resemblance of the iPad to my tablet prototype demonstrated in the video lit up the blogosphere and soon embroiled me, reluctantly, in a global patent war between Apple and Samsung.

Some bloggers posited that I must have been angry with Apple and Jobs for stealing my idea and not giving me credit. I wasn't. Nor was I envious of Jobs for becoming a billionaire and achieving lasting fame. That never was my ambition. To have the tablet of my dreams finally realized and widely adopted for reading digital newspapers and countless other uses was reward enough. Happiness with my life meant more to me than money and fame.

While my pursuit of tablets and other mobile display devices received the most media attention, it represents only one of the many overlapping chapters in my life and career, as well as in the epic saga of how Knight-Ridder, one of the largest and most distinguished American newspaper chains, helped launch the digital publishing revolution that ultimately contributed to its demise and the rapid decline of daily newspapers around the world.

Those chapters, which I have recalled in this book, encompass three distinct eras in the evolution of print and newspaper publishing since the end of the Second World War. The first era from 1945 to 1970 (chapters one and two) defines the apogee of industrial-age newspaper publishing. The second era from 1970 to 2000 (chapters three through eight) brackets the first stage of the digital publishing revolution, which initiated the computerization of print and birth of online media. The third era from 2000 to 2020 (chapters nine and ten) represents the current stage of this revolution — the rise of internet and mobile publishing. My thoughts about what the next stage might hold for newspapers and journalism are included in the epilogue.

In addition to providing behind-the-scenes accounts of my experiences at the forefront of the digital conversion of newspaper production and development of online news media, I have interwoven the personal backstory of perseverance and resilience that have been the hallmarks of my life's journey, which has spanned all three of the eras just mentioned. That narrative serves as a contextual thread for my singular odyssey through the turbulent years of galvanic digital innovations in the latter third of the twentieth century and maiden decades of the twenty-first century that spawned the greatest transformation in human communication systems and society since the emergence of mechanized printing and print media.

―――――――

My life's journey began during the Second World War at the Mount Vernon General Hospital in the State of Washington on January 21, 1943. Like so many other "war babies," I owe my existence to an intimate encounter and hasty marriage between two mismatched strangers.

My father, Frank Fidler, was a 30-year-old Army sergeant stationed on Whidbey Island about 30 miles north of Seattle. He was born in Cleveland, Ohio, but when he was two years old his parents decided to take him and his four siblings back to their ancestral home in Bohemia, which then was part of the Austro-Hungarian Empire. Their ship departed from New York City in August 1914, just as World War One broke out in Europe. His father was arrested as soon as he disembarked and sent to a French prisoner of war camp. (He was wounded while escaping and spent the remainder of the war recuperating in Switzerland.) The family went on to Bohemia where the children were separated and placed with different families for the duration of the war. When my father was 16 years old, he returned from Czechoslovakia (formed after the war by combining Bohemia with the lands of Moravia and Slovakia) to claim his U.S. citizenship. Prior to enlisting in the National Guard in 1940, he worked as a butcher and mechanic.

His encounter with my mother, Marjorie McLaughlin, who was 27 years old at the time, occurred soon after a USO dance where they met. She was born in Dillon, Montana, to parents of Irish descent. Her father, who had been a conductor on the Union Pacific Railroad, owned a hardware store and gas station in Sedro-Woolley, Washington, where she lived with her older sister. Her mother had been a mail-order bride from Kansas.

After the war's end, my father worked at a shipyard in Oakland, California, before taking us to Cleveland where three of his siblings had settled with their families. He soon found a job as a machinist with Harris-Seybold, a printing press manufacturer. We lived initially above my uncle's bakery and then in a four-family house near the factory where he worked. A few years later, he was able to purchase a new house on an acre of wooded land in the Bohemian-German suburb of Parma.

I would be their only child. They tried several times to have more children, but all were stillborn due to an Rh-factor incompatibility. While I have many happy memories from my early childhood, few involved my parents. I never developed a strong bond with either of them.

My father was a perfectionist who preferred to work alone; a trait that I would inherit. He always seemed unhappy with his life and disappointed with me. In addition to being skinny and left-handed, which he abhorred, I had an eye disorder that affected my vision and caused me to be accident prone. An experimental surgery at the Cleveland Clinic when I was five years old only temporarily corrected the problem.

My mother felt isolated within the Bohemian community and suffered from lingering bouts of depression. After each stillbirth, she would have a "nervous breakdown" that at least once required hospitalization. After we moved to Parma, she worked as a waitress. Because she never learned to cook and often was not at home during the daytime, my father hired an elderly Bohemian woman to prepare our meals and do chores.

Around Christmas in 1952, my parents took me to see *The Day the Earth Stood Still*. The experience left me with a lasting memory, but it wasn't just the movie that I would not forget. On the way to the lobby to buy popcorn and sodas, my father pulled me aside and asked: "If you had to choose between your mother and me, who would you choose?" All I could think to say was, "Why would I have to choose?" I didn't get an answer.

A short while later, the choice was made for me when my grandmother arrived at our house soon after my father left for work. She immediately helped my mother to finish packing our clothes and personal items. They then hurriedly loaded the suitcases along with me into the waiting taxi that took us to the Cleveland terminal where we would board a train for Eugene, Oregon. I didn't protest.

We could not afford to rent a place of our own for several months, so we stayed in my aunt's home. My involvement with newspapers began in the summer of '53 as a paperboy for the *Register-Guard*. I was ten years old. The money my mother earned at the Del Monte cannery barely covered our basic expenses, so my earnings were needed to help out. For several years, I would also earn money during summers picking strawberries and pole beans.

Despite our limited means and Spartan existence after the divorce, I never thought of myself as poor and downtrodden.

And, even though I was on my own for much of the time, I don't recall ever feeling lonely or sad. When I wasn't in school or working, I enjoyed my freedom to explore and daydream. On rainy days, an old radio and books were my companions. (We would not have our own TV or phone until the early sixties.)

During my four years as an "independent carrier," the *Register-Guard* was a second home to me. The roar of the rolling presses often enticed me to probe the paper's inner sanctum. I always found the compositors, printers, and journalists to be friendly and willing to show "The Kid" around and answer questions. My fascination with the world of newspapers inspired me to become a "newspaper man" and launch my own paper in the summer of '54 using a discarded mimeograph machine.

My early newspaper career, however, succumbed a few years later to a passion for stargazing that I acquired while delivering papers after sunset and before dawn. By my junior year in high school, I was president of the Eugene Astronomical League, which I had co-founded, and fully committed to becoming an astronomer. But that was not to be.

A debilitating disease that wracked my body in my senior year would profoundly alter the course of my life. After graduation, I spent most of the summer of '61 in hospitals and recuperating at home. Despite a close brush with death and the likelihood of living with frequent, potentially life-threatening flare-ups, I was determined not to let the disease prevent me from leading a fulfilling life.

That fall, I took a job at a small community newspaper doing a little bit of everything. Within a few weeks, I decided that if I could not be an astronomer, I would try becoming a science writer. So, at the age of 18, I convinced the editor to pay me extra to write a weekly column I called "Layman's Astronomy."

By the beginning of '62, I thought I was healthy enough to enroll for spring semester at the University of Oregon. I had been awarded a scholarship that covered tuition, but I still needed to work part-time in order to buy books and help with living expenses while continuing to live with my mother. I was too optimistic. In less than two months, I had another severe flare-up and once more was hospitalized for several weeks.

Upon leaving the hospital, my doctor firmly told me that if I didn't avoid stress for at least a year, I could have another major flare-up from which I might not survive. Luckily, I was able to get a job that summer in the *Register-Guard's* advertising department. The job qualified as the lowest stress position at the newspaper, but it had the advantage of affording me opportunities to again explore the production departments and newsroom. By the end of my year without stress, I was feeling better and eager to re-enroll at the university.

I could not continue working full-time during the day, so I went to the managing editor with a proposal to revive my weekly astronomy column. He accepted. Within a year, I taught myself how to create graphics for a new column I called "Earth and the Sky" and was producing maps and graphics for the paper as its freelance news artist. Also, within that year, I dated a journalism coed whom I would marry in the spring of '65.

Flare-ups of my disease continued to interrupt my life. While none was severe enough to require hospitalization, they often forced me to miss classes for extended periods, which trashed my GPA and delayed graduation. At the end of spring semester in 1966, we decided to drop out and spend the summer living like nomads in the outback of Oregon and Washington. I had hoped to get a full-time job as a science writer in the fall, but it was my skills producing maps and graphics that opened doors.

After a few months as a reporter and news artist for *The Daily Herald* in Everett, Washington, I responded to an ad in a newspaper trade magazine for an art director who was strong on maps. That led to my working at *Pacific Stars and Stripes* in Tokyo for nearly four years. During those years, my health improved and I became the father of two children.

When we returned to Oregon, by way of the Soviet Union and northern Europe at the beginning of 1971, the United States was in the midst of a recession, and newspaper jobs in locations that interested us were scarce. I finally took a job in March, just as our money was running out, as a features desk editor at the *St. Petersburg Times* (later renamed *Tampa Bay Times*) in Florida. My three years at the *Times* was a punishing ordeal that honed my skills as a newspaper designer and editor but had damaging consequences for my marriage.

In May 1974, the *Detroit Free Press*, then a Knight Newspaper, hired me to fill a newly created graphics editor position. Five months after I arrived, Knight acquired Ridder Publications. The combined company would then be the largest American newspaper publisher.

Around the same time, the *Free Press* purchased two first-generation video display terminals for remotely entering and editing text. One was placed next to my desk. This simple word-processing computer would be my introduction to the digital future of newspapers and the beginning of my 40-year odyssey that would distinguish me as a post-television new media pioneer and visionary. For more than half of those years, I had the unique opportunity to participate in nearly all of Knight-Ridder's digital and online publishing initiatives.

In February 1979, James K. Batten, then corporate vice president for news, recruited me for a team he was secretly assembling to develop an electronic newspaper. That initiative, called Viewtron, would become America's first commercial online service, a forerunner of America OnLine and the web.

Throughout the eighties and early nineties, Batten encouraged me and others to innovate and create new businesses. With his support, I founded and headed two successful companies — Knight-Ridder Graphics Network and PressLink — that introduced newspapers worldwide to computer graphics, electronic networking, e-mail, and the Apple Macintosh.

While my career was ascendant in the early eighties, my private life was in the pits. All of my achievements had come at a high personal cost — the dissolution of two marriages and estrangement from my two children. A star-crossed relationship soon after my second divorce nearly derailed my career. With help, I finally confronted the demons from my past that had contributed to my health and relationship problems, but my work still dominated my life — until a fateful encounter with a Latina journalist who was assigned to be my interpreter during a conference in Peru. What followed was a redemptive love story.

After I completed a fellowship at Columbia University in the summer of '92, Batten, who by then was Knight-Ridder's chairman and chief executive, named me as the director of new media development and authorized me to establish the Information Design Laboratory in Boulder, Colorado. At the IDL, I brought together media and tech leaders to touch the future of print while pursuing my tablet newspaper vision.

Then two years later, just as the newspaper industry was about to be confronted by the disruptive powers of the internet and web, Batten was diagnosed with a malignant brain tumor. After undergoing surgery and treatments, he died in June 1995 at the age of 59. His death marked a major turning point for

Knight-Ridder and my life. After 21 years, I decided it was time to take an "early retirement" from the company, but that would not be the end of my involvement with tablets and the digital future of newspapers.

I spent the following year consulting and speaking internationally while completing the book I began to write when I was a Freedom Forum Fellow. The book, *Mediamorphosis: Understanding New Media*, was published by Sage in 1997.

One of my speaking invitations in the spring of '96 led to my working in academia for the next two decades, first as a journalism and information design professor at Kent State University in Ohio, and then as the program director for digital publishing at the Missouri School of Journalism's Donald W. Reynolds Journalism Institute in Columbia. During those chapters of my life, I continued to pursue my vision of tablet newspapers while teaching and conducting research on the use of mobile media for news.

My retirement from academia at the beginning of 2015 provided relaxed time for reflecting on my life's journey and contemplating how the digital publishing revolution has transformed newspapers and communication media. This book is the fruit of my ruminations.

Author's notes

Samsung used me and the so-called "Fidler tablet" in 2012 to defend itself against Apple's lawsuit for alleged design patent infringement, arguing that my 1994 *Tablet Newspaper* video had put the flat, round-corner design Apple used for its iPhone and iPad in the public domain and therefore was not patentable. A judge agreed and ruled in Samsung's favor. But that was not the end of their patent war. Several more skirmishes ensued before they finally were able to resolve the issue.

CHAPTER ONE

Gutenberg's Legacy

The newspaper world I got to know as a boy in the 1950s was a complex, magical place permeated with the pungent smells of hot molten lead, oil-based ink, and tobacco smoke.

Every day of the week, hundreds of workers, each with specialized skills, cooperated to transform a profusion of words and images into arrays of lead pages, assembled through frenetic newsroom editing and "back shop" composing processes, that would be mounted on the cylinders of massive rotary letterpresses capable of churning out tens of thousands of copies per hour. After the last edition was printed, bundled, and distributed to the carriers, cleaning crews would sweep up the strata of accumulated waste paper and dump all of the press plates and chases composed of lead type into hot cauldrons where the metal would be melted for reuse the next day. Newspaper journalists would call this "The Daily Miracle."

Practically everything used and done in this world contained the DNA of printing technologies and methods invented by Johann Gutenberg five centuries earlier. None realized then that his industrial-age legacy would soon, out of economic necessity, succumb to the technologies and methods of a new age defined by computers.

When I started working as a journalist in the 1960s, newspaper companies were just beginning to install computers in their business departments. Their seemingly innocuous introduction belied the world-changing publishing revolution they would launch.

The seductive roar of the press

One of my earliest memories is of my father taking me to the Harris-Seybold factory where he worked as a machinist in Cleveland, Ohio. His job was to fabricate parts for the massive sheet-fed presses used to print the color comics sections that newspapers would insert into their Sunday editions. On that day, one of the presses he had helped to assemble would be fully tested on the factory floor. I was five years old in 1948 when that huge mechanical beast came to life, and I heard for the first time the awesome roar of a printing press.

Five years later, I would hear that roar again. This time, larger presses were printing the *Register-Guard*, the evening newspaper in Eugene, Oregon. I had moved to Eugene with my mother in January 1953 when she separated from my father. We had only the clothes and few possessions she brought with us on the train from Cleveland. For a short while, we lived with my aunt, who had a five-year-old daughter, and grandmother. Both were recently divorced.

Money was tight. So, to help out, I got a *Register-Guard* paper route that summer. For young boys like me, delivering newspapers would be our first paying job and a formative experience that taught us the importance of being responsible and reliable. As "independent carriers" our routes were our businesses. To be successful, we had to serve our customers by making sure they got their papers when and where they expected them and in a dry, readable condition. And we had to satisfy our supplier — the newspaper company — by collecting the subscription fees and repaying the amount we owed for the papers we delivered.

I couldn't afford a bicycle, but walking the route carrying rolled papers in shoulder bags was not too difficult, even for a skinny 10-year-old boy. In the fifties, nearly every household and business subscribed to the *Register-Guard,* which typically had only two sections. In-town routes with around 50 customers only required covering a few square blocks and took less than an hour to complete on weekdays and Saturdays.

The Sunday morning papers were more difficult to carry and took more time to deliver because they were thicker and heavier, which meant I had to make several trips back to the loading docks to refill my bags. And, they had to be delivered by 6 a.m., so I needed to get up around four in the morning. Fortunately, my mother had moved us into a small basement apartment a few blocks from the office.

The *Register-Guard* soon became much more for me than just a place to pick up the papers for my route. Most afternoons, I would arrive early so I could feel the seductive, adrenalized roar of the rolling presses. While waiting for the bundles of papers assigned to my route, I often would visit the newsroom to talk with the reporters and editors who I came to admire.

Growing pains

Science fiction and astronomy became my passions in junior high school. Reading stories by Isaac Asimov, Arthur C. Clarke, and Robert Heinlein stimulated my imagination and afforded me with my first inducements to touch the future.

My interest in stargazing I owed to the years of delivering newspapers after sunset and before dawn. Eugene in the fifties still was a small college town with minimal air and light pollution. Most nights, the moon and starlight were bright enough to illuminate my surroundings, and the Milky Way shone like a river of diamonds.

On one of my last predawn deliveries in October 1957, I met a subscriber who, with several of his neighbors and friends, was observing Earth's moon with a homemade 12-inch Newtonian telescope while waiting for Russia's new moon — Sputnik — to pass overhead. His invitation to join their "star party" would be the beginning of a friendship and collaboration that would lead to my becoming a dedicated amateur astronomer and a co-founder of the Eugene Astronomical League (later renamed Eugene Astralites).

By the time I was a junior at South Eugene High School, I had firmly committed to the goal of becoming a professional astronomer. I had built my first telescope, organized dozens of public star parties, and convinced the Northwest Regional Astronomical League to let our club host its annual convention in Eugene on July 30-31, 1960. (The small print shop where I was working that summer allowed me to typeset and print the convention programs.)

I no longer delivered newspapers then, but now I was occasionally quoted in them. Whenever reporters from the

Register-Guard were writing stories about meteor showers, lunar eclipses, and other night sky events, I was the person they most frequently interviewed.

That fall I was working as a Western Union messenger after school and on weekends when I felt the first signs of health problems that would profoundly alter my life and ambitions. They began as acute intestinal cramps and painful swellings of my knees. My doctor initially concluded these were just "growing pains" and recommended that I drink more milk and ride my bicycle less often. By December, the cramps and swellings had become so severe that I had to quit my messenger job. They also were affecting my school work.

In the winter, my doctor began draining my swollen knees with a long needle and giving me medications for my bouts of diarrhea. He had no idea what was causing my problems.

Despite the discomfort, I continued to pursue my interest in astronomy. I sold my first telescope to buy parts for a new instrument I built for a project that I would enter in the annual Northwest Science Fair. That May, the Oregon Museum of Science and Industry (OMSI), the fair's host, awarded me a gold medal for my "Richest-Field Astrophotography" project.

I had earned a scholarship to the University of Oregon and was looking forward to starting my freshman year in the fall. But on June 9, 1961, the morning after my high school graduation, I began passing blood. My doctor immediately checked me into Sacred Heart Hospital. Unable to determine the cause or staunch the bleeding, the doctors arranged for my transfer to the University of Oregon Medical School Hospital in Portland.

By the end of my second week, I had gone through ten pints of blood and lost about thirty pounds. Removal of my colon was considered, but the doctors feared I was too weak.

Luckily, they got the bleeding under control without resorting to radical surgery using a new medication. After numerous X-rays and sigmoidoscopic examinations, the doctors concluded that I had chronic ulcerative colitis and rheumatoid arthritis. They told me my case had helped to confirm a suspected connection between these two autoimmune illnesses.

As I was about to be discharged, a hospital administrator and doctor came to see me with a proposition. If I would agree to letting the doctor perform an experimental surgery on my eyes in the teaching auditorium, the hospital would rescind my bill, which by then had accrued to many thousands of dollars. They knew about the surgery that I had had at the Cleveland Clinic when I was five years old to correct what commonly is referred to as "lazy eye." And, that it obviously had not resolved my problem. The doctor expressed confidence that, this time, the surgery he proposed was more likely to be successful. I had nothing to lose and everything to gain, so I accepted. A week later, I left the hospital looking like an intellectual pirate with a black patch over one lens of my glasses. I also was advised by the doctors who had treated my colitis to avoid stress for at least a year. (Within that year, my eyes returned to their lazy state.)

When I got back home at the end of July, I rested for a couple weeks and then started checking the help wanted ads. The lowest stress job I could find was for a stock clerk at the Gold Bond Stamps store. In those days, merchants gave stamps, like coupons and points today, that customers could collect in books and redeem for merchandise. The job was so low stress that in less than a month I began searching the help wanted ads again.

Another setback

My next job was as an advertising proof traveler for the *Emerald Empire News*, a small weekday-only community newspaper. The operation was more like the print shop where I had worked the previous summer than the *Register-Guard*. There were no clattering Linotype machines or hot caldrons of molten lead. The text was justified and set on paper using typewriter-like machines called Varitypers and pasted on cardboard page forms. (This was the genesis of what would be known as "cold-type" composition.) Also, its offset press used plates made of aluminum instead of lead and water-based inks instead of oil-based inks.

As a proof traveler, my assignment was to deliver "proofs" — copies of completed ads — to advertisers for their review and approval before publication. After the newspapers were printed, I would bring them "tear sheets" — the actual pages where their ads had appeared.

The newspaper was always shorthanded, so in a brief time I was doing a little bit of everything — from bundling returns and preparing press plates to pasting up pages and covering school board meetings. My coup was convincing the editor to pay me extra to write a weekly column I called "Layman's Astronomy," which first appeared on October 24, 1961.

In January, I thought I was well enough to enroll in classes at the University of Oregon while continuing to write my column and cover meetings. I was too optimistic. Less than two months into the semester my ulcerative colitis flared again with a vengeance. The bleeding, weight loss, and crippling joint swellings put me back in a Eugene hospital for several more weeks. Before releasing me, my doctor again urged me to avoid any stressful activities for at least a year. Although, this time, he firmly impressed upon me the seriousness of my illness by telling me that if I had another major flare-up within the next five years, I might not survive.

While the prospect of dying in a few years weighed on my mind as I recuperated at home, I don't remember feeling angry or depressed. I was determined not to let the limitations and interruptions imposed by my illnesses prevent me from living a meaningful life, no matter how short my life might be. But I had to recognize that not everything I might want to do would be possible. The most difficult to accept was giving up on my dream of becoming a professional astronomer.

There were other dreams, however, that I was unwilling to abandon. Foremost was my desire to visit other countries. I had had a fascination with exploring the world ever since my fifth-grade geography class. Around that time, my mother subscribed to *National Geographic*. Its visually rich stories and large maps were like siren songs for me. In high school, my cartographic interests extended beyond Earth to maps of the Moon.

As I contemplated alternatives to astronomy that I thought might be challenging and fulfilling, I could not have imagined the pivotal role that maps would play in determining the future direction of my life just two years later.

In the meantime, I vowed to follow my doctor's advice, but not working was not an option. I had hospital and doctor bills to pay. My mother had already depleted a small inheritance from her father to pay off my previous medical bills, and we had no health insurance. Her hourly wages at the Del Monte cannery just barely covered our monthly living expenses. So, when I learned that the *Register-Guard* was looking for an advertising proof traveler, I immediately applied.

A lucky break

Re-entering the world of industrial-age newspaper publishing that I had come to know as a paperboy proved to be a lucky break. Employed again as a lowly advertising proof traveler, I found myself with plenty of stress-free time to recoup my health as well as to study the production processes up close and contemplate my future. By then, I already knew my future would somehow involve newspapers, but I had no clue that this experience would ultimately lead to my involvement with the future of newspapers.

The *Register-Guard* retail advertising office I entered in the spring of '62 consisted of a director, four salesmen, two artists, a secretary, and a dispatcher. I was the only proof traveler. Delivering page proofs and tear sheets on foot was not a problem because nearly all of the advertisers were less than a dozen city blocks from the paper's downtown building. There were no shopping malls or suburban business parks around Eugene in those days.

Before long, I also was assisting the dispatcher whose job included pulling the proofs and cutting the tear sheets from each edition, and then coordinating their delivery to the advertisers. One of my more enjoyable tasks was retrieving the newspapers we would use for tear sheets. As I had done when I was a paperboy, I often arrived early to watch the pressmen as they webbed the continuous sheets of newsprint throughout the two-story press units.

The dispatcher also had responsibility for maintaining an extensive file of the zinc engravings used in ads. When the artists finished laying out ads, he would locate the zincs that would be reused and take them along with the layouts to the composing room. After each issue was printed, he would collect the zincs, clean them, and refile them for future use.

He was an elderly chain smoker who had obvious drinking and health problems. That may have been why he was delegating more of his tasks to me. Often, he would tell me he was close to retirement, and, if I did well, I might inherit his job in the near future. I never had the heart to tell him that becoming an advertising dispatcher was not my career goal.

I didn't mind delivering and gathering the zincs. It gave me an opportunity to frequently visit the back shop and watch as pages made their way through composing to the presses.

Every page began with the Linotype operators who retyped the text that had arrived from advertising and the newsroom via a pneumatic tube system. I remember that at least two of the operators were deaf. That may have been a requirement for all Linotype operators in those days because the clamorous, constant clattering of those seven-foot-high hot-metal typesetting machines would have been difficult to tolerate for anyone who was not deaf.

As the operators typed on their 90-character keyboards, the Linotypes would release brass letterform molds called "matrices" from the racks of font cases called "magazines" and assemble them in lines the width of columns. The machines would then inject molten lead into the matrices one line at a time. The lines of lead type were called "slugs." After each slug was cast, the matrices would be routed back to the magazines and reloaded into their original locations for reuse. These were the mechanical engines that drove "hot-type" composition.

(Later I learned these Rube Goldberg hot-lead "line-casting" machines were invented back in 1884 by a watchmaker named Ottmar Mergenthaler. His invention made it possible for newspapers to vastly expand the amount of content they could publish each day by semi-automating typesetting, which since the time of Gutenberg had required the labor-intensive process of manually setting all type one letter at a time.)

The number of lines that could be cast was limited by the length of the galley trays. When the tray was full or a job was completed, the galley of type would be moved to a proofing machine where a copy was made to check for errors. If errors were found, corrected lines were cast to replace the erroneous ones. The galley was then put into a storage rack called the "bank" until it was needed by the compositors. Erroneous and defective slugs as well as unused galleys would be dumped into "hell buckets" for re-melting in the hot caldron.

Linotype machines could not handle type sizes larger than 24 points (a third of an inch). Headlines and large display type required a different typesetting system that involved hand-setting lines of type the old-fashioned way — one letter at a time using brass matrices stored in wooden font cases. The matrices were assembled in composing sticks and then inserted into Ludlow machines that, like the Linotype machines, injected molten lead into the lines.

With the editors' layouts and instructions in hand, the compositors would gather the appropriate galleys from the bank and assemble them inside steel frames called "chases" that sat on sturdy metal tables with rollers called "turtles." To cushion the weight of the heavy turtles, the composing room floor was covered in thick hardwood parquetry.

Fitting all of the lead components together in the chase required solving a puzzle in which some elements were usually either too short or too long. When a column of text came up short, the compositors could use several tricks to add length.

The most common was to put thin strips of lead first between paragraphs and then, if necessary, between the lines of type. For stories too short for leading, they would insert brief items set in advance for that purpose.

When the text was too long, an editor would be called to cut it, which was the origin of the expression "cut to the chase." Editors usually stood at the top of the chase opposite the compositors, so cutting stories required them to read the text upside down and backwards.

To accommodate images, the compositors would cut lead blocks to the dimensions of the engravings and insert them where the layouts indicated. Most ads were prepared in advance and already positioned in the appropriate chases.

After all of the pieces were in place and properly fitted, the compositors would lock up the pages in their chases and slowly roll the turtles over to the proofing machine where copies would be pulled and given to the proof readers and editors.

When pages were finally released by the editors, they were taken to machines where moist papier-mâché mats were pressed over the chases to make the bendable molds needed for casting the curved-lead press plates. Men called stereotypers would inject hot lead into the mats and then rout off any imperfections and precisely trim the 40-pound plates before the pressmen attached them to the press cylinders.

During lulls in the advertising department, I would often wander into the newsroom. As much as I enjoyed watching the compositors and pressmen, the reporters and editors were the workers who interested me most. In those days, they were not far removed in appearance and actions from the newsmen of the 1930s and 1940s as portrayed in the original *Citizen Kane* and *Front Page* movies. Reporters wrote their stories on manual typewriters or would tell them to "rewrite men" who did the writing and typing for them.

Wire services — news agencies such as the Associated Press and United Press International — produced the international, national, and regional stories that arrived via dedicated telephone wires connected to teletypewriters. Wire editors would scan the continuous sheets of paper and rip off the stories they would edit for the day's editions.

Some editors still wore the green eyeshades and sleeve garters I had seen in the movies as they marked up stories with pencils, cut and rearranged paragraphs (usually moving the fourth or fifth graph to the lead), typed headlines and captions, and then pasted all the pages for each story together in long strips before rolling them up and sending them through the pneumatic tubes to composing.

If they decided to hold a story, they would "spike" it. The spikes were long nails protruding from blocks of wood. They usually sat on the edges of desks, which is why reporters and editors also got spiked occasionally.

As they worked feverishly around edition deadlines, they seemed impervious to the cacophonous background noises produced by the chattering teletypewriter machines, squawking police radios, clanging fire call bells, swooshing pneumatic tubes, and ringing telephones. Nearly all puffed purposefully and incessantly on cigars, pipes, or cigarettes; their intense concentration visibly evident as they smothered the newsroom in a dense, smoky haze.

The newsroom was a man's world back then, as were most of the other newspaper departments. The few women I saw at the *Register-Guard* worked on the features and society pages or as secretaries and receptionists.

Working in the newsroom

By the spring of '63, my year of living undangerously without stress seemed to have been an effective treatment for my colitis. I still had occasional flare-ups and painful joints, but none was serious enough to require my taking more than a day or two off from work. While I had learned a lot about newspaper publishing as a proof traveler, I recognized the time had come for me to find a new job that would allow me to re-enroll at the University of Oregon in the fall.

Now that I had awakened from my unrealizable dream of becoming a professional astronomer, I decided to focus on science writing. "Layman's Astronomy" would serve as the model for a new weekly column that I proposed to Richard Baker, the managing editor and a member of the family who owned the *Register-Guard*.

Baker had seen me hanging around the newsroom and knew about my activities as an amateur astronomer, so he didn't need convincing. He offered me $10 per column, which was generous back then. My first "Star Watchers' Guide" appeared on July 1. With his support and introductions to other editors, I would earn more money by writing science articles for the Sunday magazine and features pages. Also in July, I began teaching summer classes in astronomy for the Eugene branch of the OMSI and selling telescopes I made using war-surplus lenses purchased from the Edmund Scientific catalog.

My college scholarship was still in effect, but it only covered tuition, so I still had to work and live with my mother. In addition to the usual freshman fare, I enrolled in a geology course. Like most Oregonians, I had a keen interest in this subject. The state is considered a rock hound's heaven because of its diverse geological formations. And it has an abundance of fossils dating back to when much of the state was submerged under an inland sea and later blanketed by extensive lava flows and outpourings of pumice and ash. As a Boy Scout, I had searched for agates and collected fossils on many excursions and camping trips around the state, so the idea of writing another science column on this subject was already forming in my mind.

In November, I attended a meeting on campus where students were interviewing for positions on the *Daily Emerald*, the college newspaper. I didn't take a job with the *Emerald*, but I did take a freshman coed out to dinner who later would play an important role in my life. Her name was Lucille Gerriets.

After a long conversation over pizza, in which I learned she had been a valedictorian at her high school in Portland and was enrolled in the Honors College, we made plans to get together again at a football game and rally the following Friday. Our first date would turn out to be memorable, but not in a way we could have imagined. It was abruptly postponed by an historically traumatic event — the assassination of President John Kennedy.

In the somber days that followed, we, along with practically everyone else around the world, were captivated by the memory-searing reality episodes unfolding live on our television screens. I didn't see Lucille again until after Thanksgiving and then only briefly during finals week. Our next first date would have to wait until the beginning of spring semester.

Mapping a new career path

Before classes started in January 1964, the *Register-Guard* county editor hired me as a part-time reporter. My assignment was to cover two rural towns near Eugene. I quickly discovered that people don't always appreciate reporters from the "big city" who expose the shady practices of their officials or write stories they deem as unfavorable to their communities. The experience taught me how important it is to have editors who carefully vet stories before they are published and executives who support their reporters when they come under attack.

As a county reporter, I got to know Mirkov Pither, the news artist who created the maps that were popular with *Register-Guard* editors. Actually, I got to know his work more than the person. I don't remember much about him other than one of the editors telling me that he had been a cartographer in France before emigrating to the United States.

I never knew why he moved to Eugene, but, for whatever reason, the *Register-Guard* was lucky to have him. In the 1960s, few newspapers employed news artists; even fewer had artists who possessed his talents. Most local locator maps published in newspapers, including major metros like the *Oregonian*, were crudely drawn by reporters using ballpoint pens.

The tiny office Pither occupied had a window that allowed visual contact with the newsroom editors without exposing him to the smog of deadlines. Like me, he was a non-smoker. His well-worn, oak drafting table, and small utility stand abutted the window. An adjustable-arm desk lamp with a magnifying lens stretched from one side of the table. Several plastic triangles and templates hung along with a T-square on the opposite side. A set of technical pens, a couple of razor knives, a wooden burnisher, and an assortment of other tools sat neatly organized on top of the utility stand. In the drawers of the utility stand he kept sheets of rub-down type and adhesive masking film for shading. His chair was a simple wooden bar stool.

Whenever I brought him one of my stories that required a map, I would watch as he meticulously traced roads and meandering rivers on translucent plastic sheets with his pens. On another sheet overlain on the inked layer, he would use a razor knife to carefully cut a piece of amber-colored masking film to fill in the outlines of the rivers and then use his burnisher to adhere it smoothly. On yet another overlay, he added the text elements using his burnisher again to apply the rub-down type. All of the layers would be photographically combined by an engraver to produce a single zinc plate.

Watching him inspired me to create graphics for my science column using the same tools and techniques he employed to create maps. The Eugene Art Supply store had everything I would need plus a bonus. The owner remembered me from when I was a proof traveler. When I told him about my plan, he offered to give me free technical drawing lessons.

By the beginning of June, I felt confident enough in my drawing ability to pitch a new illustrated science column to Baker that combined astronomy and local geology. I proposed calling it "Earth and the Sky." Once again, he didn't need much convincing. He bought the idea and doubled my payment to $20 per column. My new column replaced "Star Watch" on July 6.

Coincidentally in early June, I learned Pither planned to retire at the end of that month. I knew the editors would be in a hurry to find a replacement, so I decided to try my hand at creating a map to go with a story I was writing for the Sunday magazine. As soon as I showed my creation to Don Bonham, the city editor, he hurriedly escorted me along with Dave Emery, the magazine editor, to see Baker. I happily accepted their offer of $5 an hour to create maps for the newspaper as a freelance news artist.

(Emery and Barrie Hartman, the news desk editor who later became my principal newsroom contact for maps, not only launched me on a new career path as a news artist and carto-grapher; they also initiated friendships that have spanned more than half a century.)

Lucille and I finally had our first date during the first week of spring semester, which led to more dates and our becoming friends. In late March, she learned about my illness first-hand when it flared up again. That attack was not as severe as the previous ones, but the diarrhea and joint pain made it impossible to attend classes or cover town meetings and events for several weeks. With her help, I avoided another hospital stay but at a cost to my grades and my reporting job.

Losing my job as a county reporter, which I had enjoyed, was an emotional and financial setback; however, the satis-faction and income I gained later from producing maps and my new science column more than made up for the loss.

Lucille enrolled in summer sessions so we could have more time together, although she also admitted she had not wanted to spend the summer with her parents, especially her Teutonic elderly father. During most weekends and breaks between sessions, she would accompany me on my road trips to gather material for my column and magazine stories.

Advice from a journalism professor

Fall semester in 1964, I took the Introduction to Journalism course taught by Roy Paul Nelson. His course was held in a large lecture hall. When classes started, few seats were vacant. I didn't know any of the other students or anything about the professor, so I always sat quietly alone near an aisle. I assumed Nelson would never notice me, but I was wrong.

Around the midterm exam, he called out my name. I'm sure I was startled and more than a little anxious when he said he wanted to meet with me after the class. As I entered his office, I recall seeing several of my columns and maps lying on his desk. He first wanted to know if I was the author and artist. When I acknowledged that I was, he told me he had been following my work and had only recently connected the byline with my name on his course roster. He next wanted to know if I would have any objections to his showing some of my work during an upcoming lecture. Of course, I didn't.

He then surprised me by asking why I was taking his introductory course. I explained that I was considering a career as a science writer and illustrator, and that I had been uncertain about whether to major in journalism or physical sciences.

His advice was equally surprising. What I remember him telling me was: "Forget about taking more journalism courses. You're already getting real-world experience working at the *Register-Guard*. Concentrate on science and art courses. What the world will need more of in the future are journalists who can explain scientific discoveries and advances in ways people can understand." Nelson was right. More science writers would be needed in the future, but the events of the next two years would divert me onto a different career path.

On the first day of spring in 1965, Lucille and I were married at the Unitarian Church in Eugene. In hindsight, I realize how young and naïve we were. She was only 19, and I had just turned 22. Both of us had never had a close relationship with anyone else. My illness and the specter of dying soon undoubtedly influenced both of us. Her expressed desire to escape from her family and my eagerness to marry also contributed to our haste.

While I would enjoy writing and illustrating the column and magazine articles and creating maps for the *Register-Guard* for another 18 months, my illnesses would continue to intrude on my life and aspirations. After four years of frequently dropping courses because of flare-ups, I decided in May of '66 to put completing the requirements for my college degree on hold. Lucille also was feeling stressed-out and decided to put her graduation on hold too.

To find solace, we gave up the house we were renting and sold our nonessential possessions. For the three months of summer, we lived like nomads in the Oregon and Washington outback. So that I could continue to produce my columns and feature stories, we packed my portable typewriter, drafting tools, camera, and telescope into a cartop carrier along with our camping gear and clothes. Hiking through wilderness areas, fishing and picking wild blackberries, cooking over open fires, exploring geological formations, and gazing at the night sky did wonders for our mental and physical well-being.

The art of flying in virtual worlds

When the first cold September rains soaked our campsite, the time had come to find an indoor job. I had decided to quit my science column and freelance work for the *Register-Guard* as soon as I could secure a full-time job, preferably as a science writer for another newspaper.

My first choice was the *Seattle Times*. I had met the paper's science writer a few years earlier while attending a regional Astronomical League meeting in Seattle. He seemed quite old then, so I assumed he might be ready to retire. I had no problem getting an interview with the managing editor. He said he liked my work and would consider hiring me as soon as the science writer position opened up, but he didn't know how soon that might be. He suggested that I keep checking back because, in his words, "He won't live forever."

After leaving the *Times*, I tried the *Seattle Post Intelligencer* to no avail. We then drove about 25 miles north to Everett for an interview at the *Daily Herald*. Few newspapers had a human resources department in those days, so getting a job interview usually involved just walking in. If there was a "warm chair" and you appeared qualified to fill it, you got the job.

My interview with the paper's editor probably lasted less than 30 minutes. He had an open position, he thought I was qualified, so he offered me the job. I would occupy a warm chair the next day for $75 a week, which was a typical starting salary for reporters in the 1960s.

In my new role, I would wear multiple hats as the paper's science and feature writer, travel editor, graphic artist, and cartographer. I also was the photographer for my assignments, which required me to buy my own camera.

One of my early assignments was to write a feature story about Boeing's plan to build the world's first commercial wide-body jet — the 747 — at a factory under construction near Everett. When completed, it would be the largest building in the world by volume. My story, however, would not be about the plane or the factory. Instead, I would focus on an amazing new technology I saw demonstrated at Boeing's headquarters, then located just south of Seattle. While I no longer recall the name or title of the man I interviewed, he provided me with an unforgettable glimpse of the future.

He directed a team of Boeing designers and engineers who had just produced a video that showed a pilot's view of flying, landing, and parking a 747 at an airport terminal. Had he not told me the images were simulations, I would have believed the airplane I saw in the video in the fall of '66 was already in service. (The first commercial flight of a 747 would not be until

January 1970.) The simulations, he explained, were generated by an array of mainframe computers using a custom 3-D graphics program. At that time, the program could only produce wire-frame images, so animation artists had to be hired to manually render the images in color.

(The engineers and designers at Boeing who touched the future in 1966 would pave the way for the computer-assisted design programs and interactive virtual worlds that now run on personal computers with greater computing power than Boeing's mainframes.)

The director's passion for this technology was clearly evident; his enthusiastic vision of the digital future, infectious. He was convinced that next-generation computers would have a capacity to fully render the images in color and produce even more life-like simulations in less time, with fewer people, at a much lower cost. In his mind's eye, he could already visualize architects and interior designers using interactive computer programs to give clients virtual walk-throughs of houses and buildings before they were built.

His vision of the digital future opened my mind to the enormous potential of computers to transform the graphic arts. I remember wondering at the time when newspapers might adopt computer technologies, but the prospect of publishers investing in them anytime soon seemed highly unlikely.

Five months after occupying the warm chair at the *Herald*, I would say sayonara to Everett and the United States. During the next eight years, I would gain firsthand experience with the developments that led to the digital future of newspaper publishing.

CHAPTER TWO

Prelude to the Digital Future

By the end of the sixties, computers were becoming more versatile and affordable just as rapidly increasing production costs and declining advertising sales were putting the future of newspapers at risk. Most publishers quickly recognized their survival would require adopting entirely new electronic publishing technologies. They began by discreetly replacing their industrial-age typesetters that used mechanical processes to cast "hot type" in lead with electronic typesetters that used photographic processes to expose "cold type" on paper.

Few editors and reporters then were more than vaguely aware of, or even interested in, the technological transformations taking place within newspaper production departments and pressrooms. Initially, the transition from hot-type to cold-type composition had little impact on the news gathering and editing processes. While the walls between editorial and composing in most metropolitan newspapers were not as impervious as the ethically imposed walls between editorial and advertising, they would still serve to distance the word-smiths from the compositors and the technologies used to manufacture newspapers.

During this prelude to the digital future of newspapers, my life would be transformed as well. I would become a father and my dreams of living in another country and traveling around the world would be fulfilled while gaining experience as a news-paper art director and editor. But this would come at a high personal cost.

A map to a remote nation

Around the end of October 1966, a co-worker in the *Everett Herald* newsroom called my attention to a help-wanted ad in the *Editor and Publisher* magazine. The ad was placed anony-mously by a newspaper looking for "an art director who is strong on maps." I hadn't considered becoming an art director, but cartography now was one of my strengths and my chances of becoming a full-time science writer anytime soon seemed remote, so I applied.

A week before Thanksgiving, I received a letter from Ernie Richter, the paper's managing editor. He wrote that he was staying with his family in Portland, Oregon, for the holiday and would like to interview me in person as soon as possible, provided I would be willing to relocate … to Tokyo. The news-paper was *Pacific Stars and Stripes*.

When I told Lucille, she was as elated as I was about the prospect of our moving to Japan. We had already made plans to visit her parents in Portland and my mother in Eugene that week. I called and arranged to meet with him on the Saturday after Thanksgiving.

Richter greeted us warmly, though his craggy face and bushy mustache gave him the appearance of a curmudgeon, which he was. After reviewing my portfolio, he handed me a front page of the tabloid-size newspaper. The top story was about a typhoon that had devastated the island of Saipan. He pointed to a map that accompanied the story and asked for my opinion. At first, I thought this was a trick question because the answer was so obvious. It was not a map. It was an embarrassing waste of space. What the "map" showed was a dot labeled "Saipan." Above the dot was the word "Pacific," below was "Ocean." Wavy lines were added to suggest water. When he asked what I would have done, I explained what I thought was obvious — the importance of including adjacent countries and showing the path of the typhoon. He nodded in agreement. This was the map that he said had prompted him to place the ad. He then directed questions to Lucille regarding how she felt about moving to Japan.

By the end of the interview, he seemed satisfied but non-committal. He told us he had received more than a hundred replies to the ad. Of those, only nine, including me, remained interested after learning the job was in Tokyo. As we left, he promised to get back to us soon.

However, "soon" turned out to be nearly four weeks of nervous waiting. Finally, just before Christmas, a large manila envelope arrived. To my relief, it contained a formal offer letter from Richter and the documents I needed to sign. When Lucille returned home from her doctor's appointment, I told her I had a surprise — we're going to Tokyo in February. She responded by telling me she had a surprise, too — we're going to have a baby in July.

The timing could not have been better for us. The starting salary would more than double my *Herald* salary, and *Stripes* would provide a substantial tax-free housing allowance. Our foreign service status also would give us access to military commissaries and post exchanges as well as nearly free medical care at base hospitals and clinics.

When I informed the *Herald's* editor about the offer, his terse response was: "How could you possibly consider leaving 'God's Country' to go to that heathen land?" With that, I said sayonara to the States for what would be nearly four years.

For two young Oregonian Gullivers, whose only venture to another country had been a brief excursion across the border to Vancouver, British Columbia, the experience of traveling to a "Remote Nation of the World" on a jet plane would have been exciting enough. Actually living in a land as far off and exotic as Japan, well, let's just say we were starry-eyed.

As we prepared to leave Everett, we didn't give much thought to the risks we were taking or the challenges we would face. We had minimal knowledge about the country and we didn't speak Japanese. More importantly, Lucille was four months pregnant and we barely had enough money to get us to San Francisco where we were to catch a military charter flight from Travis Air Force Base. If anything went wrong, we had no fallback.

Fortunately, nothing did. The winter weather cooperated. Our drive to San Francisco and stay in the city were uneventful. The Boeing 707 we boarded at Travis would make a stopover in Hawaii before proceeding to the Tachikawa Air Force Base located on the outskirts of Tokyo. We landed on a cold February morning in the darkness before dawn more than 36 hours after we had departed from the Bay area.

Good morning Tokyo

Somehow, in our exhausted state, we found our way from Tachikawa to the *Stars and Stripes* compound, which then was located adjacent to the Hardy Barracks in Tokyo's Roppongi District. We aptly arrived with the rising sun.

The newsroom was bustling with activity. The news deadline was noon, so the staff had to start working each day around 4 or 5 a.m. Richter greeted us and introduced us to several of the editors. He then handed me my first paycheck, which was a relief. When I looked in my wallet, we only had about $20 left to our name. After I cashed the check and converted some of the U.S. government script to Japanese Yen (dollars were not allowed then), he arranged for a taxi to take us to the Tokyo Hilton where we would stay until we found an apartment.

Tokyo in February 1967 was in the midst of emerging from the ashes of the Second World War to become a great modern metropolis. Our hotel in the Shinjuku ward was ultra-modern. We were in awe as we explored the surrounding streets. Gleaming high-rise office towers coexisted with traditional temples, houses, and shops. Tall cranes and bamboo scaffolding surrounded dozens of buildings under construction.

Swarms of expressionless people were robotically rushing everywhere, seemingly unaware of other people and the chaos around them. About half of the women still wore kimonos and walked on wooden platform shoes called *geta*. Every car we saw appeared new and showroom spotless; all had white doilies draped over the tops of their seats. Restaurants displayed plastic replicas of their menu items. Signs in English often had unintentionally humorous translations and spellings. Brightly lit arcades were packed with men in business suits hypnotically playing noisy, upright pinball-like games called *pachinko*.

Nothing in our experiences prepared us for our first visit to the Shinjuku train station, then the busiest in the world. The concentrations of people scurrying to-and-fro overwhelmed us. During the rush hours, we risked being trampled by determined commuters scrimmaging to squeeze on and off trains. To our amusement, the commuters always politely bowed and said *domo arigatou* (thank you) when they received their tickets from the automated machines.

The apartment building where we initially settled was conveniently located in the Shibuya ward about two miles from *Stripes*. I could walk or take a streetcar to and from work. Our small studio apartment on the fifth floor had no central heating or air conditioning, but it did have a rooftop view of central Shibuya. We were thankful for the housing allowance. The monthly rent was nearly three times what we had paid in Everett for a spacious two-bedroom apartment with a panoramic view of Puget Sound and the Olympic Mountains.

The tenants, all of whom came from different countries, made us feel welcome. We quickly became close friends with Ernst and Jutta Selle, a German couple who lived across the hall from us. They were only a few years older and recently married, too. During the weekdays, Jutta and Lucille would go out shopping and sightseeing. In the evenings, we often got together for dinners in our apartments or around Tokyo. After Kristin was born, they would occasionally babysit so we could have time alone. When they returned to Germany about two years later, they invited us to visit them. We promised we would try.

Working at Pacific Stripes

American servicemen were conspicuous in the districts where nightclubs and hostess bars flourished. Tokyo was the most popular destination for troops on R&R (rest and recuperation) from the Vietnam War, where the U.S. involvement was rapidly escalating. At its peak in 1968, more than a half million American military personnel would be serving in Vietnam.

For many of them, *Stars and Stripes* would be an important source of news about the U.S. and the world, as well as the war. More than 60,000 free copies went to Vietnam daily, mostly for distribution in the field. Elsewhere in Vietnam and the Pacific region, the paper sold for a nickel. Total daily circulation in the latter half of the sixties averaged around 250,000.

(While *Stripes* is a government-authorized publication for the U.S. armed forces, it is editorially independent from the Department of Defense. Its First Amendment rights are guaranteed by Congress.)

During my three and a half years at *Stripes*, the staff in Tokyo consisted of U.S. civilians, military servicemen, and Japanese personnel. The editor-in-chief was an Army colonel, but the editors, department heads, and general manager were civilians. All reporters and photographers were servicemen.

As the art director, I supervised four Japanese and four military artists. In the first months after I arrived, the artists spent most of their time retouching wire service photos that frequently arrived with transmission flaws. We also were occasionally asked to alter elements in photos. One of my first retouching tasks was to paint bras on a group of Japanese topless dancers that appeared in a photo taken at a popular

43

Ginza nightclub. Most of my time, however, was spent creating maps.

By the third month, I was looking for more challenging work, so I proposed converting the paper's weekend feature supplement into a Sunday magazine. My proposal was quickly approved. The magazine would be composed entirely in the art department using "cold-type" paper output from a photo-typesetter and Headliner machine the newspaper had recently installed.

(These post-Gutenberg technologies, which used a beam of light to expose type onto scrolls of photographic paper, were significantly faster and more versatile than the mechanical Varitypers I had used at the *Emerald Empire News*.)

On July 14, the first issue of the *Pacific Stars and Stripes Sunday Magazine* went to press. The next morning, Lucille gave birth at the Tachikawa hospital to our first child, Kristin Mieko. She was a happy and very social baby. Whenever we took her out in her stroller, Japanese women would make a fuss over her blond hair and say *kawaii* (pretty).

I soon discovered that the artists were capable of doing much more than airbrushing photos. The magazine provided opportunities for them to demonstrate their formerly unrecognized talents as illustrators and designers.

The Japanese artists would imbue me with a lasting appreciation for their country's art, food, and culture, and on a few nighttime outings, introduce me to some of Tokyo's seamier sides. With their encouragement, I climbed Mount Fuji at night to watch a sunrise from its peak, simmered in hot springs surrounded by snow, and enjoyed being entertained and pampered at a traditional *geisha* house.

Unanticipated events

As we began the final year of my three-year contract, Lucille and I contemplated extending our stay in Japan. We were appalled and disheartened by the assassinations of Martin Luther King and Robert Kennedy in 1968, and the rioting that had rocked so many American cities. We were leery of returning to the States before the country had recovered from its traumas.

Our personal justifications for staying in Japan were equally convincing. I had lived more than five years without another major flare-up of my ulcerative colitis and with only occasional bouts of arthritic pain and stiffness, so our outlook on life was more hopeful. I was being paid well for a job I enjoyed, we had adapted comfortably to a Japanese lifestyle, and most of all we were happy. We had just moved into a larger Japanese-style house and adopted a Shetland Sheepdog. I also was working with a colleague on a book about the U.S. military bases in Japan. But again, unanticipated events interceded.

In March 1969, Lucille's father died suddenly. To help her mother and sister, she went back to Portland with Kristin for about a month. Nine months after her return, our second child, Eric Ernst, was born. Also that fall, the paper would undergo a radical change in leadership.

Colonel Peter Sweers, the Army officer who had been the editor-in-chief since shortly after I arrived at *Stripes*, retired from the military to become a journalism professor. Sweers had guided the paper through turbulent times when it often was denigrated as the "Hanoi Herald." He resisted the frequent attempts to censor stories and was a staunch defender of the paper's First Amendment protections. His support and honesty had earned the staff's respect.

The editor-in-chief who followed him, Colonel William V. Koch, could not have been more different. He was an avowed ultra-conservative, anti-communist career Army officer who had a low regard for journalists. His condescension and determination to "clean up" the newspaper demoralized most of us in the newsroom.

Midsummer 1970, I selected a *Chicago Tribune* story for the Sunday magazine that was critical of how the Army Corps of Engineers justified damming rivers. I was preparing to release the pages when Koch stormed into the art department and ordered me to kill the story. I replied that if he censored the story, I would quit; he did, and I resigned. Actually, Lucille and I already had been making plans to leave in the fall; the encounter just gave me a principled reason.

Halfway around the world in 80 days

The practical thing to do would have been to board a free military charter flight back to the States and then use our substantial savings to buy a house and new car. Instead, I convinced Lucille that we should take a western route home so we could visit with the Selles in Germany, and I could interview for a job at *European Stripes*, which was based in Darmstadt. The route we chose would follow Phileas Fogg halfway around the world in 80 days, give or take a few days.

The Marine captain charged with debriefing me and arranging my departure from *Stripes* nearly fell out of his chair when I told him I was going to the Soviet Union. He practically accused me of being a turncoat. My long hair and beard, and outspoken opposition to the war undoubtedly added to his rage. (I've always suspected that he reported me to the FBI.)

During our final two months, we sold our car, packed our possessions for shipping back to the States, and sent our dog on ahead to stay with Lucille's mother. We would need nearly all of that time to get our tourist visas for the Soviet Union and make our travel arrangements. All expenses for transportation, hotels, and meals at government-run Intourist restaurants had to be paid in advance, and our itinerary would have to be followed exactly.

Just as we had done when we left Everett to go to Japan, we didn't consider the risks, which obviously were much greater this time. Traveling across Siberia and Eastern Europe during the Cold War was risky enough; traveling with two small children, in hindsight, was crazy. Kristin was three and Eric was only nine months old when we started our journey.

Amazingly, we squeezed everything we would need for the trip into four large suitcases and two shoulder bags. One of the suitcases served a dual role as a folding bed for Eric. Two other suitcases were stuffed with disposable diapers and jars of baby food. We would also carry a folding stroller for Kristin, a backpack for Eric, and a case for my Nikon camera gear.

We departed Japan near the end of September. The first leg of our journey was on a Russian cruise ship that took us overnight from Yokohama to the Siberian port of Nakhodka. Our friends had joked that Russians would only serve us borscht — a cold beet soup. We were pleasantly surprised when we found a luxurious buffet with abundant Beluga caviar, lox, and sturgeon, and an assortment of delicious pastries. Borscht was not on the ship's menu.

As we were preparing to disembark the following morning, we hit our first snag. The immigration officer — a stern, middle-aged woman straight out of casting for a *James Bond* movie — would not allow Kristin to leave the ship. Her visa indicated she was Japanese. Even though she had blonde hair and didn't look Asian, the Russian who had entered her visa apparently assumed that if she was born in Japan and had a Japanese middle name, she must be Japanese. If the problem could not be resolved, the immigration officer threatened to send Kristin back to Japan … alone. After waiting anxiously for more than an hour, a bureaucrat finally came onboard to change her visa. We made it to the train station only minutes before the Trans-Siberian pulled out.

We had a cabin with just enough space on the floor between two rows of bunkbeds to open Eric's folding bed. Our car was reserved exclusively for foreigners. The only Russian was a young woman whose job was to tend the samovar for brewing tea and to keep an eye on us. The other passengers who emerged from their cabins were a Frenchman, two Norwegian men, and an American woman who we guessed was in her early sixties. (This was not the high-tourist season.)

Between listening to their fascinating adventures and watching the frozen Siberian landscape breeze by, Lucille and I didn't get much sleep that night. Fortunately, our children did, and we managed to catch up on our sleep the next night at a hotel in Khabarovsk before continuing on to Irkutsk.

There were too many memorable experiences on our journey to recount in this chapter. Suffice it to say, we made our way safely to the home of our friends in Lübbecke with a couple of disposable diapers to spare. During our two months with the Selles and their one-year-old son Derek Roger, we took several trips together around northern Germany and The Netherlands.

I didn't get a job with *European Stripes*, even though they had an opening I would have been qualified to fill. I suspected this was payback for my "principled resignation" from *Pacific Stripes*, but of course I had no evidence, and there was nothing I could do. So, just after Christmas, we caught a Dutch labor union charter flight from Amsterdam to New York City (that's another story).

We arrived at Kennedy airport on Sunday, December 27. I had purchased Greyhound bus tickets in Amsterdam for $90 that gave us 90 days of unlimited travel in the United States. We planned to stay a couple of days in Manhattan so I could apply for a job at *The New York Times* before going on to Portland. However, the next morning, after riding the subway from Kennedy to the Port Authority Building, which served as a hub for local and regional bus lines as well as Greyhound, and then walking down 42nd Street to Times Square, we changed our minds.

The dismal condition of the city shocked us and made us wish we had stayed in Tokyo or Amsterdam. The subway cars were dilapidated and covered with graffiti, homeless people and aggressive panhandlers surrounded the Port Authority Building, and 42nd Street was a creepy, run-down red-light district. Holiday decorations gave Times Square a somewhat cheerier appearance, but it still paled by comparison to what we had seen in Europe and Japan. Even Moscow was cleaner and appeared in better shape. Instead of staying overnight, we quickly made our way back to the Greyhound terminal and boarded the next bus heading west.

Next stop St. Petersburg, Florida

When I began my job search the first week in January 1971, the country was in a recession and newspaper jobs were scarce. I would use more than half of my 90-day Greyhound pass on several trips alone while Lucille and our children stayed in Portland with her mother. (Without the internet, job hunting in multiple states was infinitely more difficult than it is today.)

First on my list were the *Oregonian* and *Seattle Times*. Both had no openings. The editor at the *Times* let me know that the science writer I had hoped to replace in '66 was still alive and working. After a brief stopover in Eugene to visit my mother and friends at the *Register-Guard*, I set my sights on Denver to interview at the *Post* and *Rocky Mountain News*, but they, too, were not hiring. At the *Post*, the managing editor told me no one had left or joined his newsroom in more than 14 years. I would hear a similar refrain at nearly every newspaper I visited.

To conserve money, I mostly ate hot dogs and sandwiches from vending machines, slept on the buses or at YMCA's, and changed clothes in bus depot restrooms. Low-budget traveling through the southeastern states in the winter of '71 was depressing and at times frightening, especially for a casually dressed guy with long hair and a beard.

To keep my spirits up, I took photos with the Nikon camera I had carried across Siberia and pretended I was on assignment. I tried to convince myself that if all else failed, I might be able to sell the photos and stories from my adventures to magazines and newspapers. By the time I got to Atlanta, my spirits were sagging. I had interviewed at more than twenty papers. The editors always seemed impressed with my portfolio, but none could offer me a job.

At the *Atlanta Constitution*, the managing editor suggested trying the *St. Petersburg Times*. (In 2011, the newspaper changed its name to the *Tampa Bay Times*.) So, after a sleepless night at the YMCA, I decided to go south. Atlanta was in a deep freeze when the bus pulled out of the gate. But, as soon as we crossed into Florida, the sun popped out in its full glory. When I got off the bus in St. Petersburg, I immediately started sweating profusely in my heavy wool suit.

Walking down Main street to the *Times* office under the blazing sun, I passed rows of tree-shaded green benches occupied by elderly people dead to the world. My first thought was that at the age of 28 I was too young for a retirement home. The *Times*, however, proved to be nothing like what I was imagining. Most of the people in the modern newsroom appeared near my age, and to my relief the offices were refreshingly air conditioned.

Bob Haiman, the managing editor, interviewed me for about an hour before offering me a job as a copy editor on the features desk to fill a recent departure. The starting salary would be less than I had earned at *Stripes* and there would be a one-month probation period, during which I would not have health insurance and could be fired without cause. Despite my reservations, I had no choice but to accept. Our savings were running low, and I had no other prospects.

In mid-March, I returned with my family and rented a small house. By the time we moved in and I started my first day at the *Times*, we again had only about $20 to our name. I wouldn't be able to buy a car for nearly a year because the banks would not approve me for a loan. In Japan, all of our transactions had been in cash, so I had no credit rating. City buses and a bicycle would be our only means of transportation.

Working at the St. Pete Times

The features desk then consisted of a chief and three other copy editors. The chief was a married man in his late forties who had been with the *Times* for around 10 years. All of the copy editors were young women; only one was married. We would work together as a team editing stories, writing headlines, submitting art assignments, and laying out pages for the daily sections.

Each of us on the desk also had responsibility for one or two weekend sections. I was initially assigned the Saturday Leisure and Sunday Homes sections. In the first years of the seventies, the real estate market around Tampa Bay was booming. The bountiful advertising made Homes by far the largest of all *Times* sections. Most Sundays it would be split into two printed sections with as many as 64 broadsheet pages; about a third were full-page ads.

I would receive the page dummies in the afternoon on Wednesdays for Homes and Thursdays for Leisure. All copy, headlines, art, and layouts had to be delivered to the composing room before eight the following mornings.

For the first time in my professional life I felt I was in over my head. And drowning fast. All of my previous experience had been with tabloid pages; laying out broadsheet pages was a whole new ballgame. And, I had limited experience working with color, which the *Times* used extensively. Also, nearly four years in Japan speaking a mix of simple English and Japanese had eroded my vocabulary. While editing stories, I was constantly checking the *Webster Pocket Dictionary* and *AP Style Guide* that always sat no farther away from me than my coffee cup.

At the end of my probationary month, the features editor informed me that my work was unsatisfactory. He didn't give me any specifics. Nor did he recognize how much effort I had put into meeting his demands, which often were unrealistic considering the size of the sections.

No question I was burning out. On Wednesdays, I would come in at noon to start laying out the Homes section. Even with help from the desk chief and other copy editors, I would often work through the night until 3 or 4 a.m. and then return by 8 a.m. to oversee the pages as they were being made up in composing. This would take me until Thursday afternoon, just as the page dummies for Leisure arrived. I didn't get home on those nights until around midnight.

I was so tired I was almost hoping I would be fired, but I knew that would have been a financial disaster. I was relieved when he said he would give me another month of probation.

I had to figure out a way to beat the system without killing myself. The best solution, I reasoned, was to get ahead of the deadlines by editing more stories in advance and creating a file of completed layouts that I could plug into pages. To do that, I started working on weekends. Copy editors were salaried workers, so there was no overtime pay.

My long weekdays at the *Times* and the loss of weekends made life difficult for Lucille and our children, too. On many days we hardly saw each other, and when I was home, I was usually too exhausted to be of much help with chores or to participate in family activities.

The stresses would soon affect our health. Miraculously, none of us had gotten sick during our globe-trotting adventures through the fall and winter months. But, after just six-weeks of living in sunny Florida, we all came down with a flu-like illness. For Kristin, it turned into pneumonia. She would be hospitalized for nearly a week. Because of the extended probation, we had no health insurance. It would take more than a year to pay off the bills.

When my second probationary month ended, the features editor didn't fire me or extend my purgatory, although my ordeal continued. A year later, I still worked long days, but I no longer needed to go into the newsroom every weekend.

By then, I understood the realities of my job. Foremost was my realization that no one at the *Times* cared about anything in the features sections beyond the staff-written lead stories. The other stories, which we got from national syndicates and news agencies, were regarded simply as fillers around ads. Moreover, all of us on the copy desk had learned from experience that few of the newspaper's readers paid much attention to the inside feature stories.

The Homes section, for example, often had more space for editorial content than we had home-related stories. Most of the time, I could quickly fill inside pages by making "creative use of white space." On occasions when the story bank was exhausted, one of the other copy editors and I would resort to making up stories. It was amazing how creative we could be after midnight. Our "fake features" ranged from humorous to ridiculous. Often our creativity would turn risqué, like our story about how the sizes of screwdrivers mattered. We never received a complaint.

Only once in my three years at the *Times* can I recall hearing from readers. One of the staff writers had interviewed local residents to get their reactions to *All in the Family*, the first television sitcom to directly confront bigotry in the United States. The story that led the Sunday Entertainment section, which I was editing at that time, included words and expressions used by the program's main character, Archie Bunker, that were rarely printed in newspapers. All of the editors expected angry readers to flood the switchboard on the following morning.

They did, but they weren't complaining about the story. They were angry because I had reduced their popular, half-page-wide Sunday crossword by one column to accommodate the *All in the Family* story, which the features editor had insisted could not be cut. Clearly, the large crossword was more important to loyal readers than the feature stories.

Another reality of the job was that appearance mattered more than substance. The front pages of the weekend feature sections were essentially showcases for the paper's writers, photographers, and illustrators, and for its use of color. The *Times* had several award-winning visual journalists, so I would often display their work extra-large with a catchy headline even when the main story was weak. Invariably, if the pages looked good, the writers would get praised by the senior editors and publisher. Copy editors rarely got praised.

One step forward, two steps back

By the summer of '72, things were looking up. My section fronts were being regularly shown at the American Press Institute as examples of creative feature page layout and color usage, which pleased Nelson Poynter, the owner and publisher, and Eugene Patterson, who had recently joined the *Times* as executive editor and president. Their praising memos boosted my status with the features editor. I no longer was his whipping boy.

Lucille and I also were feeling more in control of our lives although we were still struggling financially. We had accumulated credit card debts, which apparently pleased the bank because it finally granted me a loan to purchase a used car. With the car, we gained more freedom to explore Florida and more time to do shopping and other activities as a family. Giving up the bicycle that I was using to get to and from the office also relieved some of the arthritic pain in my legs that had returned.

We were just beginning to settle into a manageable routine when Lucille's mother called. She wanted to know if she and Lucille's sister could come live with us until they could find a place of their own in St. Petersburg. She said their landlord had sold the house they were leasing, and they were about to be evicted. Of course, we couldn't say no. So, we immediately arranged for shipping their possessions and for sending us our dog and their dog by air.

With four adults, two young children, and two dogs, the three-bedroom, one-bathroom bungalow felt like a sardine can. Even with minimal furniture, the rooms were cramped and the thin walls made privacy impossible. Our situation was reminiscent of Japan where several generations shared small houses and slept in rooms separated by moveable rice-paper walls.

To cover the costs for moving Lucille's mother and sister, and then caring for them, we maxed out our credit cards. Their ability to support themselves on her mother's Social Security, much less afford to rent a house of their own, was a remote prospect. Her mother was elderly with physical limitations and her sister, who was two years older, was mentally impaired; a severe case of measles when she was young had left her brain damaged.

That fall, Kristin started kindergarten and Lucille took a job at a print shop as a proof reader and assistant to the owner, who required her to work on Saturdays. She also found a job for her sister with the Goodwill store. While that reduced our financial stresses somewhat, it increased our marital stresses. Lucille and I would have even less time together. The conjugal happiness we had enjoyed in Japan was now a distant memory. Our jobs became our escape.

(Both of us would find comfort and intimacy outside of our marriage and later suffer the emotional consequences. In the libido-liberating seventies, satisfying carnal needs was easy, especially in hormone-charged pressure cookers like the *Times* newsroom.)

The dawning of electronic publishing

Around the beginning of '73, the *Times* installed state-of-the-art computerized typesetters to complete its conversion to all cold-type composition. The features department would be given the dubious honor of being the first to use an optical character reader (OCR) system that connected directly to the new photo-typesetters. These early editorial systems, which newspapers across the country were adopting, marked the dawning of electronic publishing.

In theory, scanner technologies would improve efficiency and reduce costs by eliminating the need to re-keyboard staff-written stories in composing. That assumed reporters would be able to type their stories perfectly on their IBM Selectric typewriters. Few could. Corrections and changes were frequent and frustrating to make; editors often had to retype whole pages before they could be scanned.

To handle the additional workload on the features desk, the *Times* hired another copy editor. Even then, most of our editing continued to be done the old-fashioned way with pencils on the typewritten letter-size sheets of newsprint provided by the reporters. Mercifully, the OCR systems were short lived in newsrooms. Their use by newspapers would be relegated to scanning stories that had been printed in the newspaper for storage and access in electronic archives.

That spring, Poynter instructed Haiman to create a task force to redesign the *Times*. He assigned the features editor to lead the project with me as the designer. For several months that would be my sole responsibility. The newspaper was not unionized, so I was free to work on prototype pages in the back shop alongside the compositors.

There I saw, for the first time, compositors using computers to communicate directly with the phototypesetters. Unlike the OCR system, operators could display text on small green screens as they typed. Corrections and changes were easily made. I remember wondering at the time why computers weren't being used in the newsroom instead of the clunky OCR system. I guessed that it was because electric typewriters were cheaper than computers.

In July, the features editor and I (though not friends, we had come to respect each other's talents) presented my proposed redesign to Poynter and Patterson. They approved it with minor changes and authorized us to put together a plan for its implementation. Poynter implored us to launch the redesign gradually to avoid upsetting the paper's loyal older readers.

We had just begun to introduce elements of the redesign when events a world away put everything on hold. At the beginning of October, on the Jewish Yom Kipper holiday, several Arab nations launched a surprise attack on Israel. Soon after, the Arab oil producers imposed an embargo on all shipments of petroleum to the United States in retaliation for supporting Israel. The resulting shortages, combined with increases in the price of gasoline and products that used petroleum, had a sudden and profound impact on the country.

The newspaper industry was hit hard. Printing and distributing newspapers required huge amounts of energy, nearly all of which was derived from oil. Producers of newsprint and inks also were huge consumers of petroleum. Consequently, costs rose steeply within a few months. The price of newsprint and inks jumped by more than fifty percent, and utility companies added hefty surcharges. Gasoline rationing and price increases at the pump hampered deliveries and made servicing routes more expensive.

Revenues declined just as steeply. Nearly every enterprise cut back on its advertising, and a significant percentage of the paper's subscribers cancelled their home deliveries. Cancellations were especially high among the paper's loyal subscribers — retirees on fixed incomes and so-called "snow birds" who decided to forego flying south for the winter.

The *Times*, along with most other American newspapers, immediately shifted into crisis mode. All attention focused on cost cutting. The highest priority was given to reducing newsprint consumption. That was not too difficult because the reductions in the amount of advertising also reduced the number of pages in each section. The *Times* went further by reducing the percentage of space allocated for editorial content, making headlines and art smaller, and minimizing the use of white space. I don't recall any newsroom layoffs.

A greater reduction required more time and expense. Until 1973, most American broadsheet newspapers had a 15-inch page width with an eight-column format. Publishers recognized that reducing the page width by a couple of inches and adopting a six-column format would afford significant savings. But this would entail expensive modifications to their presses as well as all equipment from the newsprint roll handlers to the platemaking machines. The crisis also accelerated the conversion from letterpress to more economical offset printing. The resulting savings, however, would have an editorial consequence — less space for news on each page.

Early in 1974, the *Times* decided to adopt a narrower page width. The conversion was estimated to take about a year to complete. In the meantime, my redesign would have to be modified for the narrower pages. That project would be left to another editor.

Breaking out and moving on

Around the same time, Lucille and I met with a marriage counselor. After several sessions, we agreed the only hope for us as a couple and a family was to break out of our deep, emotionally destructive rut. That would require leaving St. Petersburg.

In mid-March, I found an ad in the *Editor and Publisher* magazine for a graphics editor. The newspaper was the *Detroit Free Press*. I applied and within a couple of weeks I was on a red-eye flight to Detroit for an interview. When I arrived at 8 a.m., the personnel director immediately took me to a small conference room to begin taking a battery of tests. I was exhausted and excited at the same time. I had had a long day at the *Times* and had not been able to sleep that night on the plane or in the hotel, but the prospect of a new beginning gave me a rush of adrenaline.

Every hour or so, the personnel director would escort me to meetings with editors. The first editors I met were Bill Baker, the features editor, and David Dolson, the Sunday editor. Both were congenial and gave my portfolio a thorough review. The features department, which occupied the fifth floor of the *Free Press* building, appeared as if it had not changed, or been thoroughly cleaned, since the end of the Second World War. The only similarity to the modern *Times* newsroom was the IBM Selectric typewriters on the desks.

By the end of the day, I had endured about six hours of intelligence, aptitude, and psychological tests and met with five or six editors. My last meeting was with Kurt Luedtke. At age 34, he was the youngest executive editor of an American metropolitan newspaper. (Five years later he would leave the *Free Press* to become a successful Hollywood screen writer.)

Luedtke was not one to waste time on small talk. He asked pointed questions about my experience and goals as he studied my portfolio. His cool demeanor gave no clues as to his thoughts. After about an hour, I left his office without any sense of how he perceived me. The personnel director met me on the way out and assured me he would be in touch soon.

I didn't have long to wait. Toward the end of April, I received a formal offer letter from Baker and immediately submitted my resignation. My last assignment for the *Times* would be to lay out a 46-page broadsheet special section that contained the entire, unedited text of the transcripts from President Nixon's Watergate tapes that were released on April 30. The section was printed on the sixth of May. The following day I started my drive north to Detroit ... alone.

Lucille and I had agreed that we needed time apart to sort out our feelings for each other and to determine the paths we wanted to follow. I would spend nearly three months in Detroit residing at "Mother Wishwell's" boarding house for single men.

In July, we met at a Detroit hotel and decided we would try to put our marriage back together. The following month, we moved with our two children into an apartment not far from the *Free Press* building. Lucille's mother and sister would stay in Florida with our dogs. By then, both were working at Goodwill and able to afford the rent for a small house. After three years in a dark pit of despair, Detroit afforded us a ray of hope and the prospect of a happier future.

CHAPTER THREE

Computerizing the Free Press

The mating of phototypesetters with newsroom computers in the early seventies set in motion a momentous clash between the old and new worlds of publishing. With the resulting computerization of print, the newspaper industry would unwittingly help to launch the greatest transformation in human communication systems since the invention of mechanized printing — the digital publishing revolution.

By the end of that decade, authority over page composition would be transferred from the composing room to the newsroom, whole segments of the newspaper production process would be eliminated, and long-established divisions of labor would be reordered. While computerization afforded solutions to the mounting financial problems associated with labor-intensive industrial-age publishing, transitioning would prove to be a formidable task, especially for unionized metropolitan papers such as the *Detroit Free Press*.

Over the course of some three and a half centuries, newspapers had evolved into complex amalgamations of fiefdoms that jealously guarded their specialized crafts and jurisdictions. Resistance to change was deeply ingrained in the culture. Efforts to introduce new technologies and methods had often resulted in prolonged labor disputes, lockouts, shutdowns, and costly strikes, which occasionally became violent. During my five years at the *Free Press*, I would be embroiled in the conflicts and hostilities that would arise from the paper's transition.

Detroit and the Free Press at their apex

When I joined the *Free Press* in May 1974, Detroit was an industrial-age leviathan that supported two highly regarded, fiercely competitive daily newspapers — the morning *Free Press* and the evening *News*. In that decade, the *Free Press* was the fifth largest American newspaper with a circulation of more than 600,000 on weekdays and 800,000 on Sundays.

They occupied landmark buildings separated by only two city blocks on West Lafayette Boulevard. Both were designed in the first decades of the twentieth century by Albert Kahn, the foremost industrial architect of his time. The *Free Press* was owned by Knight Newspapers; the *News* was the flagship of Booth Newspapers.

Like nearly all other companies in Detroit, both papers were unionized. At least a half-dozen different unions represented the nonmanagement employees. On day one, I was enrolled as a dues-paying member of the Newspaper Guild for the first time.

The features staff occupied a narrow, mostly undivided space that spanned the full length of the fifth floor on the north side of the building overlooking Lafayette Boulevard. Bill Baker, the features editor and my boss, had the only enclosed office.

I sat directly across from the magazine editor who was between me and an open window, undoubtedly the source of the dust and soot that coated everything. There was no air conditioning then, so open windows provided the only ventilation and relief from the oppressive summer heat waves.

My grey steel desk and swivel chair had seen better days. The associate Sunday magazine editor sat on my right. On my left stood a tall wooden file cabinet that appeared to have not been used for more than a decade. Leaning against the cabinet, a stack of yellowing newspapers at least four feet high served as an effective barricade.

My initial assignment as the paper's first graphics editor was to design covers and lay out pages for the Detroit Sunday magazine while creating prototypes for its redesign. The magazine and TV guide were the first sections to be produced entirely with cold type.

Learning union shop rules

The production department was not too different from the *Eugene Register-Guard* back in the 1950s, except for being much larger, with around 600 workers, and, as I would discover, much less friendly. Union rules prevented me from touching the type and pages. Baker had warned me to keep my hands in my pockets whenever I was in the composing room. Any breach of the rules, he said, could result in a "chapel call" — a costly temporary shutdown, or worse.

On my visits to this latter-day Gutenberg-era page factory, I had to carefully navigate around clattering Linotype machines, scurrying compositors, and rolling "turtles" carrying heavy page "chases" filled with lead type, always cognizant of Baker's admonition. The easel tables used for pasting up the magazine and TV guide pages were located along a far wall. Nearby was the brightly lit, air-conditioned, glass-enclosed room where the newspaper had recently installed two computerized phototypesetters.

All of the compositors were burly men uniformly dressed in blue coveralls with black ink smudges. Each kept a red shop rag stuffed into a pocket for wiping sweat from his face and ink from his hands. Most wore traditional printers' hats folded from discarded newsprint.

Everything in hot-metal composition was precisely controlled. Column widths, type sizes and styles for headlines, body text, captions, and other text elements were all standardized. The spacing between columns, paragraphs, and lines of type, as well as the spacing between headlines and body text were defined by regularized lead spacing strips and historically imposed typographic rules.

The half-size page-dummy forms typically used by editors to sketch layouts and provide basic instructions were sufficient for assembling broadsheet and tabloid pages with hot type. Compositors had always been given considerable leeway to interpret and adjust layouts. Editors depended on the compositors' skills and judgements to make everything fit properly in the metal chases. Often the final pages bore little resemblance to the editors' original layouts.

Making up pages with cold type required an entirely different set of skills and judgements — more like those of a draftsman or graphic artist. While the standards and rules still applied, adhering to them was more difficult. Positioning elements required visual judgements as well as technical skills. Even with the blue-line grids printed on the page forms, nothing prevented the paper text elements and artwork from floating or even inadvertently overlapping other elements.

Moreover, all of the tools used for cold-type pages — razor knives, waxers, T-squares, straight edges, and tape rules for lines and boxes — were antithetical to the "masculine" hot-type world. Most compositors considered cold-type make up demeaning "women's work."

After several frustrating months, during which compositors rarely followed my layouts and instructions, I decided to take a different approach. I would lay out pages on the same forms the compositors used for the magazine. And instead of sketching layouts, I would paste copies of the text and art exactly where I wanted them to appear.

The printed pages finally conformed to my layouts — until a union steward complained. He argued that I was intimidating the compositors with my precise full-size page dummies.

This was the first of many confrontations I would have with the International Typographers Union (ITU). In this one, management prevailed, and I was allowed to continue pasting up full-size page dummies for the magazine issues and prototypes — so long as I stayed away from the compositors while they were working on my pages.

I was not inherently hostile toward unions. I had grown up in a blue-collar family believing unions played a vital role by representing workers' interests in conflicts and negotiations with management. Breaking unions was never my intention. I only objected when their rules inhibited progress and embraced mediocrity.

Life and career changing developments

By the summer of '74, I had put the depressing St. Petersburg experiences described in the previous chapter behind me. I was feeling confident and happy again. After more than three months apart, Lucille and I reconciled and moved with our two children into a spacious, modern apartment in Lafayette Park, a new urban complex of residential buildings that surrounded a large green space. Our apartment was conveniently located within walking distance of Detroit's thriving downtown department stores, famed Greektown, and the *Free Press* building.

I was now working regular 8-to-5 hours, five days a week, so we were able to enjoy family activities and outings more often than had been possible in Florida. For Lucille and me, the respite provided a chance to rekindle our relationship and reconnect with our children.

Two developments in the fall, however, would profoundly affect the rest of my life and career. In October, Knight Newspapers acquired Ridder Publications. The combined company — Knight-Ridder Newspapers — would be the largest American newspaper chain in terms of total circulation. Most of the corporate executives were former journalists who had been mentored by John ("Jack") and James Knight, the company's distinguished co-founders. All shared their stalwart commitment to quality journalism and public service. They also were forward looking and willing to invest in the future of newspapers. I would be a beneficiary of their vision.

Around the same time, Baker told me the file cabinet and stack of old newspapers next to my desk would have to be cleared out to make room for a new "thing" the *Free Press* had just purchased. He said the thing was being evaluated as a possible replacement for the optical character reader (OCR) system that the paper had been using for several years. The thing that filled the newly emptied space came mounted on a pedestal with wheels.

The installer called it a 6200-model Hendrix VDT (video display terminal). Hendrix was one of the early developers of newspaper "front-end" systems (computers intended for use by the originators of content). These first-generation VDTs were essentially stand-alone word processors designed specifically for remotely entering and editing text, and for outputting punch tape suitable for reading by the typesetters. They could only handle about 8,000 characters (8K). When the limit was reached, the operator had to punch a tape. If there was a power failure or the electric plug was pulled before the tape was punched, all was lost; the 6200 models had no internal storage memory whatsoever. Nevertheless, they were a major improvement over the OCR system. Editing on the screen was much easier and faster than it was on paper. And the saved tapes could be quickly reloaded if changes had to be made.

Unlike my colleagues who tended to be technophobic, I didn't need any encouragement to begin "playing" with the computer on wheels stationed beside me. Within a few days, I had mastered the required coding and was successfully setting type for the magazine. This would be my first occasion to touch the digital future of newspaper publishing.

A promotion without a job description

On March 16, 1975, I launched the Sunday magazine redesign. In the same time frame, the *Free Press* installed a more advanced editorial front-end system. The Hendrix 6400 was a multi-terminal system built around a refrigerator-size DEC mini-computer. It had a five-megabyte hard drive and was linked directly to the typesetters, so tapes were no longer required.

Terminals were placed in the features department for the magazine and TV guide, and in the sports department, which was just beginning its conversion to cold type. All were linked to the minicomputer housed in a small fourth-floor storeroom with a new window air conditioner. Cables snaked across the floors and up the walls. All were taped down, but even that didn't prevent people from occasionally tripping over them or accidentally pulling them off the walls.

Kurt Luedtke, the executive editor, had no interest in technology. Initially, he assumed day-to-day management of the editorial system could be left to the individuals who used the terminals. That approach didn't work out so well.

While the new VDTs were relatively simple to operate, the minicomputer was not. None of us was familiar with computer terminology, much less the hexadecimal language the minicomputer understood. Interactions with the system were done through a teletypewriter and a row of toggle switches.

At the end of each workday, the last person to leave was expected to do an "orderly shutdown" of the minicomputer. In the morning, the first person to arrive was charged with "rebooting" the system. Whenever it "hung up," which was not infrequent, whoever was on duty at the time was supposed to interpret the cryptic error messages printed by the teletypewriter and take whatever action was required to get the system back up and running.

After a number of snafus that resulted in corrupted files and the infuriating erasures of the hard drive, Luedtke reluctantly agreed that fall to designate someone as the "unofficial" systems manager. I was the "lucky" someone.

That designation immediately ran afoul of the Guild. The tensions between management and the Guild had been steadily escalating ever since the first VDTs were installed. Management saw the computers merely as new tools that would improve efficiency and reduce costs by eliminating the re-keyboarding of content in the composing room. From the Guild's perspective, management was exploiting its members by forcing them to take on extra responsibilities for which they were not being paid. I didn't feel exploited. Learning to use the computers, in my view, was all about adapting to the future of publishing.

Luedtke's resolution of the conflict was to move me into a non-union management position. My new title would be graphics editor *and* editorial systems manager. The promotion didn't come with a job description or much of a salary increase. His only instructions were to keep the editorial front-end system running without problems and to assist the editors and users whenever they needed help, which meant carrying an annoying beeper and being on 24-hour call. I would still have all of my magazine responsibilities.

Before starting my new role, I arranged to have a Hendrix technician teach me more about maintaining and troubleshooting the system. At the top of my priority list was finding a way to eliminate the daily routine of shutting down the minicomputer every evening and rebooting it in the mornings.

Relying on whomever happened to be the last user to leave and the first to arrive had been a factor in nearly all of the snafus. Moreover, I wasn't eager to return every day in the middle of the night to personally execute these procedures. To my relief, the technician assured me the routine was no longer necessary; the minicomputer could now operate continuously without a problem.

A few weeks later, the minicomputer had a problem. It died sometime during the night, and all of my efforts to restart it in the morning failed. Even the technician could not restart it, so he proceeded to perform exploratory surgery. In short order, every part was spread out on the floor. By the end of the morning, he looked haggard. He couldn't find anything wrong. Then by chance, he looked behind the teletypewriter stand. There he found the source of the problem. The computer and teletypewriter had been unplugged, most likely by a cleaning person. Thus, I learned the cardinal rule of computer trouble-shooting — before doing anything, always make sure the computer and its ancillary devices are plugged into live electrical outlets.

I soon discovered that the new system's typesetting codes could control much more than the basic text parameters. They also could be used to position type on the rolls of photographic paper and to draw horizontal and vertical rules of any thickness. By mastering the power of the codes, I reasoned that I could restore the controls over spacing and alignment that had been lost in the conversion from lead to paper. And I could eliminate the crooked lines compositors often put down with tape rules.

Learning how to apply these capabilities was challenging. The manipulated type could not be previewed on the VDT's screen before it was output from the phototypesetter, so I had to learn by trial and error.

My errors always delighted the compositors, especially when I would forget to insert a code after a headline that changed the type back to the body text size. On those occasions, they would stand pridefully in front of my desk and dramatically unroll across the room 20 to 30 feet of exposed photographic paper with an entire story set in half-inch-tall or larger headline type.

My successes, however, did not delight the compositors. As soon as I understood how to position type, I decided to try partially "paginating" (assembling) a couple of the magazine pages. Lots of coding and calculations were required to accurately position all of the text elements and rules.

Less than an hour after the files emerged from the photo-typesetter, Baker escorted me into a meeting with the VP for operations. On the VP's desk were the pages I had paginated with everything positioned exactly as I had intended. The VP looked at the pages and then at me. After an uncomfortably long period of silence, he said: "Nice work Roger. Do not do this again," with extra emphasis on "not."

Baker later told me the union steward had threatened a shut-down of the composing room when he saw the files. The VP had to convince him that I had not been authorized to paginate pages and that the incident would not be repeated. That decree, however, didn't prevent me from continuing to use the codes for controlling spaces and inserting lines and boxes within single columns of text. Only multicolumn output was verboten.

Another confrontation with the ITU soon followed. I was happy to have a young compositor assigned to the magazine who actually enjoyed working with cold type and took pride in his work. I made a point of letting him know how much I appreciated his attention to details. One afternoon, I was in composing as he was finishing the last spread for the issue. He had only one more element to place when the "cleanup" bell rang. Under the terms of the ITU contract, all work had to stop 30 minutes before the end of each shift to give the compositors time to clean up and change clothes. He told me he didn't want to leave the spread for the evening crews, so he continued working a few minutes past the bell.

Unfortunately, someone reported him to the union steward. Later I learned the steward had pulled him off the magazine and assigned him for a month to the galley bank, which was considered the lowliest position in composing, and hit him with a fine. Such were the rewards for being competent and dedicated.

Las Vegas happenings

Around the beginning of 1976, Luedtke took me to lunch at the London Chop House behind the *Free Press* building on West Congress Street. This fabled restaurant, where Henry Ford II and other Detroit tycoon families frequently dined, was one of his favorite lunchtime haunts. But it wasn't the prime rib and well-stocked wine cellar that attracted him; it was the martinis. He was notorious for his three-martini lunch meetings. No one ever saw him eat. Amazingly, no one ever saw him drunk either.

While he sipped his first martini, he informed me that Knight-Ridder had agreed to purchase a new editorial system in the following year that would support VDTs in all departments. When the system was operational, corporate expected the *Free Press* to be composed entirely with cold type and printed with offset presses.

Luedtke then told me, as he downed his second martini, that he was promoting me and giving me a raise. I would keep the same title and desk, but I would no longer be responsible for laying out the magazine; a new graphics editor would be hired. Now I would report directly to him and devote most of my time to assisting in the planning for the new system. Without allowing me time to respond, he ordered his third martini and gave me my first assignment.

He said he had just come from a meeting with Jack Knight. Even though Knight was 81 years old and no longer chairman and CEO, he still maintained a watchful and critical eye over "his" newspapers. Editors would frequently receive tear sheets with errors, weak headlines, and other transgressions circled and annotated in his dreaded green ink.

Knight had an exacting eye for typography too, which he demonstrated during the meeting Luedtke attended. He had brought with him enlargements of several headlines he found in the sports section, which had just begun its conversion to cold type, to compare with the same size headlines he found in the front section, which still was composed with hot type. The comparison revealed they were not identical. For Knight, this was unacceptable. Someone had to fix this problem. Once again, I was the "lucky" someone.

That summer, Luedtke requested that I go with the VP for operations and other production department managers to the American Newspaper Publishers Association (ANPA) Annual Production Conference and Exhibition in Las Vegas. He wanted me to, as he put it, "kick the tires" on all of the systems and then give him a detailed comparison and evaluation.

(In the 1970s, ANPA was the preeminent newspaper trade organization representing nearly all daily newspapers. Its research institute was a major force in the development of new printing and production technologies. In 1992, the ANPA merged with seven other newspaper industry associations to form the Newspaper Association of America [NAA]. In 2016, its name was changed to the News Media Alliance [NMA], reflecting the declining fortunes of printed newspapers.)

This would be my first visit to Las Vegas. And it would be my most unforgettable. I remember landing with the production contingent in the late afternoon. Walking across the tarmac, my senses were overwhelmed by the blinding sunlight and oppressive heat. Entering the terminal, my senses were again assaulted — first by a blast of frigid air and then by the bright artificial lights, kitschy decor, and oddly alluring sounds of slot machines.

When we arrived at the Hilton Hotel, the lobby was packed with guests checking in. After waiting for over an hour, I finally got to the front desk only to discover I had been bumped. The hotel was overbooked and Luedtke's secretary had not guaranteed my room. The operations VP came to my rescue. He was a frequent Hilton guest and pulled enough weight with the manager to get me one of the rooms that Vegas hotels typically hold for their high rollers and most loyal customers who arrive without reservations.

Before going to our rooms, the VP took us to dinner on his expense account. After a gourmet meal and several glasses of wine, I opted not to go out on the town with the group. I was tired, and, to be honest, I didn't have much money of my own to spend. I assumed my room would be just like every other hotel room I had stayed in. It wasn't. It was a honeymoon suite overlooking the Strip with a round rotating bed, mirrored ceiling, and a huge Jacuzzi. Being alone in this hedonistic den felt like a cruel joke. I wondered if it actually was a joke perpetrated by the VP, especially during our gathering for breakfast the next morning when he asked me, with a wry smile, if I had "enjoyed" the room.

The Las Vegas Convention Center was mercifully linked to the hotel by an air-conditioned corridor. A sign at the entrance proclaimed the ANPA conference to be the largest exhibition of newspaper technologies in the world. More than 30,000 people from around the world were registered that year. I don't recall seeing any women in attendance from newspapers but, as I would discover, there was no shortage of women. Scantily clad young models and showgirls were employed by many of the vendors to demonstrate products while exhibiting their physical assets. After all, this was Sin City in the uninhibited seventies and most of their prospective customers were middle-aged men alone and hundreds of miles from home.

The Convention Center had more than 100 meeting rooms on two levels and a theater large enough to seat 2,000 people. Just beyond the meeting rooms, the building opened into the enormous exhibition hall where I would kick tires for five days. The cavernous space with extra high ceilings was jam-packed with vendors displaying every conceivable component of newspaper production including locomotive-size printing presses. Electronic editorial and advertising front-end system vendors were clustered together in a small fraction of the space.

Only four companies demonstrated editorial systems that summer — Hendrix, Atex, CSI, and SDC. To capture all of the information I would need for my report to Luedtke, I had prepared a 30-page packet of forms with more than 200 items to be checked on each system.

I would spend the better part of each day exercising my fingers on keyboards and taking notes. I can only imagine what the attractive women working in the booths must have thought about the thin bearded nerd who paid more attention to the computers than to them. I've never forgotten one of the women at the Hendrix booth who had unzipped her top almost to the navel. Whenever she would lean over in front of me, her ample unfettered software invited inspection. Needless to say, my attention often drifted between the display on the VDT and the display above it.

As I was preparing to leave the booth, she handed me an invitation to a cocktail party Hendrix was hosting that evening in one of the hotel's hospitality suites and coyly informed me she would be there. Later, I learned that all of the vendors hosted invitation-only cocktail parties every night of the conference.

For prospective customers, the parties were typically followed by dinners at fancy restaurants with the vendors' executives. The *Free Press* production managers and I were invited to all of the four systems vendors' parties and dinners.

The woman from Hendrix did attend the company's party. I was out of my comfort zone, but she was able to put me at ease as we spoke. Her gentle voice and breadth of knowledge about the newspaper business surprised me. Before I left the party, she let me know the source of her insights — a lawyer for one of the local papers who also happened to be her fiancé.

Not long after I returned to Detroit, Luedtke informed me that my work had been for naught. Corporate was considering a vendor that wasn't present at the ANPA exhibition to provide systems for nearly all of the company's newspapers, including the *Free Press*. The vendor was Systems Integrators Inc. (SII).

Worlds in collision

Knight-Ridder signed a contract with SII early in 1977. The first VDTs were scheduled to arrive in the spring along with next-generation phototypesetters. Before they could be installed, the *Free Press* building had to undergo major renovations.

Raised flooring and power poles to hide the proliferation of cables were the first signs of the changes to come. A collateral benefit of computerization came next. After sweating through hot, humid summers and coping with dirty air for nearly fifty years, the building would finally get what its occupants had long wished for — air conditioning. The justification for the expense, however, had little to do with improving the working environment for humans. It was because computers had less tolerance than humans for high temperatures and humidity, and even less for dust and soot.

While air conditioning was welcomed by the editors and reporters, most were not enthused about the prospect of having VDTs replace their trusty typewriters. They also were not eager to take on the typesetting functions that historically had been relegated to the "back shop." For many, the reordering of responsibilities entailed by the new front-end system was an affront to the journalism profession. They believed the changes would detrimentally affect the quality of their reporting and editing as well as diminish their status. Some declared that the day computers appeared on their desks, they would immediately resign.

For the compositors, the transition had far more serious implications — the loss of their jobs. During the renovations, relations with the composing room became increasingly contentious. The removal of a couple of Linotype machines and the addition of more easel tables for cold-type pages served to aggravate tensions to the point of open hostility.

A sleazy bar across from the *Free Press's* main entrance, appropriately nicknamed the "Green Latrine," provided the accelerants for their growing anger. More than a few compositors would return from their breaks with unsteady hands and breath reeking of alcohol.

When the first terminals and minicomputers arrived, Luedtke again promoted me without changing my title. But, this time the change came with a substantial raise and something else — an office in the *Free Press* tower. My promotion, however, also came with much greater responsibilities and challenges … and risks.

I would now be responsible for overseeing the installation of terminals in the main newsroom and several other departments as well as features. The sports editor would oversee the installation in his department. Additionally, I was tasked with writing styles (programs that contained the strings of codes required to typeset headlines, body type, and all of the other text elements) and training the editors and reporters. The DEC minicomputers would be housed in a secured room adjacent to the phototypesetters in composing and would be overseen by the information technology (IT) director who reported to the VP for operations.

After outlining my responsibilities for the editorial system, Luedtke told me this was only half of my new job — the other half would involve redesigning the *Free Press*. I could hardly contain myself. Redesigning the paper had been my ambition since I arrived. Now I would have an opportunity to take full advantage of the new system and cold-type composition.

To put a damper on my obvious excitement, Luedtke stressed that the redesign would get close scrutiny from Lee Hills, a former *Free Press* executive editor and publisher who then was the chain's chairman, and other corporate executives, including Jack Knight. He also told me that the redesign would have to be completed by the spring of '78 when the paper was scheduled to make the switch to all cold-type composition and offset printing, and that he was assigning Bill Baker, the features editor, to provide oversight.

As if that wasn't enough pressure, Luedtke made a point of telling me to be extra careful. He affirmed that the ITU already considered me its number-one enemy, and the editors were none too fond of me either. In their mindsets, I was the villain who was about to destroy their familiar industrial-age world and replace it with an alien computerized one.

He also informed me that contract negotiations with the ITU had broken down, so my work on typesetting styles and redesign prototypes would have to be done in secrecy to avoid triggering a strike. This was Luedtke's main reason for moving me from a desk in the features department to a secure office in the tower. Before the Knights relocated the company's headquarters to Miami, the tower was used for executive offices and meeting rooms. Security had been a prime concern, so operating the private elevator and accessing the stairwell required a key, and all offices had locks.

My new office on the eighth floor obviously had been unoccupied for some time. It was musty and Spartan, more like a large storage room than an executive suite. The walls needed a fresh coat of paint and the floor had a gaping hole to bring in cables for power and connections to the photo-typesetters and minicomputers.

The recently added drafting table, utility cabinet, desk, and closet filled most of the room. All were antiques, which made the VDT seem all the more like an alien technology. The office's saving graces were two north-facing windows, which afforded a slightly better view of downtown Detroit than I had had in the features department, and a new air conditioner that had been installed in one of the windows.

The tower was mostly vacant. The creaky floors and rattling elevator gave it a spooky quality, especially after dark. The only other office on my floor was occupied by someone I assumed was not employed by the *Free Press*. The sign on the door read, "Private Investigator." I never saw anyone; I only heard the door open and close once in a while.

Soon after I moved in, I met with the IT director and one of his cold-type managers away from the office to ensure privacy. The manager was responsible for maintaining the photo-typesetters and minicomputers at night. Our objective was to set up the clandestine procedures we would use for testing styles and setting type I would need for the redesign.

The plan we agreed on was to have all files from my tower VDT stored in a queue that only the cold-type manager could access. Every weeknight after all of the compositors had gone home, he would send the files to the phototypesetters and then put the output into an envelope that he would slip under my office door.

The procedures worked well for several months. By the end of summer, the prototype pages I created were approved, and I began to introduce the new fonts and typographic style changes. On the technology front, the terminals were up and running in the features and sports departments, and preparations were underway for installing them in the main newsroom and other departments.

Then all hell broke loose. Somehow the compositors got tipped off about what I was doing. (I remember wondering at the time if the private investigator across the hall from my office might have been hired by the unions.) My first hint of the troubles that were brewing came in the envelope I opened one morning. The cold-type manager had inserted a poster he found circulating in the composing room. In his note to me, he said one of the other managers had seen another one taped to the dart board in the Green Latrine. The poster was a photo of me with a bullseye across my face. The text positioned below my face read "Tower Rat."

I promptly took the poster to Luedtke's office. He also had a copy and was seemingly as alarmed as I; however, his advice did little to calm my nerves. Keep your door locked at all times he said, which I already had been doing. He also urged me to stay out of sight by making sure I didn't arrive or depart during meal breaks and shift changes. I was already doing that. What about having a security guard escort me out of the building? We both decided that was a bad idea as it would only draw more attention to me as the unions' Public Enemy Number One.

In short, I was on my own. The situation made me jumpy, especially when walking between the office and my home. Fortunately, there was only one serious incident. A man, whom I assumed was a compositor, verbally threatened to break my kneecaps as he was leaving the Green Latrine, but luckily his friends prevented him from carrying out his threat.

I wasn't the only target of the compositors' anger. Luedtke along with the sports editor, IT director, cold-type managers, and others involved with the conversion also received threats. I didn't know until then that negotiations were entering a new, more confrontational phase.

The *Free Press* was offering production department buy-outs and moving aggressively to complete the conversion to all cold-type composition. Resistance from the ITU was evident in the frequent slowdowns and increasing harassment of editors. On a number of occasions, photos were altered provocatively on cold-type pages just before they went to press. A few managed to make it all the way through the print run to readers' doorsteps.

Resistance from newsroom editors and the Guild also was mounting but not to the degree of the compositors and ITU. Mostly it took the form of delaying tactics. At one point, the Guild proposed hiring some of the displaced compositors to work as VDT operators and typesetters alongside editors in the newsroom. That idea was quickly nixed ... by the ITU.

To avoid disrupting the main newsroom, we installed the terminals early on a Sunday morning. When the senior news editor, who had been with the *Free Press* for decades and had become something of a legend, arrived the next day, he was true to his word. As soon as he saw the terminal on his desk, he submitted his prepared resignation to the managing editor and walked out.

Reporters were none too happy with the terminals either. But their complaint wasn't so much about the VDTs on their desks; it was about the VDTs that were NOT on their desks. Someone in corporate had decided that four reporters could share one terminal. Contention for the limited number of mobile reporter terminals often came close to resulting in fist-fights and got Luedtke's attention. Within a few months, all of the reporters had terminals.

The job that didn't exist

By spring of '78, the new electronic publishing system was fully operational and the conversion to cold-type composition and offset printing was complete. The last elements of the redesign appeared on the third of April. Hills and Knight had expressed some concerns about the extra-bold typeface and rules I used for logos and flags but otherwise seemed pleased with the new look. Luedtke apparently was pleased, too, because he changed my title to design director and put me in charge of the art and photo departments. The editorial system would no longer be my responsibility although I would continue to write style programs.

What a difference four years made. The features depart-ment where I began now was clean and uncluttered; there were no stacks of old newspapers, the new desks with VDTs were orderly, and all windows were closed. Few vestiges of the old office could be seen. The same was true for the main news-room and most other editorial departments.

While the makeover gave the offices a more modern, organized appearance, it did not please everyone. Many of the editors and reporters lamented that they now felt as if they were working in a dreary insurance office, nothing like their former untidy, noisy, exciting, and wonderful old newsroom. I had to agree. But, as with all transitions, some things were lost. That could not be avoided. For the newspaper industry, computerization was a matter of survival.

What was lost in the production departments, however, was far more painful for the workers. The caldron of molten lead along with the Linotype machines, turtles, and chases were all gone; as were nearly three quarters of the compositors. The cavernous space with neat rows of easel tables now was as quiet as a library reading room. The pungent smells of hot lead, ink, and sweat were a fading memory. Shallow ruts in the parquet flooring were the only remaining hints of the heavy-metal world that was.

A few weeks after I assumed my new position, Luedtke and Baker arranged for me to participate in the company's program for evaluating potential future executives. It involved two days of role-playing and problem-solving exercises in addition to taking a battery of tests in Miami. The program culminated in an interview with Ivan Jones, the director of personnel.

After reviewing my performance, Jones told me my intelligence, creativity, and tenacity rankings were among the highest he had seen, but I exhibited strong altruistic tendencies and tended to avoid conflicts. I wasn't sure if he considered my willingness to help others achieve their goals was a good or bad quality. He also said he worried about my ability to manage time efficiently. This was based on his observation that I hadn't worn a watch.

Despite these concerns, he said I qualified for a management track that could ultimately lead to my becoming an executive editor at one of the chain's newspapers. He obviously was taken back when I thanked him and then said I wasn't interested in going that route. He seemed even more perplexed when I told him of my goal to become a newspaper design and technology consultant, either on my own or for a chain. All he could say before sending me on my way was: "That title doesn't exist."

I assumed Jones must have shared my evaluation and contrarian goal with Baker and Luedtke because when I returned from Miami, Baker told me he had a consulting job for me. Larry Allison, the editor of Knight-Ridder's two former Ridder papers in Long Beach, California — the morning *Independent* and evening *Press-Telegram*, had inquired about having me assist with their redesign projects. Other newspapers soon followed with requests for my assistance. All across the country, newspaper designers suddenly were in demand.

This surge of redesign projects didn't come as a complete surprise. I had been anticipating it since my final year at the *St. Petersburg Times*. While I was working on the redesign that Nelson Poynter, the owner and publisher, had requested, I remembered him telling the staff how important it was for newspapers to change with the times. He was right. As Bob Dylan foretold a decade earlier, the times were indeed a-changin'.

The societal upheavals of the sixties and the economic and political turmoil of the early seventies had set the stage for radical changes in lifestyles that would confront publishers just as the leading edge of the baby boom generation was coming of age. Coincidentally, the transition to cold-type composition and installation of electronic publishing systems had provided the impetus and the means for newspapers to at least change the way they presented their contents. With hot-type composition, typography and design had always been constrained by the industrial-age technologies. Lead type had inalterable attributes. Rigid rules defined by machines and compositors severely restricted page layouts.

Cold-type composition and electronic publishing systems did away with most of the former constraints and uncorked a wellspring of creativity. Computerized phototypesetters afforded the freedom to alter the attributes of type in ways that previously were inconceivable. By transferring authority over page production from composing to the newsroom, the old rules could be broken and layouts could take almost any imaginable form (for better or for worse).

As I became more involved in redesign projects, I saw a need for a newsletter about newspaper design and graphics. Toward the end of the year, I incorporated Source Publications, with Luedtke's and Baker's approval, and began gathering material for a bimonthly newsletter that I titled the *Newspaper Design Notebook*. I published the first issue at the beginning of January 1979. It attracted several hundred paying subscribers and an invitation to participate later that month in the founding meeting of the Society of Newspaper Design.

On the last day of the meeting, I received an enigmatic call. It was from James K. Batten, the Knight-Ridder vice-president for news. He politely but firmly requested that I grab the first available flight to Miami. All he revealed was that he urgently needed to meet with me about a matter of great importance to the company. Little did I realize that I was about to embark on an adventure that would involve me in the next stage in the computerizing of newspapers — the development of digital alternatives to ink printed on paper and the birth of online media.

Author's notes

My marriage to Lucille and relationship with our two children, which had been on the mend during my first years at the *Free Press*, faltered again as I became more engaged in the digital future of newspapers. The root cause was time — the increasing amount I was devoting to my work and taking from my family. This also had been the source of our marital problems during my years at the *St. Petersburg Times*. However, the personal reasons in Detroit were quite different from those that had inflicted so much emotional damage in Florida.

At the *Times*, the boot-camp ordeal I endured had demanded nearly all of my time with few rewards other than keeping my job. In addition to depriving me of time with my family and damaging my marriage, it sapped my confidence and sense of self-worth. At the *Free Press*, I had volunteered my time because the assignments were challenging and exciting, and they gave me a renewed sense of purpose and accomplishment. However, my indomitable drive to please and prove my worth professionally soon overshadowed my personal life.

My dogged involvement with the *Free Press* editorial system and redesign project, combined with frequent traveling for Knight-Ridder during my last three years in Detroit, took a toll on my marriage and relationship with my children. Lucille and I grew apart again. Only once in those years did we take a family vacation together.

CHAPTER FOUR

Online Media's Premature Birth

By the end of the seventies, television — the new media of that time — had already vanquished most of the visually rich, large-format national magazines, such as *Life, Look,* and *Saturday Evening Post,* that once were read by millions of Americans each week. With the launch of Ted Turner's Cable News Network (CNN) — the first 24/7 news channel — on June 1, 1980, cable TV in the United States emerged from the shadows cast by the big-three broadcast networks — ABC, CBS, and NBC — to become an even more formidable competitor to print media.

While computerization had significantly reduced the fixed costs of publishing and improved the newspaper industry's overall financial health, publishers reluctantly had to accept that they were still losing their battle for the attention and dollars of increasingly television-centric news consumers and advertisers. And, if that wasn't worrisome enough, a new electronic publishing technology was emerging that could circumvent newspapers by providing direct on-demand access to vast stores of news and information via telephone lines connected to television sets.

In 1979, Knight-Ridder decided to confront this potential threat head-on by secretly recruiting a team to field test the technology and then launching what would be America's first consumer online service. Even though the chain's costly, pioneering effort to commercialize this new media ultimately failed, it paved the way for widespread adoption of the internet and web that, by the turn of the century, would have dire consequences for daily newspapers.

'What You Want — When You Want It'

The sign above the kiosk in the Miami mall declared "The Waiting is Over... What You Want — When You Want It," and urged shoppers to "Touch the Future." The "future" resided in an unassuming rectangular white plastic box with a black faceplate called the "Sceptre" that was connected to a telephone line and an ordinary color television set.

A salesperson with a small wireless keypad mesmerized the gathered shoppers by magically calling up pages of text and images on the TV screen. In addition to displaying the latest news stories and weather reports, the salesperson demonstrated how the Sceptre could be used for shopping, banking, playing games, and communicating with electronic mail, as well as for accessing libraries, airline schedules, restaurant menus, movie guides, and much more.

The date was October 30, 1983. This was the public debut of Viewtron, the first consumer videotex service in America and a harbinger of the online media future. It was the culmination of more than five years of research and development by

Knight-Ridder and AT&T, then the largest telecommunications company in the world. I was an original member of Knight-Ridder's Viewtron development team.

At the time, nearly all of those who had participated in the gestation of Viewtron felt certain they were touching the future. Marketing firms and securities analysts tended to agree with them. Most optimistically predicted that videotex services would become ubiquitous, hugely profitable businesses by the end of the century, though some foresaw a more ominous future in which this new media would diminish or even supplant printed newspapers.

Both predictions proved to be correct; only the underlying technologies and online business models were wrong. All of the videotex services operated by newspaper companies, including Viewtron, failed to attract large enough audiences to make them profitable and consequently were shut down within a few years. Today, videotex technologies and the commercial services they spawned have been reduced to footnotes in the history of online media.

Nonetheless, the notion of "What You Want— When You Want It" and practically all of the content categories and services developed for Viewtron lived on — first with America OnLine (AOL) and Prodigy, and then with the commercial internet and web. Many of the more than 250 people who had been employed by Viewtron went on to work for companies that were developing more advanced online media technologies. And many of the more than 20,000 early adopters who had subscribed to Viewtron went on to become the evangelists, developers, and customers for the next generations of online services.

An offer I couldn't refuse

My involvement with Viewtron began with a Sunday afternoon phone call on my 36th birthday — January 21, 1979.
That weekend I was participating in the founding meeting of
the Society of Newspaper Design at the Buck Hill Inn, a resort
in the Poconos near Allentown, Pennsylvania. The caller was
James K. Batten, then Knight-Ridder's vice president for
news. He wasn't calling to wish me a happy birthday. He was
calling to request my presence at corporate headquarters in
Miami for an urgent meeting. He wouldn't divulge what it was
about but insisted that I get there ASAP. The following
morning, I drove through a snowstorm to catch my flight back
to Detroit, where I was living at the time, and then hopped a
red-eye flight to Miami.

The corporate headquarters was on the sixth floor of the
Miami Herald building. Batten's office, like those of the other
senior executives, faced east overlooking Biscayne Bay and the
Venetian Isles. The view could not have been more different
than the view of grey buildings and parking lots from my office
in the *Detroit Free Press* building. With the brilliant morning
sunlight sparkling on the placid turquoise water below and the
lush green tropical foliage crowning the islands in the distance,
I had to remind myself it was still mid-winter.

My initial nervousness was alleviated by Batten's warm
greeting. I had met him on several occasions but never had an
opportunity to converse with him. After a few minutes of casual
banter to put me at ease, he informed me in a serious tone that
what he was about to tell me was highly confidential, not be
shared with anyone, not even my wife.

Knight-Ridder, he said, was secretly embarking on a venture that could have profound implications for the future of the company and the newspaper business. He called it Knight-Ridder's "Manhattan Project," evoking the top-secret U.S. project that developed the atomic bomb during the Second World War.

Before revealing anything about the venture, Batten wanted to know if I would have a problem with traveling to England in the next week or two and with relocating to Miami. I was enthralled by the prospect of participating in a secret project that had something to do with the future of newspapers and by the opportunity to travel to England, so no way was I going to decline even though I knew moving to Miami could pose a problem for my marriage.

Once I accepted Batten's preconditions, he explained that Dr. Norman Morrison, the corporate director of information systems, had alerted him to a new technology developed by the British Post Office (BPO) called videotex that could connect television sets to electronic warehouses of news and information via phone lines. He said he had gone to England the previous summer with Morrison and several other Knight-Ridder executives to learn more about this technology and Prestel, a public videotex service the BPO was preparing to launch in the upcoming spring. Publishers, advertising firms, travel agencies, and education institutions were being actively recruited to serve as "information providers" for the Prestel service.

(Later I learned the BPO in those days was a government monopoly that, in addition to the mail services, controlled all telephone lines and television cables and leased nearly all telephones and television sets throughout the United Kingdom.

Its telecommunications division, which was spun off in 1981 to become British Telecom, had research laboratories comparable to AT&T's Bell Labs in the United States. The BPO originally called the technology viewdata, but videotex, without the final "t", soon became the more widely adopted term.)

Batten admitted they saw videotex more as a potential threat than as an opportunity. After meeting with their counterparts at the Eastern Counties Newspapers Group in Norwich, one of the first newspaper companies to sign on as a Prestel information provider, they concluded that whatever the future might hold, proactive action was needed. Instead of waiting for other companies to exploit this technology, they proposed that Knight-Ridder should act quickly to preempt possible competitors.

Their first act after returning to Miami, he said, was to commission a short video to show board members and potential partners how a commercial videotex service might be used by American families. Upon securing board approval, Batten began assembling a team, headed by Morrison, to develop a Prestel-like service. Batten informed me that John Woolley, the *Free Press* business editor, would be responsible for all content as the team's senior editor.

My role, Batten said, would be to oversee the creation of content pages as the team's "graphics guy." He instructed me, as he had the other team members, not to reveal my involvement with the videotex project. To provide cover, he said he would name me as the corporate design and newsroom technology consultant for the company's newspapers. I was happily surprised because the title he chose was the same one the company's personnel director said didn't exist when I suggested it the previous year during my interview in Miami.

In this position, Batten thought I would only need to spend about half of my time, at least initially, on the videotex project. The other half would be spent working with Knight-Ridder's newspapers on design, graphics, and electronic publishing projects as I had been doing since 1976. I accepted the dual-hat arrangement without a second thought.

The secret mission

Ten days later I was on a plane to London. It was early morning on Saturday, February 3, when the bus from Heathrow airport arrived at Victoria Station. The weather was brisk as I made my way to the nearby taxi stand. A lone man with a large suitcase and heavy topcoat was waiting there. He appeared to be about my age. My first thought was that he might be one of the other videotex team members. I knew it was a long shot, but I decided to ask him anyway if he was going to the Portman Hotel, where the team had reservations for the night. After a brief hesitation, he said yes and then asked me if I worked for Knight-Ridder. That's how Mort Goldstrom, the team's advertising consultant, and I met for the first time. In the taxi, I learned he was an advertising executive with Knight-Ridder Newspaper Sales based in New York City.

When we arrived at the hotel, John was waiting for us with Kebby Kebschall, the *Miami Herald's* operations manager who would be the team's production consultant. At check-in, Mort and I discovered he was registered as "Adlai Adguy" and I was registered as "Desi Artguy." With a wink, John whispered these were the secret code names Batten had chosen for us.

The Portman Hotel was selected because it was the first hotel in England to provide guests with access to Prestel. This was to be our introduction to the world of videotex before moving on to Norwich, where we were to receive hands-on training. That was not to be. The service was down for routine maintenance that weekend.

But not all was lost. In our rooms, we discovered the TV sets had been recently adapted to access two teletext services — Ceefax and Oracle. These services used an interactive broadcast technology, also developed by the BPO, to display text on TV screens in a fashion similar to videotex. Teletext took advantage of the empty spaces that separated video frames for display on television systems, called vertical blanking intervals or VBIs, to sequentially broadcast several hundred frame-size pages of textual content in continuous loops.

With a special decoder and a numeric keypad, viewers could request a specific frame of information by entering the appropriate page number, much like changing channels with a remote control. As soon as the page ran past the decoder, it was grabbed and displayed. The page would stay on the screen until the viewer requested another page or switched back to regular television programming. This technology was relatively inexpensive and easy to implement as well as uncomplicated and simple to use. But, to achieve this level of simplicity and efficiency, the content and presentation had to be severely restricted.

We spent most of our first day in London playing with these services. The pages provided snippets of information, such as weather forecasts, airline schedules, sports scores, and brief news items. The crudeness of the graphics troubled me; most were just decorations.

The next day, as we journeyed by train through the English countryside to Norwich, we were frequently looking over our shoulders, suspicious of everyone. James Bonds we were not.

We arrived at dusk. Our hotel was located in the heart of the city near the Norwich Castle, just a short walk from the train station. Kebby had whet our appetites for a traditional English dinner by suggesting that we should find a public house where we could dine on Beef Wellington or cottage pie. To our dismay, we learned all pubs were closed on Sundays.

On Monday morning, we began our training session at the Eastern Counties Newspapers Group headquarters. My assignment was to master the frame creation terminal (FCT) and then produce pages for a Miami tourism site. Knight-Ridder had committed to be a Prestel information provider in partnership with the Norwich group not long after Batten's visit.

As with the teletext pages, content and graphics were necessarily constrained by the low resolution of standard television screens. Videotex pages had the added constraint of slow, error-prone data transmissions across standard phone lines. Each page in this early presentation format, called alpha-mosaic, had a maximum of 20 lines of text in only one type size and style. Each line was limited to 40 characters. Small colored squares called tiles were used to construct the graphics.

All of the pages were first drawn on quad-ruled paper using colored pencils and then placed on storyboards. Videotex systems organized pages in a logic-tree structure with hierarchical menus that had numbered options between 0 and 9. Each option linked to a branch of sequential pages, which often included more menus.

Creating graphics with the FCT was challenging, but by the end of the day I was already turning out acceptable pages. I'm a perfectionist, so, if I didn't like a page, I would not hesitate to delete it and create a new one. This surprised my colleagues who later told Batten how I had deleted a page that a Norwich artist had worked on for several hours and then recreated a better page in less than 30 minutes. This somewhat embellished story of how I quickly transitioned from student to teacher became one of Batten's and John's favorite stories to tell about me, especially after we learned that our Miami tourism site was officially recognized as one of the most popular on the Prestel service in 1979.

Upon our return from England, Knight-Ridder quietly formed a joint-venture relationship with AT&T to launch a commercial service. In addition to providing communications, AT&T's Bell Labs was to develop the FCTs and customer terminals. Knight-Ridder was to be responsible for the content, host computers, management, and marketing.

Within a few weeks, Knight-Ridder created a wholly owned subsidiary called Viewdata Corporation of America (VCA), named Hal Jurgensmeyer (the visionary VP for operations who had initiated the computerizing of KR newspapers) as VCA's president, and began making plans for a market trial that Morrison code named "Bowsprit." (He and many of the other Knight-Ridder executives owned sailboats; hence the use of a sailing term meant to suggest moving forward.) To accommodate the host computers and staff that would be required for the trial, the company leased space on the second and third floors of the 1444 Building on Biscayne Boulevard about two blocks west of the *Miami Herald*.

A new career path with consequences

I wouldn't be needed on the videotex project until after the move into the new offices was completed and the computers were installed, so I put on my new corporate newspaper consultant hat and went back to winter in Detroit. In the three weeks I had been away, the direction of my life and career had taken a sudden, unexpected turn. Now I had to deal with how moving to Miami would affect my wife and children.

My agreement with Batten prevented me from telling Lucille about the videotex project. All I could share with her was my promotion to a new role as a corporate consultant, and that it required my relocating to the Knight-Ridder head-quarters. She wasn't surprised. She knew that was my goal but was adamant about not returning to Florida; too many bad memories remained from the three years I spent working for the *St. Petersburg Times*. She asserted that if I was determined to move to Miami, staying in Detroit was not an option for her and our two children. Our compromise was to find a college town where there were good public schools and she could find fulfilling work.

A decision on the location would have to wait until Lucille finished her last semester at Wayne State University and our children started their summer break. I also would need time away to complete several KR newspaper projects before I could take vacation time.

In May, Lucille graduated with a bachelor's degree in public relations and was inducted into the Phi Beta Kappa Honor Society. This was now 12 years after we had both dropped out of the University of Oregon. I was too focused on my California projects to attend her graduation.

The following month, we visited prospective college towns in several Southern states with our children. She finally decided on Chapel Hill, North Carolina. During our follow-up visit, we made a down payment on a townhouse. Owning a house in a small town with a university and community newspaper where we could work was Lucille's dream, but not mine.

After moving our possessions from Detroit and settling in the new home, we amicably agreed on a separation with the provisos that I would remain involved in our children's lives and would continue to provide financial support. Even though we both understood there would be no reconciliation this time, she insisted that we not tell our children about our separation and not file for a divorce until they were older; a decision we would later regret.

When I returned to Miami in September, the videotex team had already moved into its new offices and the programmers were busy bringing the computers online. My task was to hire and train the graphic artists who would work with me to create pages for the market trial.

Preparing for the Viewtron market trial

Near the end of 1979, Albert Gillen, the head of Knight-Ridder's television division, was named president of VCA to replace Jurgensmeyer, whose health was declining. Gillen had joined Knight-Ridder in 1977 when the company acquired Poole Broadcasting where he had been a senior executive. His television perspective would have a significant influence on the company's assumptions about how the videotex service would be perceived and used by customers.

One of Gillen's first priorities was to give a name to the service. In typical corporate fashion, he formed a naming committee, which included me along with the other original team members. After a couple of weeks, we still had not come up with a name he liked. Then, at what would be our last committee meeting, he abruptly walked into the room and told us the name had come to him in a dream — it would be "Viewtron." And, with that said, he immediately dismissed us.

Now that we had a name for the service, production ramped up. Our goal was to offer more than 10,000 pages of news, information, and ads every day from 6 a.m. to midnight. Only about a third of the pages would have to be created manually by the artists before the launch. These were called "cold" pages because their content was unlikely to change during the course of the trial. They included travel guides, restaurant menus, health care manuals, Spanish lessons, and games. The so-called "hot" pages included news stories, weather forecasts, sports scores, airline schedules, shopping items, and all other content that was likely to change frequently. For these pages, the computer would flow text into predesigned templates.

At one of our first planning meetings, Batten implored us to make sure the database of pages had depth as well as breadth. He worried about creating, as he put it, "a large pie with a beautiful, enticing crust and no filling." He also wanted us to make it easy for participants to find what they wanted. Providing deep content was not too difficult; making it easy for participants to navigate was.

Unlike newspapers, videotex services could not be easily browsed, and unlike the future World Wide Web, they could not be searched. The hierarchical menu system, which was originally conceived to simplify navigation and reduce access time, more often than not only succeeded in confounding subscribers and extending their time online. The logic tree was so large that navigating from the main menu to a page of interest could require working through seven or eight layers of menus. With ten options to choose from on each menu, the process was more like taking a multiple-choice quiz than reading a newspaper.

The only way participants could get directly to a specific page with Viewtron was by keying in its unique system number. But listing all of the pages or even just the menus with their system numbers in an online directory would not have been practical or useful. Our workaround was to give participants a printed directory that categorized and listed the branch menus with information about the contents of each branch. This solution not only made locating pages of interest somewhat easier, it also generated additional advertising revenue from printed ads.

The trial and the verdict

The original Bowsprit plan called for placing modified color TV sets in 150-160 homes in Coral Gables, an affluent suburb of Miami, over a six-month period beginning in the spring of 1980. AT&T would supply the TV sets with built-in videotex controllers and modems (devices used to transmit computer data via phone lines). They were essentially "dumb" personal computers that could not be used for anything other than accessing the Viewtron service.

Only those families judged as most likely to become early adopters were selected. Researchers led by Dr. Philip Meyer, the corporate director for news research, reasoned that if people who already were predisposed to buying and using new technologies disliked the service, it would have little chance of succeeding in the consumer market. If the opposite were true, they believed the service at least had a fair chance of becoming a profitable business.

When the trial finally launched on July 14, 1980, 34 families had Viewtron TV sets. They would be given free access for between two and three months, after which the TV sets would be given to another 34 families. At the end of the trial 14 months later, 204 families had used the Viewtron service that by then would have more than 15,000 pages of accessible content.

Throughout the trial, Meyer and his research team conducted frequent interviews and analyzed volumes of usage data captured by the Viewtron mainframe computers. Their main objectives were to understand how the selected families used the service and to learn how much they might be willing to pay if it became commercially available.

Feedback from the families always was encouraging. They told us they liked what the service offered, especially all the news and shopping information. And they were genuinely sad when they had to give up their Viewtron TV sets and free access.

For those of us who had midwifed Bowsprit, the experience provided important lessons about market research as well as about human nature and electronic publishing. The crucial lesson became obvious when the information garnered from personal interviews was compared with the actual usage data — In the real-world people do not always want what they say they want, or do what they say they do.

Comparing what was said in interviews with actual usage was an alarming wake-up call. Participants were using the service far more for communicating with other participants than for gaining access to news, general information, and advertising. Meyer's team found that users rarely spent more than a few minutes reading content on their TV screens, and they almost always did it alone. Here was a clear case where market research debunked preconceived notions, but those notions were too deeply embedded in the corporate mindset.

Nearly everyone at Knight-Ridder who came from a newspaper background envisioned Viewtron as an advertiser-supported electronic newspaper that subscribers would use to consume content much as they did with printed newspapers. And they saw VCA centrally controlling content, presentation, and distribution in the same way that newspapers controlled everything.

In Gillen's alternative TV-shaped view, family members would share and use Viewtron the way he believed they watched television in those days — happily sitting around the TV set and casually discussing what they saw on the screen. This unreal interactive television image would be replicated visually in almost all of Viewtron's marketing materials.

The researchers concluded that both notions were wrong. Viewtron was neither an electronic newspaper nor an interactive television. They surmised that it actually was more of a social medium. Their conclusions were ignored. After Meyer submitted his final Bowsprit reports, he resigned to become a journalism professor at the University of North Carolina in Chapel Hill. Jenny Fielder would take over his role and later become the VP for research.

Back in the print world

In the period between the Bowsprit launch and the ramp up for the commercial service, only a few artists were needed to create frames. Those who were not needed were assigned to customer support services. In addition to answering questions and helping solve problems, they were used to purchase merchandise, shop for groceries, make deliveries, and perform a host of other tasks to fulfill the orders and requests that Viewtron subscribers made online.

I wasn't needed at VCA most of that time either, so I went back to consulting on newspaper projects. Actually, I had already begun working on projects for the *Wall Street Journal* and the *Miami Herald* toward the end of 1979.

The *WSJ*, then owned by Dow Jones, had grown to be the largest daily newspaper in the United States with more than 1.6 million mostly affluent readers all across the country. On many days, demand from national advertisers for space would push the historically one-section broadsheet newspaper to its maximum printing capacity of 64 pages. To accommodate more advertising, the owners decided to add a second section.

I was one of five design consultants retained by the *WSJ* to create prototypes for the new section front. Knight-Ridder and the *WSJ* were not competitors, so Batten approved. After more than six months and several iterations, they finally launched the two-section *WSJ* on June 23, 1980. The final design was a synthesis of elements from several prototypes including mine. (The paper later added more sections.)

The *Miami Herald* redesign project was initiated in a more typical newspaper manner. After seeing a presentation of my *Free Press* redesign at a Knight-Ridder editors meeting, John McMullan, the *Herald's* executive editor, and Bob Ingle, the managing editor, asked me to create prototypes for a redesign. My work with Viewtron and *WSJ* would consume most of my time in the first half of 1980, so I recruited Rolf Rehe, a typography consultant, to assist me.

As with the *Free Press*, the prototypes were reviewed by Lee Hills, then Knight-Ridder's chairman. He had initiated a major redesign of the *Herald* in the early fifties when he was the paper's managing editor. This was my first opportunity to meet Hills. Like Batten, he was personable and unpretentious.

While he had a keen interest in typography and my design concepts, he also was politely inquisitive about my life and goals.

After Hills gave his stamp of approval, Ingle put together a plan for incrementally introducing the redesign to readers. The first section to display the new look would be a weekly business tabloid called "Business Monday."

As was typical of newspapers in those days, this new section was conceived by editors without consulting the advertising department or conducting market research. Using content suggested by the business editors, I created a 16-page prototype. Several hundred copies were printed and given to the advertising staff for use as sales tools. They initially argued that there would not be enough new advertising to support it. In this case, they were proven wrong. The section launched in September 1980 with 54 pages. Nearly 70 percent of the space was ads; most were new.

The financial success of the *Herald's* Business Monday encouraged other KR papers to launch similar sections; nearly all were profitable. That was not typical. Most new sections were launched by KR editors to fill perceived needs without considering profitability.

As the *Herald's* editors gained confidence with the design, the formatted elements were stepped into the rest of the paper over a four-month period. The last to change was the front page in January 1981. I would not be in Miami most of that time. Batten had diverted me to work on two projects he said had higher priority: A redesign of the Fort Wayne, Indiana, *News Sentinel*, which Knight-Ridder had just purchased, and implementation of the chain's first fully integrated pagination system at the *Star-News* in Pasadena, California.

One of the perks was the opportunity to occasionally fly with Batten in the corporate jet to the locations where I would be consulting. During those flights and our meals together, we got to know each other on a personal level. What developed was a bond based on trust and mutual respect that was as close to an honest friendship as a corporate executive can afford to have with a subordinate.

The man I found behind the friendly but stoic executive mask was much more complex and introspective than his public persona revealed. After a while, Batten confided that he had been happiest during his tenure as the editor of the *Charlotte Observer* in North Carolina. In those years, he said, he believed he knew what he was doing and where newspapers were heading; now, with all of the changes being wrought by new technologies and the growing emphasis on profits, he wasn't so sure. He intimated that he often felt as if he was wandering in uncharted territory where, with every step he took, he risked falling into quicksand.

The Batten I got to know in '80 and '81 also was much more pessimistic about the future of newspapers in private than he conveyed publicly. During one of our late-evening meals at a nearly deserted diner in Fort Wayne, he openly vented his animosity toward those he saw endangering newspapers and journalism, as well as democracy, through their insatiable greed.

He told me that when Jack Knight lured him to Miami in 1975 to be the newly merged company's vice president for news, he thought he would be in a position to protect the core values of Knight Newspapers — quality journalism and public service — from the "bad guys." I assumed he meant the former Ridder Publications executives who were known for caring more about profits than journalism. While Batten understood his role in a public corporation required him to balance the demands of journalism and business, he said he soon realized he was outgunned by a more formidable and dangerous external adversary — Wall Street analysts who demanded year-over-year profit growth at the expense of Knight's core values. In his view, they represented the lowest form of life and the greatest threat to the future of newspapers.

Retooling for the commercial service

A few months before the Bowsprit trial concluded, Knight-Ridder leased the top floors of a new office building on Lincoln Road in the Art Deco district of South Miami Beach to accommodate the much larger array of computers and staff that VCA would need to support the commercial service. The roll out was tentatively planned for the spring of '83.

Around September 1981, the Knight-Ridder and AT&T executives made a fateful decision. They moved to adopt a new, more advanced videotex technology called the North American Presentation Layer Protocol Standard. The main advantage of NAPLPS (pronounced nap-lips) was its ability to eliminate the coarse appearance of Bowsprit pages. Instead of constructing pages with tiles, artists would be able to create more sophisticated graphics using a variety of geometric shapes and employ more than one type style and size.

All of us believed these enhancements would make Viewtron more appealing to both subscribers and advertisers, but the perceived benefits would come at a high price. Changing to the NAPLS alpha-geometric format would require a time-consuming and costly do-over because none of the software and pages created for the Bowsprit trial would be usable for the commercial service. And, as should have been expected, not all would go smoothly.

When AT&T delivered the first frame creation terminal (FCT) that fall, we were elated by its capabilities but not by its $42,000 price tag, which was nearly an order of magnitude more than originally budgeted. Despite the initial sticker shock, we had to acknowledge that the FCT was a remarkable computer graphics system for its time. Engineers from Bell Labs were justly proud of its advanced drawing tools, but most of all they were excited by its color palette that allowed artists to choose from 64-million combinations of hues, shades, and intensities.

No one seemed concerned that the low-resolution NTSC television standard used in American home TV sets could not distinguish more than about 100 colors. Or that unlike the FCTs with their high-resolution RGB monitors, the colors on home television picture tubes could not be precisely controlled. For reasons unknown to us, Bell Labs would take nearly a year longer than anticipated to finalize the customer terminal design and start production. Consequently, we had no way of knowing how the pages we were creating would appear on subscribers' home TV sets.

We could not afford to delay page creation until AT&T delivered a customer terminal. So, because they were available on the FCTs, we used all of the tools and colors at our disposal to create spectacular pages. As slides for presentations they were fabulous; as videotex pages they would be a disaster.

The disconnect between the Bell Labs engineers who designed the FCT and the engineers assigned to the customer terminal should have troubled us much earlier than it did. From the beginning of our planning for Viewtron's commercial launch, it was apparent that AT&T did not have a grasp on how the customer terminal should be designed.

For the Bowsprit trial, AT&T had modified standard color TV sets. At one point, AT&T proposed a hybrid videophone, but that was not considered a viable option for the commercial service. The VCA's preferred concept was a console similar to the ones used for video games that could be easily plugged into existing home TV sets and telephone lines.

When we finally received the first shipment of Sceptre customer terminals in the summer of '82, we discovered just how blinded we had been by our great expectations. In anticipation, we had set up about a dozen color TV sets of different brands and sizes in a small conference room. We expected some problems, but none of us was prepared for what we saw.

We were speechless. Most of the contrasting colors we had so carefully chosen on the FCTs for the text and backgrounds could not be differentiated on home TV sets. Additionally, all our efforts to match the colors used in corporate logos, sports insignias, and the like had been for naught. A blue logo on the FCT might appear green on some home TV sets and purple on others.

Even more troubling were the graphics. On the FCTs, they had displayed quickly, so none of us gave much thought to how much time they would require to display on home TV sets. Our first tests revealed that even simple graphics could take 10-20 seconds; some graphics took up to a minute, which felt like an eternity. We were faced with the hard truth that much of our work had been wasted effort. Most of the graphics would need to be simplified or deleted in order to accommodate the Sceptre's limitations. (In the early eighties, its data transfer rate of 1,200 bits per second was considered fast. Today, even a million bits per second is considered slow.)

Disappointments with the Sceptre, however, were not confined to color and graphics. All business planning with AT&T had assumed that home terminals would cost less than $200, which is what our researchers had determined was the maximum subscribers would be willing to pay. But soon after we received the first Sceptres, AT&T revealed the actual price would be closer to $1,000.

After some intense negotiations, AT&T finally agreed to let VCA sell it below its cost for $600. This would be in addition to the $12 monthly subscription price for the Viewtron service. (In May 1984, VCA switched from selling Sceptres to renting them. The monthly subscription price for new customers was raised to $39.95 to include the rental fee.)

Even though Knight-Ridder's executives had misgivings, they felt the company was too deeply committed to do anything other than proceed. The launch date, which was planned for March, had to be postponed twice, mainly due to problems with the Sceptre, but AT&T's legal problems also contributed to the delays. In 1983, it was preparing for the court-ordered breakup of the Bell System monopoly.

The reckoning

When the service finally went public on October 30, 1983, Knight-Ridder and AT&T acted quickly with much fanfare to make Viewtron a household name in South Florida. The staff, which had grown from around 30 during the Bowsprit trial to more the 250, was exuberant. All were certain they were embarking on twenty-first-century careers.

As with so many promising ventures, the future took a different path. Even after the company introduced Viewtron in multiple cities and made its services accessible on personal computers, VCA showed no signs of being able to turn a profit. The money subscribers and advertisers were willing to pay in the eighties proved to be inadequate to cover the unexpectedly high production and marketing costs.

Early in 1986, John Woolley presented Knight-Ridder with an eleventh-hour plan to abandon the Sceptre terminal and convert Viewtron into a smaller computer-based online service focused on PC users, but it was too late. When the research confirmed again that subscribers were using the service mostly for email and text messaging rather than news feeds, regardless if they were using a Sceptre or PC, Viewtron's fate was sealed. Knight-Ridder pulled the plug on March 31, 1986. Gateway, another major American videotex service launched in 1984 by the Times Mirror chain in Southern California, met the same fate earlier that month.

Many reasons have been given for the failure of these early commercial online services, but the simple truth is they were too ambitious for their time. From today's vantage point, it's obvious that the technologies and markets for electronic access to news and information in the eighties were not ready.

Most phones were still hardwired to walls. Transferring data across home telephone lines was excruciatingly slow and error-prone. Television sets and personal computer monitors relied on low-resolution picture tubes that were not designed for reading. And the videotex menu structure was not suitable for conveniently retrieving content from large databases.

While personal computers would provide a more robust technology for online services, they had only just begun to penetrate the consumer market. Most people associated them with work and saw little need for them in their private lives. Even after Steve Jobs introduced the Apple Macintosh in 1984, the market for home computers remained small. Emerging dial-up bulletin board services, such as CompuServe and Quantum Link (the predecessor of America OnLine) mostly served small cadres of dedicated PC users and electronic-game aficionados.

Moreover, one of Viewtron's gravest errors from a marketing standpoint was promising to provide subscribers with anything they wanted, whenever they wanted it. The centrally controlled system simply was incapable of anticipating, much less quickly and economically providing everything users might want at any point in time.

The failure of Viewtron, however, does not diminish its seminal role as the vanguard of online media. Within a decade, the commercial internet and web would revitalize and expand upon Knight-Ridder's original vision but with unintended consequences. By the beginning of the new century, online media would begin to rapidly and massively disrupt all established media companies and most other enterprises and institutions much more profoundly than anyone could have imagined in the eighties.

Author's notes

About a year before Viewtron's public debut, my involvement ended. I had spent nearly four years juggling my two hats — one for VCA and the other for KR newspapers — that Batten had handed me in February 1979. My position was unique during those years. No other members of the development team divided their time between Viewtron and KR newspapers. Additionally, I was the only one, other than Gillen, who reported directly to Batten, so the VCA executives and managers tended to treat me with suspicion as an outsider. Gillen and Morrison were especially distrustful of me. One of my colleagues told me they had always regarded me as a spy for Batten and were eager to replace me.

In October 1982, they got their wish. At Batten's request, I handed all of my remaining Viewtron projects to a new art director and embarked on another venture. While I would continue to assist KR newspapers with design and technology projects, Batten had a different mission for me that took precedence — to improve the quality and quantity of news graphics that appeared in the chain's newspapers. That mission would lead to my founding of the industry's first computerized news graphics service and global online network.

After the shutdown, Morrison took early retirement and Woolley took a management position with Knight-Ridder's Vu/Text venture, a newspaper information retrieval service based in Philadelphia. Goldstrom left Viewtron in 1984 to become the *Herald's* retail advertising manager. Around the same time, Kebschall and Gillen retired. Batten went on to become Knight-Ridder's chief executive and chairman.

CHAPTER FIVE

The Golden Decade of Print

Newspaper publishers and print journalists would come to regard the eighties as a golden decade. By 1980, the digital publishing revolution clearly was on the verge of eliminating the last vestiges of the Gutenberg era. Nearly all newspapers had completed their conversion to cold-type composition, VDT front-end systems, and offset printing. Computerization had transferred authority over page production from the composing room to the newsroom. All of the lead and most of the burly hot-type compositors were gone. The few men who had remained now worked alongside women pasting up cold-type pages and making lightweight offset press plates in greatly diminished composing rooms.

With the substantial cost savings accruing from this transition, most publishers put greater portions of their growing profits into making qualitative and quantitative improvements in their newspapers. To compete more effectively with television, the nation's newspapers in this decade increased their newsroom staffing by about a thousand workers per year.

As a result, investigative and explanatory journalism flourished, minority representation grew, new sections appeared, space for news expanded, and more bureaus were established. Nearly all newspapers redesigned their pages to make them more appealing to the baby boom generation, which created a growing demand for information graphics. To meet that demand, I founded the first computer graphics service and global intranet for newspapers.

USA Today and the rise of graphics

In the first years of the 1980s, America's two largest newspaper chains — Knight-Ridder and Gannett — placed large bets on decidedly different strategies for attracting television-centric news consumers and countering the steady decline in readers and advertisers. Knight-Ridder chose to put newspapers in television; Gannett opted to put television in newspapers. Both would invest tens of millions of dollars in their divergent visions.

Knight-Ridder's bet on the online future of newspapers, called Viewtron, was prescient but premature. Its efforts to create a new business around displaying newspaper content on television screens, as I described in the previous chapter, was declared a failure and shuttered in 1986, less than three years after its public debut.

Gannett's bet on the ink-on-paper future of newspapers, called *USA Today*, proved to be perceptive and perfectly timed. Launched a year before Viewtron on September 15, 1982, the national newspaper for the television generation, as envisioned by the company's chairman Allen Neuharth, adopted a concise, short-form style for stories more akin to television news than traditional newspapers. At a time when newspapers were typically staid and mostly black-and-white, *USA Today* was colorful and visually arresting with large photos and graphics. By the end of 1985, *USA Today* had surpassed *The New York Times* to become the second largest American paper with a daily circulation of 1.4 million. (The *Wall Street Journal* had the largest circulation.)

While mainstream newspapers initially mocked *USA Today* as the "McPaper," they didn't wait long to begin copying elements of its design. Editors had been redesigning their pages and adopting more modern typographic styles since the early seventies. Now they were incentivized to add more color, shorten stories, and enlarge photos. Within a year of the launch, dozens of newspapers introduced their own versions of *USA Today's* distinctive weather page. One element, however, proved to be more difficult to emulate — information graphics.

Before *USA Today*, *The New York Times* was one of the few American newspapers to frequently put information graphics on its news pages, and then only in black-and-white. The reasons for the dearth of information graphics in newspapers prior to *USA Today* involved both human and economic constraints.

Visualizing and rendering information in the forms of charts, graphs, diagrams, plots, and maps that could be easily understood by a majority of newspaper readers required artists who possessed technical drawing and drafting skills, as well as a basic knowledge of statistics and the appropriate uses for each graphic form. Artists with those talents were rare.

A lack of qualified artists was not the only human constraint. Newspaper editors who appreciated and understood information graphics were in short supply too. Statistics and data visualizations were topics that most journalists avoided.

For newspaper publishers, adding information graphics involved making a substantial investment. Qualified artists commanded higher salaries than were typically paid for news artists. The graphics also tended to be much more time-consuming and expensive to produce than ordinary illustrations and cartoons.

Consequently, the demand for information graphics after the launch of *USA Today* far exceeded the supply of qualified news artists. What resulted was an extended period in which newspapers frequently published colorful charts and graphs, often just for the sake of adding color and graphics, that were poorly executed, oversized, and more decorative than informational. A solution ironically would be drawn from Viewtron.

The first nationally distributed news graphics package

Within a couple weeks of *USA Today's* launch, Jim Batten, who had been recently promoted to president of Knight-Ridder, called me into his office. He wanted to know how quickly I could conclude my work at Viewtron. His eyes and the tone of his voice clearly communicated that the only answer he expected was immediately.

In the nearly four years since Batten recruited me to be the "graphics guy" with the videotex development team, I had been dividing my time between Viewtron and Knight-Ridder newspapers. At that moment, my work with the online project was essentially done, so I wasn't surprised when Batten politely instructed me to hang up my Viewtron hat and help the chain's newspapers make more extensive and better use of graphics.

In addition to a new title — corporate director of graphics and newsroom technology — and a new office, Batten told me

I also would be reporting to the two vice presidents for news who had just been appointed to fill his former role — Bill Baker, the features editor who had been my first boss at the *Detroit Free Press*, and Larry Jinks, the *San Jose Mercury News* editor. When I asked how that would work, he explained that he still wanted me to keep him informed, but Baker would handle my expenses as well as coordinate meetings with editors at Knight-Ridder's smaller community newspapers; Jinks would handle contracts and coordinate my meetings with editors at the chain's larger metropolitan newspapers and Washington Bureau.

Batten then informed me that Robert Boyd, the chain's Washington Bureau Chief, had requested my help to create graphics for stories the bureau's reporters were writing about the alarming growth of the federal deficit under President Reagan. In a matter of days, I handed over my remaining Viewtron projects to a newly appointed art director and flew to Washington, D.C.

Boyd and I immediately connected. From the start, we agreed that the text and graphics for the deficit package should fit on a single broadsheet newspaper page. That required unusually close coordination between the story elements and the graphics. Together we decided on the content and amount of space we would allocate for each module. I then set to work manually creating each graphic as he edited the story elements to fit the available space.

The outcome was the first nationally distributed full-page news graphics package. The text for the stories would be sent electronically to all of the chain's newspapers via the Knight-Ridder/Tribune (KRT) News Agency on October 25, 1982. Printed copies of the graphics, along with my suggested page layout, had to be sent by way of the U.S. Postal Service. About two-thirds of the newspapers published the complete package as we had intended. Responses from the editors and their newspapers' readers were overwhelmingly positive. Batten did much more than just express his enthusiasm for the project. In a memo he sent to Boyd and me, he wrote:

> "My enthusiasm extends beyond the subject matter of this particular project. In an era when newsprint is precious, and more particularly when many readers' attention spans are short, I believe it's critically important to hone our ability to present complicated material in compact, clearly illustrated packages. As a company, we have not emphasized that as much as we should. The deficit-project model ought to stimulate our thinking in that regard."

The deficit project did stimulate thinking that would lead to my creating more national graphics packages in collaboration with the Washington Bureau. But, more significantly, his memo also set in motion my thinking and efforts that would result in the founding of the newspaper industry's first computerized news graphics service and global online network.

Around this time, I had my first meeting with Larry Jinks. Like Batten and Lee Hills, he was affable and unpretentious. After graciously welcoming me into his new office, he somewhat sheepishly said "I don't know what you do, but I'm told that whatever you do, you do well."

Computerizing full-page makeup

By the beginning of the eighties, the future I had touched in 1966 when I saw Boeing's groundbreaking computer graphics system appeared tantalizingly close. In 1981, just as Knight-Ridder was concluding its Viewtron market trial, the company decided to take the next bold step in the computerization of newspaper production — electronic full-page makeup, commonly referred to as pagination. The goal was to bypass the composing room entirely so completed pages could flow directly from the newsrooms to the presses.

Knight-Ridder contracted with Information International Inc. (Triple-I), a company best known then for its work with the movie industry, to develop a pagination system for its former Ridder newspaper in Southern California — the *Pasadena Star-News*. I spent several weeks learning to use the system and training the editors. When the first pagination terminals were installed in the newsroom, they stood out like *Star Trek* consoles on a *Citizen Kane* movie set. The antique wooden desks they sat on actually appeared to predate the *Citizen Kane* era.

The pagination terminals were huge — more than twice the size of the editorial VDTs. Their large displays had low contrast and brightness, so the window shades had to be drawn and new lighting with a pinkish glow had to be installed. The editors joked that it gave the newsroom the look of a high-tech brothel.

When the installation was completed the following year, the *Star-News* would become the first American newspaper to produce all of its pages electronically. With the marriage of pagination and editing systems, publishers took a giant step toward their goal of fully computerizing page composition, but the conversion still wasn't complete. Two news departments remained untouched by computers — art and photo.

While the Triple-I pagination terminal technically was a computer graphics system, it could not be used to create graphics. The AT&T frame creation terminal (FCT) developed in 1981 for Viewtron, however, did have that capability.

With its vector-based drawing tools, we could create maps and most forms of information graphics using an array of geometric shapes. But output devices capable of making high-quality prints of video images on paper were not yet available. The only option then was to photograph the FCT screens.

Regardless of the method, capturing continuous-tone images of information graphics that could only conform to the resolution and shape of a computer monitor would not have been appropriate for use in print media. What would be needed is a computer system that allowed graphics to be created in any size and shape, and to be output as camera-ready line art complete with text and fill patterns. To produce the graphics, news artists would need precision tools for measuring and positioning elements, controlling attributes of lines and fill patterns, and managing colors. They also would need typesetter-quality scalable fonts.

The search for a graphics system

When I began my search at the beginning of 1983, no commercially available computer graphics systems met my criteria. Several companies had released business and research software for mainframes and personal computers that could be used to create accurate charts and graphs, but the graphics were still confined to the shape of the monitor and could not be visually edited or typographically enhanced on the screen.

Moreover, the only compatible output devices were dot-matrix printers and plotters that produced crude, low-resolution black-and-white prints of the screen images. While some newspapers did publish the jaggy printouts of computer-drawn charts and graphs, most used the printouts as templates for artists to manually re-create the graphics.

During the summer, I met with representatives from HP, Xerox, IBM, and several other companies that were beginning to market systems with graphics capabilities. All were obviously eager to make a sale to a company they believed could open the door to the whole newspaper industry. However, despite their promises, it was apparent their systems were unlikely to be useful for creating publication-quality information graphics in the short term.

I wasn't alone in the search. The Associated Press, the world's oldest and largest news agency, also was struggling to meet the growing demands for information graphics from its newspaper members. For nearly 50 years, the agency had employed news artists to manually create simple maps and charts that it would scan and transmit to newspapers world-wide via its Wirephoto service. The underlying technology, however, was designed for delivering photos — continuous-tone images — not for line art. Consequently, the graphics that newspapers received through this service were of low quality and more often than not required redrawing.

By 1983, the AP understood that computers would be needed to speed up the production of graphics. Instead of waiting for a tech company to introduce a suitable graphics computer, the AP decided to fund the development of its own proprietary system.

Not long after I saw an early iteration of the AP system in New York, the art director at the *Philadelphia Inquirer*, a Knight-Ridder newspaper, invited me to see a demonstration of Compugraphic's new Personal Composition System (PCS) that he was proposing to purchase. This would prove to be my eureka moment. Almost as soon as I began playing with the PCS, I knew I had found the computer system I was seeking.

Compugraphic had married Apple's recently introduced Lisa computer, the predecessor of the Macintosh, with its popular mini-phototypesetter. The PCS was much more than just another computer-to-typesetter hookup; it represented a major advancement. It would be the first commercial publishing system capable of outputting camera-ready hard copies of graphics that included vector-based geometric shapes as well as text and fill patterns.

The PCS also was one of the first publishing systems to adopt the so-called WYSIWYG (what-you-see-is-what-you-get) interface technology, originally developed at Xerox PARC in the mid 1970s. Unlike the VDT systems, users didn't have to learn typesetting codes. The WYSIWYG interface translated everything on the Lisa's screen into instructions the typesetter understood.

The Apple Lisa represented a major advancement in its own right. It would be the first mass-market personal computer to employ two other technologies developed at Xerox PARC in the mid-seventies — a mouse and a "point-and-click" graphical user interface. With Apple's drawing applications — LisaDraw and LisaGraph — nontechnical users could create and manipulate complex vector graphics on the computer screen in any size or shape, enter and edit text, and select from any of Lisa's scalable font styles.

The Knight-Ridder graphics service

As soon as I returned to Miami, I submitted a request to purchase a PCS with two Lisas along with a proposal to launch a graphics service for KR newspapers. The service I envisioned would initially deliver weekly packets of timely graphics created with the PCS as well as provide copies of artwork manually created by artists at the chain's newspapers.

Batten and Jinks not only quickly approved the purchase and my proposal, but they did so without requiring me to write the usual mandatory business plan. In January 1984, Compugraphic installed the system in my corporate office, just days before Steve Jobs introduced Apple's new Macintosh computer.

"The computer for the rest of us," as Jobs described the it, generated lots of excitement, especially after the spectacular "1984" commercial Apple ran during Super Bowl XVIII. It also caused some second-guessing within Knight-Ridder about my decision to purchase the PCS. I overcame the doubters by pointing out that with only 128K of RAM and MacPaint as its only drawing program, the first-generation Macintosh was no match for the Lisa as a computer graphics workstation.

I had had only a couple of weeks to play with the PCS when Barrie Hartman called Baker to request my help with graphics for a major investigative report the *Daily Camera* was preparing to publish on the use of cocaine in Boulder County, Colorado. Hartman and I had met and become friends twenty years earlier when he was a news desk editor at the *Eugene Register-Guard*. In the previous year, he had joined Knight-Ridder as the *Camera's* executive editor.

I spent several days in Boulder with Hartman and the reporter who wrote the stories roughing out the page layouts and graphics for the four-part series. Instead of manually creating the more than two dozen charts and graphs, I decided this was a job for Lisa. Back in Miami, I was able to produce all of the graphics on a Lisa and output them from the Compugraphic typesetter in two days. Manually creating the graphics would have taken at least twice as long. The series went to press in early March. These would be the graphic service's first computer graphics published in a newspaper.

In May, I conducted an audit at Batten's behest of graphics usage during one week by Knight-Ridder's 28 newspapers. The objective was to establish a baseline for evaluating the effect of my proposed service on the chain's use of graphics. The nearly 200 issues I received filled every available space in my small corporate office. Working alone, I spent several weeks tabulating the numbers, sizes, sources, locations, and types of graphics, as well as taking notes.

The report I gave Batten in June confirmed that KR newspapers made little use of graphics. The metropolitan papers averaged only about three graphics per day; the community papers averaged less than one per day. More than 90 percent were illustrations or cartoons. Nearly all of the information graphics were either locator maps or simple column charts, mostly provided by the Associate Press for use with business and financial stories. The few information graphics created by the newspapers' staff artists were generally of low quality.

That summer, I recruited Judy Treible, one of the artists I had hired for Viewtron. Working in my office alongside the PCS, we began assembling weekly packets of graphics for delivery to KR newspapers. Each packet included printed copies of around a dozen graphics. About two-thirds were graphics created on the Lisas for current national and international stories. The rest were timeless illustrations provided by artists at the chain's newspapers.

In December, Judy and I conducted the first audit of graphics usage since the launch of the service. We found, much to our delight, that the service was having a positive effect. The average number of graphics used daily by both metropolitan and community newspapers during the audited week had increased by more than 50 percent. And the percentage of information graphics grew from less than 10 percent to nearly 40 percent. The quality of staff-created information graphics, however, had not noticeably improved.

Despite the encouragement we frequently received from executives and editors, our dependence on the postal service prevented us from providing what they wanted most — timely graphics for breaking news stories. The obvious solution was an online network, but the Lisas did not have communication software or ports for connecting phone lines.

The Apple breakthroughs

Nineteen eighty-five would be a watershed year for Apple Computer, KR Graphics Service, and the computerization of news graphics. And it would be a consequential year for me, too.

In January, Steve Jobs introduced the LaserWriter printer at Apple's annual shareholders meeting. This amazing, ground-breaking printer would hold the key to making Macintosh computers the predominant platform for graphics and desktop publishing worldwide. While the resolution of the LaserWriter was less than that of the Compugraphic phototypesetter, the difference was indistinguishable without a magnifying glass.

What made this printer exceptional were two innovative components — Postscript and AppleTalk. Postscript was the brainchild of John Warnock. He had co-founded Adobe Systems with Charles Geschke in 1982 after leaving Xerox PARC to market his page-description language. When Jobs learned of Postscript, he negotiated an agreement with Warnock to license it for use with the laser printer that Apple was developing. Postscript's main advantages were its device independence and ability to greatly compress the amount of data required to render scalable text and images. AppleTalk evolved from Apple's efforts to develop a local networking solution that would allow multiple devices to be easily and inexpensively connected to its machines.

Three months earlier, Apple had released an upgraded Macintosh, nicknamed the "Fat Mac." With quadruple the memory of the original, the Macintosh finally had the capacity to compete with the Lisa as a computer graphics workstation. In the same time frame, Apple introduced MacDraw software, which essentially was LisaDraw for Macintosh computers.

The Fat Mac and MacDraw had caught my attention, but not until Jobs introduced the LaserWriter was I ready to adopt the Macintosh platform for the KR Graphics Service. As soon as it went on sale that March, I purchased one with two Fat Macs and sold off the PCS.

Several KR newspapers also were quick to purchase Macs and LaserWriters. The prospect of networking art departments now seemed feasible. Unlike the Lisas, Fat Macs had ports for connecting to modems (devices used to transmit computer data via telephone lines). All that was missing was an online service that could distribute editable MacDraw files.

Batten was intrigued with my idea of networking the Macintosh computers so that we could deliver graphics for breaking news stories. He urged me to visit Apple's headquarters in Cupertino, California, to explore the company's willingness to work with us, which I did. Our Apple sales rep arranged for me to meet with several executives and engineers. All listened but gave no indication that Apple might be working on a national or global networking solution.

A month later, an Apple executive called to tell me the company had just begun field testing an online network for employees and dealers called AppleLink. He wanted to know if I would be interested in participating. I jumped at the offer. Within a few days, I received a disk with the beta software I needed for connecting my Mac to the AppleLink network. Dial-up access was provided through a toll-free "800" phone number. Installing and launching the software took less than a minute; no instructions or technical tweaks required.

The familiar sounds of the telephone dial tone, numbers being dialed, and the shrill screech of the modem connecting to the host computer were reassuring. The screen that opened after I connected to the AppleLink network resembled the standard Macintosh desktop. There were several folder icons and a panel on one side with "Inbox" and "Outbox" icons for e-mail. As with other Mac applications, all I had to do to open a folder or mailbox was point and click with my mouse.

Apple had provided a public folder for field-test participants to use. So, the first thing I did was upload a MacDraw graphic by dragging it from my Mac desktop and dropping it into the folder. A couple of minutes later, I clicked on the file and downloaded a copy back onto my computer. I could hardly contain my excitement. I immediately told Batten that I had finally found a way to easily deliver graphics for breaking news stories to newspapers.

The graphic service goes online

The AppleLink network manager generously agreed to create a private Knight-Ridder folder I could use for uploading and storing MacDraw files. He also provided several log-on IDs I could assign to KR newspapers. By the end of August, the *Miami Herald, Journal of Commerce, Charlotte Observer,* and *San Jose Mercury News* were online. On September 7, 1985, *Editor & Publisher* magazine ran a story announcing that

Knight-Ridder had launched a Mac-based computer graphics network that would connect all of the chain's newspapers in the following year. The article established that KR Graphics was the first computerized news graphics service and the first to go online nationally. The Associated Press and the other major newspaper graphics services still had not adopted the Macintosh platform.

The *E&P* also reported that more than 1,000 newspapers in the U.S. had already purchased or planned to purchase Macintosh systems, according to a Society of Newspaper Design survey. My own poll of KR editors, however, revealed less than half were likely to have Macintosh systems installed before the end of the year; only a few indicated they planned to include them in their 1986 budget proposals.

I obviously had my work cut out for me if I was going to connect all KR newspapers to the graphics service by the following June (the goal I had conveyed to Batten). Soon after the E&P article appeared, I recruited another artist from Viewtron so that I could be free to take a Mac on the road for onsite demos and training seminars at KR newspapers.

Nearly all of the art departments I visited were stuck in the past. At the *San Jose Mercury News*, a lone Mac computer was sitting on a well-worn wooden drafting table. Even more troubling was its connection to an old and slow Bell modem acoustically coupled to a telephone handset. That explained why I was getting complaints from the art director about the inordinate length of time required to download graphics.

The technology was not the only problem I encountered. To my surprise, several editors and art directors at the chain's metro newspapers let me know they had serious concerns about using the service. Mostly, they expressed fears that corporate would use the service to justify eliminating their news art departments. I had to reassure them that reducing the number of news artists was not corporate's intent. The motivation for the service, I explained, was to increase the availability of timely news graphics for national and international stories, as well as to provide local news artists with the computer tools and training they needed to produce high-quality graphics for local and regional stories.

Most overcame their skepticism when I showed them how quickly and easily the MacDraw graphics they received from the service could be updated, modified, and localized, as well as edited to conform to their newspapers' typographic styles. Another convincing selling point for the computer graphics system was its ability to print complete, camera-ready graphics that could be placed directly on cold-type pages without going through the time-consuming and costly processes of applying text in composing and combining layers photographically.

The greatest resistance to using the service, however, came from the news artists. While they were understandably afraid of losing their jobs, they mostly were afraid of touching the digital future. The tools and techniques they used had not changed significantly in their lifetimes. Few had ever used a computer or could even imagine using one to create graphics.

For most of the older artists, the Macs and AppleLink were too intimidating and frustrating to use. More often than not, it was young photographers and reporters who gravitated to the Macintosh and became the graphic artists at newspapers. The *Miami Herald* was one of the exceptions. The paper had updated its art department when it installed the Macintosh systems and recruited two artists from Viewtron. Both became frequent contributors to the service.

The birth of PressLink

Around the beginning of November 1985, the AppleLink network manager informed me that Knight-Ridder would no longer have free access after the field-test concluded at the end of the year. AppleLink had become vital to the service's future, so I took the initiative to inquire if Apple would be willing to license the software to Knight-Ridder and allow us to rebrand it for use by newspapers. The name I proposed was PressLink.

Later that month, I flew to Cupertino with Jinks to discuss a licensing agreement. To our amazement, Apple agreed to license the AppleLink software to Knight-Ridder and authorized us to rebrand it; all for free. However, there was a catch. To use it, we would need to negotiate a separate agreement with the General Electric Information Services Company. GEISCO was hosting AppleLink on its timesharing mainframe computers and providing access through its global network.

A GEISCO sales rep met with us in Miami a few days after we returned. The voluminous contract he brought would keep lawyers busy for several months. Nevertheless, we managed to sign an interim agreement that would allow the graphics service to continue using the software and network without interruption.

Early in January 1986, Knight-Ridder incorporated PressLink as a subsidiary and named me as its president. Even though only seven of the 28 KR newspapers were connected that month, I remained confident I could bring all online by June and begin marketing the service, which I had renamed the Knight-Ridder Graphics Network (KRGN), outside of the chain by that fall.

In the same time frame, Batten and Jinks accepted my proposal to move from Miami to Washington, DC. The new location, I had argued, would make it possible for the graphics team to work more closely with the Washington Bureau and KRT News Agency, as well as give KRGN more credibility outside of Knight-Ridder. Fortuitously, office space would become available in March adjacent to KRT on the same floor as the Bureau in the National Press Building.

On January 28, the KRGN artists and PressLink proved their worth when a tragic news story broke. As soon as news that the Space Shuttle Challenger had disintegrated shortly after liftoff began spreading through the corporate offices, I descended with the KRGN artists to the *Miami Herald* newsroom, one floor below, to gather the material we would need to begin creating graphics. That afternoon we posted four detailed Challenger graphics on PressLink.

On February 4, I sent a memo to all KR editors and publishers. I intended it to show the newspapers that had not yet connected to PressLink what they had missed. My memo included all of the Challenger graphics, as well as those for two other major breaking news stories that KRGN had created and posted in the previous week. That did the trick. Within a few months, all of the chain's papers purchased Mac systems and were connecting to PressLink.

Around the end of March, just as Knight-Ridder was shuttering Viewtron, I moved the KRGN team into our new National Press Building office and soon after hired three more artists. I had planned to start creating and posting graphics daily on the first of June, but another tragic event interceded a few weeks earlier. On April 27, the Chernobyl nuclear reactor caught fire and exploded. The breaking news graphics we created launched our daily service.

That summer, Jinks and I negotiated an agreement with Tribune Media Services (TMS), the international syndicate that marketed the KRT News Agency, to also market KRGN. The agreement authorized TMS to handle subscriptions and billing for KRGN, but not PressLink, which I argued had potential to provide online services for more than the graphics service.

In September, the *Arizona Republic* became the first non-Knight-Ridder subscriber. A year later, KRGN would have more than 100 paying customers in the U.S. and Canada connected via PressLink. European papers would soon follow.

The final graphics-usage audit conducted in the spring of '87 revealed that the metros then were averaging more than eight graphics per day; the average usage by community papers had increased to nearly three per day. More than 90 percent were information graphics.

The separation

In October 1987, Batten acknowledged at a meeting in Washington that KRGN and PressLink were accomplishing the goal he had set for me five years earlier of helping KR newspapers make more extensive and better use of graphics. But, he also saw that to evolve and grow PressLink as a business, it would need to be managerially separated from KRGN.

I had come to the same conclusion. While I was proud of the graphics that had been created and distributed under my leadership, I knew the time had come to hand over the reins of KRGN to a new director who had more artistic talent. My talents had been attuned to creating accurate maps and charts, as well as to solving technical problems and developing the techniques artists could use to minimize file sizes for fast online distribution.

During the meeting with Batten, I suggested that Knight-Ridder should try to lure George Rorick away from Gannett. Rorick had designed the full-color *USA Today* weather page and was manually creating impressive illustrated information graphics at the *Detroit News*, then a Gannett newspaper. When I spoke with Rorick at a seminar that summer, he admitted that he had been skeptical about using Macintosh computers but had become a believer after seeing some of the creative work done by KRGN artists.

Batten and Jinks met with Rorick in November and made him an offer, which he initially accepted and then rejected when Gannett made a counteroffer. I had to convince them not to give up on Rorick. After agreeing to a higher salary offer, he finally assumed the KRGN director's role in February 1988 and began building a graphics team second to none.

The delay meant I could not be in Washington when Rorick took over. I had to return to Miami on New Year's Day to take possession of a condo and await the movers. While I had reservations about leaving without a confirmed successor, I had confidence in the ability of the staff to maintain the service in my absence. I would need to devote all of my time to growing PressLink as a business independent from KRGN.

Later that year, the Chicago Tribune Graphics Service, which had been the dominant national provider of news graphics, merged with KRGN. At its peak, the Tribune service had around 600 newspaper subscribers that received weekly mailed packets of graphics produced manually by the *Chicago Tribune's* news artists. By the time of the merger, KRGN had already surpassed it. The new entity was integrated with the

KRT News Agency as KRT Graphics under Knight-Ridder's leadership. Around that time, the AP abandoned its efforts to develop and market a proprietary computer graphics system and adopted the Macintosh platform.

For most customers, KRGN and PressLink had been synonymous, so separation caused a serious identity crisis. Working alone for nearly all of 1988, I focused on adding new customers and services, as well as on promoting an independent PressLink identity. In that year, the number of active customers grew by more than 50 percent, from 466 to 693, and monthly usage more than doubled from about 8,000 hours to more than 18,000 hours. Tribune TV Listings, Weather Central, United Media, Chronicle Features, and Multi-Ad were among the services I added. I also extended PressLink across the Atlantic to 24 European newspapers.

While growth remained strong in the first quarter of 1989, problems were brewing. Apple was nearly a year behind in the release of upgraded AppleLink software and GEISCO could not make its version for PCs work with our network. To make matters worse, a new company, Connect Inc., was beginning to compete with us. It was marketing more advanced software for both Macs and PCs at a lower hourly rate.

I was spread far too thin. Even after hiring two assistants, it was impossible to keep up with the demands of the rapidly growing company. I was managing PressLink in crisis mode every day. By February 1989, I concluded that GEISCO's delays and pricing were putting PressLink in serious jeopardy. The following month, I made several visits to Silicon Valley to evaluate the Connect network and discuss a possible contract. After meeting with Rorick and Baker, we agreed that moving off GEISCO was in everyone's best interest.

The initial response from our customers to the new software was positive. However, within a few months, we began experiencing system failures that resulted in long periods when customers could not connect to PressLink. Implementing workarounds quickly overwhelmed our three-person operation. That summer, I also discovered that Connect could not provide us with timely usage data or reliably manage billing.

In August, I voiced my concerns to Batten about PressLink's precarious position. He and Ridder agreed to a new three-year plan that included hiring more staff and a general manager. We finally selected Rick Blair, but he was immediately reassigned to temporarily oversee another project.

In December, PressLink's position became even more precarious. Connect announced that it was nearly out of money and looking for a buyer. We were told that if a buyer was not found, the company would probably shut down in February or March. To save PressLink, I had to quickly negotiate a new contract with GEISCO, reconcile seven months of customer invoices, create and implement a Mac-based PressLink billing and information management system, and arrange to buy back our receivables, while doing everything within my power to keep Connect alive long enough to convert back to GEISCO.

System reliability had become so bad by this time that Tom Priddy, the assistant I hired from *The State*, a KR newspaper in South Carolina, to be PressLink's managing editor, was working around the clock putting out fires and trying to convince angry customers not to give up on PressLink. Without his selfless dedication, PressLink would not have survived.

The switch back to GEISCO began in March 1990. When Blair rejoined us in June, PressLink was just getting back to where it was before the transition to Connect. For all essential purposes, we had lost a year. But, more importantly, we had lost much of our credibility within Knight-Ridder and with our customers. Rebuilding our image and regaining our momentum became my highest priorities.

In September, GEISCO finally delivered the software for PCs, which made it possible to restart corporate communications on PressLink. By the summer of '91, when I stepped down to become a fellow at Columbia University and Blair became president, the network was back in the black. PressLink would soon also become the online network of choice for photo-journalists who were adopting digital technologies as well as for international photo agencies and archives.

While KRT Graphics and PressLink were profitable multi-million-dollar ventures, their contributions in their best years to the bottom line of Knight-Ridder, which then was a three billion-dollar enterprise, were relatively insignificant. However, Batten and most other corporate officers recognized that their true value to the company could not be measured in revenues and profits alone. The return on investment mostly was found in their intangibles.

By taking the lead in the computerization of news graphics, KRT Graphics and PressLink had enhanced Knight-Ridder's prestige as an innovative and farsighted company. They also made the chain's name more well-known and respected around the world. This had a positive influence on analysts and share-holders, which helped to increase the company's share prices.

Through my efforts and emphasis on quality, they set the standards by which all computer news graphics would be measured and attracted most of the best news artists to the chain's papers. The computerization of news graphics also would have a much greater influence on newspapers and journalism than just improving the quality of information graphics. At newspapers that had editorial art departments, staff artists were generally held in low regard, which was reflected in their depressed salaries. As papers began installing Mac systems, artists who used them to create and edit information graphics were quickly integrated into the newsroom, often working alongside editors and reporters. By the beginning of the 1990s, most newspapers had elevated their Mac artists to a status and pay grade at least equivalent to that of reporters and photographers.

PressLink, for its part, introduced many journalists and artists to electronic mail and networking, and helped prepare them for the online future of publishing. Prior to the emergence of the commercial internet and web, PressLink also would acquaint them with another online service that employed a similar AppleLink front end — America OnLine (AOL).

Reinventing newspapers for baby boomers

The payoff for publishers who had invested in enhancing their newspapers' editorial quality during the eighties was mostly positive. After falling steadily since the emergence of radio and television, daily newspaper circulation in the U.S. leveled off at around 62 million throughout the decade. Annual surveys revealed that the percentage of adults who said they read a newspaper once a week or more also had stabilized, averaging about 86 percent.

Despite these encouraging numbers, publishers were still worried about one trend that had not changed significantly — the lagging newspaper readership by people born between 1946 and 1964, known collectively as the baby boom generation.

In years past, most people tended to become frequent newspaper readers when they entered their thirties and started families. That was not happening with boomers who had been weaned on television.

Gannett had had some success attracting them by adopting a more television-like presentation for its papers and launching *USA Today*. In 1989, Batten and Tony Ridder conceded the time had come for Knight-Ridder to invest in a bold initiative of its own to reinvent newspapers for the baby boom generation. They named it the "25-43 Project" for the target age bracket. Ridder recruited editors from within the chain and hired consultants to create prototypes and test them with focus groups. He decided to use *The News*, a small KR newspaper in the affluent South Florida enclave of Boca Raton, as a lab for evaluating the new concepts under live daily conditions. (I was only peripherally involved in this project.)

When the completely revamped *News*, which sported a large pink flamingo in its nameplate, debuted on October 11, 1990, the paper fielded hundreds of calls. Most were from subscribers who thought they had received another newspaper by mistake. It soon became apparent that the "newspaper of the future," as it was called in the promotions, did not work for many of the Boca Raton residents; a majority of whom were older professionals, retirees, and "snow birds" from urban areas in northern states.

While some of the changes were genuinely innovative, most were seen as derivative of *USA Today*. Surveys of the boomer-age residents, who made up about 20 percent of the market, found that most liked the changes, but few said they were more inclined to become frequent *News* readers. Accurately assessing the impact of the project on the paper's circulation proved to be impossible. For years, the circulation directors had been padding the numbers with thousands of free copies.

The following year, Knight-Ridder phased out its funding for the 25-43 Project. From that point, the paper's lean newsroom staff was on its own, without any of the additional resources or help Knight-Ridder had provided during the project. Consequently, most of the design's new features had to be scaled back or abandoned. Gathering and distilling the content for each component, along with condensing stories and creating graphics took far more time and resources than the little paper could justify.

Despite corporate's efforts to spin the project as a learning experience, no one could articulate what exactly was learned. While editors at a couple of KR newspapers said they saw a few innovations they might try to adapt for their markets, I could find no evidence that they actually made changes based on what they saw in the *Boca Raton News*. Most of the editors I spoke with expressed concerns that the company was heading in the wrong direction.

After corporate support for the project ended in '91, *The News* ceased to be a topic of discussion within the chain. In the following years, readership of the "newspaper of the future" declined steadily. Obviously, the radical redesign had not saved the paper, although, to be fair, no one at corporate had ever claimed the project's goal was to save *The News*. In 1997, Knight-Ridder sold it to Community Newspaper Holdings.

Author's notes

In 1983, after living more than 800 miles apart for four years, Lucille initiated the formal one-year legal separation required by the state of North Carolina before a divorce could be granted.

Despite opting not to contest the financially punishing settlement drafted by her lawyer, the process dragged on until early 1985. During that time, we maintained a reasonably civil relationship, but not so with our children. My connection with them became more estranged.

Getting married for a second time soon after the divorce was final to the daughter of a wealthy Miami businessman, who I had been dating for about a year, undoubtedly was one of my worst life decisions. My children's obvious hostility during their separate visits a few weeks after our marriage did not bode well.

Within a couple of months, my professional life again overwhelmed my private life. The more time I spent traveling alone for meetings and working late at the office, the more irrationally jealous she became. On several occasions she threatened divorce. When I told her in January 1986 that we would be moving to Washington, D.C., she seemed excited. Even when we went apartment hunting a month later, she gave no hint of being unhappy. But just as we were preparing to move in March, she balked and again threatened divorce. This time, I said okay and drove north … distraught and alone again.

CHAPTER SIX

Conceiving the Tablet Vision

The future course of my odyssey would be revealed in the fall of '81 by an essay I wrote and illustrated for an Associated Press Managing Editors special report titled *Newspapers in the Year 2000*; though I wouldn't know it from my colleagues' dismissive responses. Most regarded my vision of digital newspapers delivered online and read on portable, lightweight flat-panel displays by the turn of the century as either a sci-fi fantasy or a "whack-ball idea."

While my work on the three digital-age online publishing ventures described in the previous two chapters — Viewtron, Knight-Ridder Graphics Network, and PressLink — consumed most of my time and creative energy during the eighties, I didn't abandon my tablet newspaper vision. Many nights I would lie awake imagining tablets and the ways broadsheet newspapers could be adapted for reading on their letter-size screens. Toward the end of that decade, I would get another opportunity to articulate my vision for an American Press Institute seminar and report on the future of newspapers. For this event, I created a scenario to describe how I thought tablets might be used for reading digital newspapers in the year 2000. I had hopes that it would get a more positive response from colleagues than I got in '81. It didn't.

Their quick dismissal without any justifications surprised me, but again it didn't deter me from continuing to advance my vision. Whatever disappointment I felt was quickly dispelled by the events that followed a fateful, life-changing encounter at a conference in Peru.

Christmas morning in April 2010

After a restless night, I awoke early on Saturday, April 3, 2010, feeling like a hyperactive child on Christmas morning. On this day, the waiting that began in January would be over, but I still had to wait a few anxious hours longer for the arrival of Santa's sleigh in the form of a UPS truck.

Just before noon, a driver came to my front door with a package that contained a thin white box unembellished except for a small Apple logo. Inside was the object I hoped would finally realize the vision I had been pursuing for thirty years — an iPad tablet.

I wasn't disappointed. With the touch of a solitary round button, the lightweight tablet instantly came alive. Except for its larger size, the iPad was not too different from my iPhone in its functional simplicity. Apple had introduced its trend-setting smartphone three years earlier. Both had multi-touch, finger-sensitive screens and ran on a new operating system Apple developed for mobile devices called "iOS".

Their similarity led critics to deride the iPad, soon after Steve Jobs introduced it on January 27, as merely a super-sized iPhone that no one needed or would want. Many were certain it would be his first failure since his return to Apple. Instead, Apple sold more than a million iPads in the first month and went on to sell more than 250 million in the first five years. The critics had failed to recognize that the larger touchscreen was what made the iPad such a popular new device. It also was what made the iPad so important to fulfilling my tablet vision.

What is an electronic newspaper?

My vision began to take shape in the summer of 1980, around the time Knight-Ridder launched the Viewtron market trial. All of us on the development team had been intensely focused on the project for nearly a year. During that period, we never questioned our initial assumption about the nascent online media we were creating. It had textual news, classified and retail advertising, and subscribers, so we had accepted that it must be a newspaper. All it lacked was paper, or so we thought.

However, by the time of the launch, some of us were having doubts about the validity of that assumption. The reading experience just didn't feel anything like a newspaper. Headline menus gave no visual clues to the relative importance of stories, content pages were all alike, and there was no way to quickly scan stories or know their length. And, unlike newspapers where advertisers gained exposure by being juxtaposed with stories, advertisers with Viewtron were relegated to their own menus apart from the editorial content.

Most troubling was the service's overall presentation, which was repetitious, silent, and static; nothing appeared to change from hour-to-hour or day-to-day. In other words, reading the news with Viewtron was, in all honesty, uncompelling and laborious.

Displaying the content on television screens made the experience even worse. Not only were the low-resolution television picture tubes not designed for reading large amounts of text, their landscape orientation and original motion-picture proportions predisposed subscribers to be disappointed. With television, there was an expectation of visual richness, moving images, sound, and most of all entertainment. Viewtron offered none of that.

For doubters, this begged the question: If Viewtron isn't an electronic newspaper, what is Viewtron? Jim Batten, then VP for news and the online service's corporate champion, also wrestled with this question and urged us to suggest alternative metaphors. None took hold. The notion that Viewtron was an electronic newspaper was too deeply embedded in Knight-Ridder's corporate mindset.

For me, the inverse of this question held greater interest: If an electronic newspaper isn't Viewtron, what is an electronic newspaper? This question started me thinking more deeply about the attributes of newspapers and how they might be adapted for electronic media.

The attribute that struck me as most important was the ability to comfortably hold and read a newspaper almost any-where — at the breakfast table or coffee shop, in an easy chair or bed, on a train or airplane. Obviously, portability was not one of Viewtron's attributes.

What made newspapers so portable was a lightweight, inexpensive, organic-fiber display technology that had evolved over more than two millennia — paper. I realized the prospect

146

of replacing paper with a comparable electronic display technology in the near future might be a pipe dream. But that didn't dissuade me from imagining what it would be like to read newspapers on an electronic device that I could comfortably carry and hold in my hands.

Visualizing this hypothetical paper-like device in my mind's eye, I could see that an electronic display as large as a broadsheet newspaper page would be impractical. Even if it could be folded or rolled up like a printed newspaper, it would still be unwieldy to hold.

Moreover, I could not see myself wanting to own a display device that could only be used for reading large-format newspapers. To be widely adopted, I reasoned the device would have to be suitable for reading all kinds of publications and documents. Since the vast majority closely conformed to a letter-size format, I deduced the dimensions should be around 9 inches wide by 12 inches tall to accommodate the American and international standards.

Coincidentally, this was the inverse of the standard TV screen's 4-by-3 proportions. In other words, the device I imagined would have the screen turned on its side, so it would be taller than it was wide (3-by-4). The reason seemed obvious: TV screens were designed for viewing three-dimensional moving images in a landscape orientation; most publications and documents were designed for reading two-dimensional static text in a portrait orientation.

Unbeknownst to me at that time, scientists and engineers at Xerox's famed Palo Alto Research Center (PARC), a few years earlier, had built the world's first personal computer designed for nontechnical users — the Alto. Their decision to employ a portrait monitor made sense for an enterprise that billed itself as "The Document Company." They anticipated that most office workers would use PCs primarily for writing and editing letter-size documents, and that they would want to see those documents on letter-size screens.

When I moved to Miami in 1979, executive secretaries in the Knight-Ridder corporate offices were already using dedicated word-processing workstations with letter-size, portrait monitors, so I knew that turning screens on their side was possible. My vision of a portable reading device, however, was constrained by a much bigger problem with the screen. The only electronic display technology available in 1980 was the bulky, power-hungry cathode ray tube (CRT) used in TV sets and computer terminals. Still, I felt confident that a more suitable display for portable devices would be developed; it was just a matter of when.

An invitation to touch the future

During the following year, Batten diverted my attention onto other Knight-Ridder projects, so I wasn't able to give much more thought to the device or how broadsheet newspapers might adapt to a letter-size display. But two things happened almost simultaneously in the summer of '81 that would bring my vision into focus.

One was an invitation from the Associated Press Managing Editors (APME) association to write and illustrate a brief essay about what I thought newspapers might be like at the beginning of the twenty-first century. The APME had sent the invitation to several dozen prominent North American editors and designers. We were told that our essays would be published in a special report and presented that fall at the association's annual convention.

The other was the arrival of a prospectus from a start-up company called Panelvision. Batten sent it to me with a note that asked: "Is this what you're thinking about?" He recalled that I had shared my idea of reading news on portable displays during one of our visits to KR newspapers. The prospectus included a description of a handheld device that the company's founder, Dr. Peter Brody, proposed to manufacture and market.

It would use a revolutionary display technology that he had invented in the mid-seventies while working as a researcher at the Westinghouse Laboratory in Pittsburgh. He called it an "active-matrix liquid crystal display" (AM-LCD). This is the technology that would beget laptops and tablets as well as flat-panel TV sets and computer monitors.

In those years, the Westinghouse Electric Corporation was a leader in the design and manufacture of household electrical products that included radios, TV sets, and other audio/video equipment. Its independent science-based research laboratory was world-renowned for developing innovative new technologies and products.

For Westinghouse's executives, however, Brody's invention was too revolutionary. They had correctly surmised that manufacturing AM-LCDs would not only require a huge upfront investment; it would also threaten the company's enormously profitable CRT business. When they cancelled the liquid crystal research program in 1979, Brody resigned. A year later he formed Panelvision to continue his flat-panel research. While the device he described was only about the size of today's smartphones, he suggested that larger devices would soon follow.

With the limitations of CRTs no longer constraining my vision of a portable device, I gained the confidence I would need to continue pursuing this digital alternative to ink printed on paper. My challenge now was to conceptualize a newspaper optimized for reading on letter-size flat-panel displays. The deadline imposed by APME for submitting an illustrated essay energized me to put my thoughts in writing and to create page mockups.

This would be the first time my tablet newspaper vision would be published. I was excited though mildly apprehensive. I hoped my essay would stimulate discussions about electronic newspapers and alternatives to ink printed on paper, but I was concerned that the notion of reading news on portable display devices might be viewed as too futuristic to be taken seriously. In 1981, nothing like it existed.

I finally decided not to worry. After all, the APME had urged all of us to touch the future, and the beginning of the twenty-first century seemed light-years away. Recalling the technological advances of the previous two decades convinced me that even more surprising developments could be expected in the next two.

The whack-ball idea

I began my conceptualizing from a reader's perspective with the premise that electronic newspapers should be as effortless and enjoyable to read as the printed versions. That meant whatever new digital capabilities I might imagine could not encumber reading or navigating the content. Simplicity would be my guiding principle.

I initially considered adopting a magazine format, which obviously could be more readily adapted to a letter-size display than a broadsheet newspaper format. But I quickly dropped that idea. As a publication designer, I had come to appreciate the characteristics that differentiated newspapers from news-magazines. Those characteristics are essentially the same today as they were in 1981. To begin with, daily newspapers typically contain many more stories on a wider array of topics and convey a much greater sense of immediacy.

The ways people read them also are quite different. With magazines, stories are typically organized for reading and browsing sequentially and predictably from front to back, one story after the other. Not so with newspapers. The stories are organized more like smorgasbords for reading and browsing nonsequentially and selectively. Their locations on pages and headline sizes, however, are not random. They are assigned by editors to provide readers with visual clues to their relative importance. While most readers will at least scan a news-paper's front page before beginning to select and read stories, many will bypass it and go directly to the elements that are of most interest to them, such as the sports and comics pages, or crossword puzzle and horoscope.

As soon as I began giving serious thought to how these characteristics might be retained within a letter-size electronic newspaper, I realized the enormity of the challenge. Metro-politan newspapers in the eighties averaged about 48 pages on weekdays. Broadsheet pages had four times the space of my envisioned electronic newspaper pages. So, just to match the physical space available in an average weekday print edition, the electronic edition would need around 200 pages. Sunday editions with their inserted preprinted sections usually had twice as many pages.

I had no way to accurately estimate the amount of memory that would be required for a 200-page edition. The best I could do was make a guesstimate based on my assumption that the pages would average about 50 kilobytes. That worked out to 10 megabytes. Back then, this was a very large file. At the beginning of the eighties, hard drives with a 10-megabyte storage capacity were expensive and about the size of today's countertop microwave ovens. Obviously, that wouldn't work for portable devices, but I trusted that memory would become cheaper and smaller before the end of the century. (I could not imagine then just how cheap and tiny memory would become.)

My more immediate concern was how readers would navigate several hundred pages on a letter-size display. The teletext services I had played with at the Portman Hotel in London two years earlier came to mind. Each held around 300 pages. Users could access specific content pages by entering their page numbers with a remote keypad. My first thought was to marry a version of that model with a newspaper-like design.

To accommodate the idiosyncratic mode of reading and navigating, I conceived three categories of pages — browsing, reading, and index. Browsing pages were the equivalent of Viewtron's menu pages. But instead of only listing headlines, they would include story summaries I called capsules laid out like newspaper pages within sections — news, sports, business, entertainment, etc.

As with printed newspapers, I presumed editors would curate the content and place the stories they considered most important on the first browsing page of each section. The reading pages would present stories laid out in a multi-column format. I also presumed that advertising would appear within browsing and reading pages. The index pages would list headlines and advertisers with their corresponding page numbers.

I quickly recognized that the only way this concept could be made to work on a portable device would be if the pages had embedded hyperlinks and the display had a finger-sensitive touchscreen. This would not only simplify navigation; it also would eliminate the need to add a physical keypad. I imagined that the device would only require one physical button to turn it on and off like a radio or TV set. All of the operational buttons for "turning" pages, accessing indexes, and other actions would be virtual. To call up stories, readers would simply touch the capsules or headlines on the browsing pages or touch their page numbers on index pages.

(I knew from articles I had read in *Scientific American*, my favorite magazine in those years, that several types of touchscreens had been invented in the seventies. So again, I assumed it was only a matter of time before they would be developed for use with portable display devices.)

The last technical issue I had to address for my essay was how newspapers might be loaded on the devices. There were no broadband mobile telephone services or Wi-Fi networks in the early eighties, and the transmission of digital data across standard telephone lines was slow and error-prone. The engineers I spoke with at AT&T's Bell Labs assured me that telephone lines would have the capacity to reliably transmit 10-megabyte data files in less than a minute by the beginning of the new century. But they were not too optimistic about transmitting large data files over wireless networks. I decided to hedge my bets by suggesting in my essay that newspapers would be loaded via an information outlet without specifying what I thought that might be. I also alluded to updating electronic newspapers throughout the day.

I was in Miami hosting the Society of Newspaper Design Workshop that October when the APME distributed the special report at its annual conference in Toronto. I heard nothing from APME about my tablet vision; however, I did hear from some of my colleagues after the report circulated within Knight-Ridder. In my presence, they politely dismissed it as an "interesting" sci-fi fantasy although I suspected many shared the critical opinion of one senior Viewtron manager who called it a "whack-ball idea." The only encouraging words came from Batten who sent me a supportive handwritten note attached to a copy of the report.

The best of times and worst of times

In the six years that followed, the tablet newspaper vision remained on my mind but mostly in a dormant state. After leaving Viewtron in the fall of '82, nurturing Knight-Ridder Graphics and PressLink through their start-up phases had absorbed nearly all of my time and creative energy.

Both ventures grew rapidly and attracted worldwide attention. Apple gave Knight-Ridder a huge boost in the months following the shuttering of Viewtron in March 1986 by including the computer graphics service and online network in its print advertising and marketing materials. Articles about them were featured in *The New York Times, Wall Street Journal,* and dozens of other newspapers and magazines. As a result, I suddenly found myself in demand as a speaker at newspaper conferences and meetings where Apple Macintosh systems and computer graphics had become hot topics.

With apologies to Charles Dickens, it was the best of times for me professionally and the worst of times personally. Within Knight-Ridder and the newspaper industry, my star was ascending; I was now recognized as a budding entrepreneur and media visionary. While outwardly I appeared happy and hopeful, inwardly I was struggling with sadness and despair.

The anguish of failing twice in marriage and acknowledging my shortcomings as a father cast me into a mental hell bucket. I was totally alone in my despair. Throughout my career, I had effectively compartmentalized my private life and managed to keep the turmoil from affecting my work and professional relationships, but the membrane that separated my personal and professional universes was beginning to fray. Soon after my second marriage ended in divorce, my loneliness and search for redemption drove me into another destructive relationship that nearly derailed my career and finally forced me to confront my inner demons.

By the spring of '87, I was close to a meltdown. I recognized that I could not continue hiding my personal conflicts. When I finally opened up to Batten and Baker, they were stunned. They had no inkling of my troubled life. I sensed they were disappointed, but no more so than I was in myself. I thought they might fire me, but they showed compassion. One of their conditions for keeping my job was to meet with a psychologist.

After several months of sessions and introspection, I saw how unresolved issues from my childhood had contributed to my inability to bond with people as well as my drive to prove my worth. Fortunately, even in my worst periods, I was able to resist the seductive lure of alcohol or drugs; giving up on life never occurred to me.

To move on, the psychologist helped me to recognize that if I didn't want to live alone for the rest of my life, which I didn't, I would have to become more astute at choosing a partner and committed to involving her in my life and myself in hers. After all I had been through, however, I was too emotionally drained that summer to even imagine becoming involved with another woman, much less getting married again.

ROGER FIDLER

Seven days in September

Around the middle of August 1987, fate sent me a letter that
would change the course of my life. It contained an invitation
from the Inter American Press Association (IAPA) to speak at
its annual technology conference in September. The venue
was in another "Remote Nation of the World" that excited my
inner-Gulliver — Peru. This would be my first venture below
the equator to a South American country as well as a much-
needed vacation from my troubles.

The three-day conference, which began on September 21,
the beginning of spring in the southern hemisphere, attracted
newspaper executives from throughout Latin America. I didn't
speak Spanish or know much about the country. Fortunately,
the IAPA's Chilean executive director and *Miami Herald's*
Cuban-born VP for operations who traveled with me were
bilingual and had been to Peru several times. They told me on
the flight that *El Comercio*, the host paper, had recruited inter-
preters for me and would provide airfare and lodging so that
I could visit Cusco and the Inca citadel of Machu Picchu.

We arrived at the El Pardo Hotel in the affluent Miraflores
district of Lima about one in the morning. I was too excited to
get much sleep. At dawn, I walked along the manicured alameda
that led from the hotel through the district's commercial
center to the high bluffs overlooking the Pacific Ocean. The
view was as startling as it was spectacular.

Clinging to the barren escarpments all the way down to the
beaches were about a dozen shanties that appeared to be made
mostly from driftwood, cardboard, and newspapers (a use I had
never contemplated). I watched as several women filled buckets
with water from a drinking fountain in the overlook park and

carried them down the steep slope. Their abject poverty stood in stark contrast to the conspicuous wealth that towered above them.

Back in my hotel room, those images were still haunting me when the phone rang exactly at 8 a.m. The caller was a woman who identified herself as my interpreter and said she was waiting for me in the lobby. She spoke too fast for me to catch her name, so I inquired at the registration desk. The secretaries didn't speak English but recognized me as the "gringo" and pointed to a slender woman in a red dress standing with her back to me at a nearby table.

After introducing myself, she said her name was Ada Vigo and then coolly but politely instructed me to sit down while she finished collating and stapling the pages of my speech. I could see that she still had quite a few pages remaining and seemed perturbed. So, I offered to help, which took her by surprise. As we worked together, I learned she was a reporter for *El Comercio* who, because of her faculty with languages, had been assigned by the editor on short notice to translate my speech and to be my interpreter and guide. When I described the shanties and women I had seen, and how they had affected me, her demeanor softened. Covering Lima's shanty towns, she said, was her beat.

We were assembling the last copies of my speech when a secretary told her a driver was waiting for us. Ada had arranged to borrow a Macintosh computer from the Xerox office for my demos. (In those days, Xerox held the franchise for Apple products in Latin America.) Along the way, she asked if I would like a tour of Lima's historic central district; I told her I would. With each colonial-era church we visited, she became visibly happier and friendlier.

After retrieving the Macintosh, I gave Ada a brief demo. At her request, I drew a likeness of a bear. When she told me it reminded her of the large stuffed bear she loved as a child that had been taken from her by a thief, I sensed her emotional pain. But before I could think of something touching to say in response, she was gone. I wouldn't get to see her again until the following morning because of scheduled events that afternoon and a private dinner that evening with the publisher, Dr. Alejandro Miro Quesada, and his wife at their home. All the while, I couldn't get this engaging woman in the red dress out of my mind. My inner voice, however, kept warning me not to get involved; to keep my distance.

We spent nearly all of the next day offering to demonstrate KR Graphics. As it turned out, only a few of the participants requested a demo, and those who did were more curious about the Macintosh than the Knight-Ridder service, so we had time to get to know each other.

Ada proved to be a skilled and very personable interpreter. Through her, I learned that the participants considered the service too advanced for their newspapers, which had only recently started to install electronic publishing systems. Even *El Comercio*, the largest and most influential newspaper in Peru, was just beginning to use editing terminals in its newsroom. By the end of the day, my inner voice was a wreck.

That evening, I was taken to a reception at the paper's new printing plant. Ada attended, but she wasn't there to be my interpreter. She had been assigned another role — to sing several romantic Peruvian songs. Her sensuous voice captivated me and, from what I could observe, all of the other male guests who were also admiring her exotic beauty.

The next day, I sat through several presentations without the benefit of an interpreter. I was nervous. This was my first speech at an international conference, and I didn't feel confident working with the man assigned to be my simultaneous interpreter. I was the last speaker on the program. By the time I got up to speak, about half of the seats were empty. I was anticipating that. I had seen quite a few participants carrying their suitcases to the afternoon sessions and leaving early.

What I hadn't anticipated were the questions. Nearly all were about my tablet newspaper vision, which I had included as an afterthought. I learned that in Peru, and most other Latin American countries, newsprint had to be imported and was expensive. And that some governments used their control over price and distribution to influence what newspapers published. So, the notion of paperless newspapers that could be read on tablets had a strong appeal, even if the technologies required to make the vision possible might be far in the future.

After my speech, Ada gave me the airline ticket for Cusco with firm instructions to be at the airport two hours before the departure time, which was early the next morning. My return flight was scheduled for Saturday morning in time to catch my flight back to Miami. She then told me I was invited to an informal after-dinner party that evening. I accepted when she told me she would accompany me.

The party was at a relatively low-decibel salsa disco that *El Comercio* had reserved exclusively for the remaining participants and newspaper staffers who had assisted. For this occasion, Ada wore another elegant, backless red dress that accented her flawless cinnamon-colored skin. The Peruvian music was new to me. I hesitated to dance, but she didn't. With her encouragement and guidance, we made frequent trips to the dance floor. Nearly all of the revelers were men, so we attracted lots of attention. The party was still going strong when we left just before midnight. At the hotel, sadness was plainly visible on both of our faces as we said goodbye, believing we would not see each other again before I returned to the States.

Fate had different plans. I missed my flight to Cusco. Embarrassed, I called the *El Comercio* office and asked for Ada. The receptionist spoke limited English, but after several awkward minutes she told me that Ada had not yet arrived. To my relief, she understood my predicament and arranged for a driver to pick me up and bring me to the newspaper.

Finding me drinking coffee in the paper's canteen caught Ada completely off guard. Her startled expression quickly dissolved into a warm smile. After I explained how I had mis-read the departure time, she called the airline to reschedule my flight for the next morning. With only one night in Cusco, she told me I might not have enough time to visit Machu Picchu.

Coincidentally, that day was the birthday of the editor, Alejo, who was Dr. Miro Quesada's son. So, after Ada gave me a tour of the ornate building, she guided me to a Chinese restaurant for a lunch birthday party with the editors and office staff. Sitting close together and obviously enjoying each other's company, we again were the center of attention.

(Sometime later, Ada told me that everyone at the paper assumed something must have happened between us after we left the disco party, which had caused me to miss my flight and her to arrive late for work. No one, she said, believed her honest denials.)

Upon our return to the newspaper, we learned that fate had intervened again. Alejo's secretary told us my reservation, along with those of my two travel companions, for our flight back to the States on Saturday morning had been cancelled due to a booking error. New reservations were made for me to depart late on Sunday evening. That meant I would have to spend two more days in Lima, which did not displease me. Nor, I happily realized, Ada.

The secretary also told me I was invited to a formal birthday party for Alejo at the Miro Quesada estate that evening. Ada declined the invitation, but insisted that I attend without her.

Arriving before sunset, I had a very different view of the family's residence than I had had when I arrived after dark for dinner three days earlier. All I could recall seeing then was the entrance and interior of Alejandro's elegant house. On this occasion, a fortified womb of wealth confronted me. Armed guards stood ominously on high walls that surrounded the compound.

The IAPA director, *Herald* VP, and I were among the early arrivals. I revealed my ignorance about Peru when I asked why the publisher's residence was so heavily guarded. Our driver explained that many important people, including a former president as well as several generals and congressmen, were expected. The extra security, he said, was required to protect us from the *Sendero Luminoso*. This was the first time I had heard about the revolutionary Marxist group, known in English as the Shining Path, that was terrorizing the country with assassinations, kidnappings, and bombings. My companions added that the Miro Quesadas were among the richest and most powerful families in Peru, which made them prime targets.

From the parking area, I could see three ranch-style houses positioned around a large courtyard carpeted in lush grass, an extravagance in that arid region. Several propane-fueled grills and dozens of tables and chairs were clustered near the center of the courtyard. A bevy of black-and-white jacketed waiters awaited the guests who were emerging from a steady stream of chauffeur-driven limousines. As far as I could tell, I was the only non-Latino American.

Fortunately, the evening was uneventful, and I was able to leave well before midnight. This time, I had no problem catching my early morning flight to Cusco. After a brief rest, I joined a guided tour of the city's historic sites that concluded with a traditional Andean dance performance that evening.

Returning alone after dark, I got lost. There were few street lights and the security gates were down, so I had difficulty locating my hotel. My anxiety grew more intense when I noticed soldiers observing me warily from rooftops and armored cars. After about an hour of nervous wandering through this apparent war zone, I finally stumbled upon my hotel's entrance.

The phone rang almost as soon as I got back to my room. It was Ada. I sensed from her voice that she was really stressed. She said she had been trying to reach me for several hours and worried that something might have happened. After reassuring her I was okay, she told me *El Comercio* had purchased a ticket for me to spend the next day in Nasca, where an ancient people had inscribed enigmatic lines and glyphs in the desert. The flight would depart a few hours after I returned from Cusco, so she let me know, with a hint of sarcastic humor, that she would stay with me to make sure I didn't miss another flight. I was happy for that.

As promised, Ada greeted me at the arrival gate just as the sun peaked out from behind the Andes. This time she was casually dressed in jeans and blouse. Despite the early hour, both of us felt electrified as we made our way to the Nasca gate. Before boarding the flight, we arranged to spend Sunday, my seventh and last day in Peru, exploring Lima together.

Nasca was memorable, but thoughts of Ada occupied my mind. For the first time in years, I felt genuinely happy and emotionally unburdened. All I could think about was seeing her again the next day, even though I knew it might be for the last time.

Ada arrived mid-morning at the El Pardo Hotel. After a proper Spanish hug, she told me that when the receptionist, who had remembered seeing us together during the conference, pointed to me, she said "your husband is waiting for you over there." We laughed in unison.

Leisurely walking along Lima's winding streets, totally absorbed in each other's life stories, we paid little attention to our surroundings or the time. After a couple of hours, we realized we were lost. Ada finally stopped a *campesino* family to ask for directions. When they offered to take us to our intended destination, we didn't hesitate to jump into the bed of their old pickup truck with two small children and several bags of Peruvian corn and potatoes.

We finally made it to a couple of museums. I wanted to show Ada my appreciation, so I offered to take her to dinner at La Rosa Nautica, an elegant restaurant on Miraflores beach, before going to the airport. She accepted, but first she had to return home to change and let her mother know she would be working late. At age 31, like most unmarried women in Peru, she lived in the house where she was reared and still cared for her mother who was divorced.

At the restaurant, a waiter gave Ada a rose and asked if we were newlyweds. Later, during our three-hour wait at the airport, another couple asked us the same question. We had obviously become friends in the week we had known each other but, despite what others might have believed, our friendship had remained Platonic. We hadn't considered pursuing anything more than that. We had not even talked about getting together again after my return to the States; we were happy just living in the moment without complications or expectations.

Thinking about Ada on the red-eye flight, I realized fate had presented me with a conundrum. The comfortable friendship we shared had breached my defenses against becoming involved in a new relationship. But, given the physical distance between us, the prospects of our becoming more than friends seemed unlikely. I decided that didn't matter; I would try to stay in touch with her, even if a long-distance friendship was all that would be possible. For the first time, I noticed that my inner voice was joyfully silent. As soon as I deplaned in Miami, I wrote Ada a letter expressing how much I had enjoyed getting to know her and my hopes of seeing her again. A short while later I received her enthusiastic reply.

In January 1988, after four months of corresponding, Ada accepted my invitation to get together again in Miami. During her visit, which she extended to six weeks, we discovered that we were much more than friends. She would return to Miami two more times, and I would go to Peru twice that year. In the fall, she accompanied me on my first European speaking tour.

The more time we spent together, the more our bond of friendship and the feelings of comfort and happiness we had experienced during our first encounter in Peru grew stronger. Whatever hesitancies we might originally have had about our relationship had evaporated.

The following January, Ada took "early retirement" from *El Comercio* and moved in with me. The next month on Valentine's Day we were married by a justice of the peace in the Miami city hall. This time, I promised myself and her that there would be no barrier between my personal and professional universes; we would be equal partners involved in each other's life.

A second invitation to touch the future

In September 1988, I was one of 22 U.S. and Canadian designers and editors invited by the American Press Institute (API) to participate in roundtable discussions about what newspapers might look like and how they might evolve at the turn of the century. We also were asked, in advance, to design newspaper front pages for the first decade of the twenty-first century and to write essays about our concepts. All of our submissions, we were told, would be analyzed and critiqued by Roger Black, a distinguished New York designer, and then compiled and published by API later that year in a book titled *Newspaper Design: 2000 and Beyond*.

The opportunity to revisit my 1981 tablet newspaper vision inspired me again. This time, I presumed the notion of reading electronic newspapers on portable displays would not be viewed as a "whack-ball idea." Laptop computers, touchscreens, and hypertext were becoming mainstream technologies, and most publishers acknowledged that electronic delivery of newspaper content, in some form, would at least be an option in the not-too-distant future.

Several colleagues at Knight-Ridder, with whom I had discussed my vision and the API assignment, argued that publishers would not be willing to hire additional staff to create two completely different versions of their newspapers. They challenged me to explore alternative tablet concepts that would be less expensive to produce and more like the printed versions.

My initial thought was to use replicas of actual printed pages reduced to letter-size for the tablet browsing pages. With this approach, I envisioned that readers would be able to turn pages and scan headlines and images on the tablet's touchscreen much as they did on paper. When they found stories or advertisements of interest, they could call up reading pages, with the text and images enlarged, by touching embedded hyperlink buttons.

For publishers, this approach had potential to reduce the cost of producing and delivering electronic editions for personal computers and ultimately tablets. I assumed that by the time tablets were available, the process of adding hyperlinks to screen replicas of printed pages and flowing text and images into reading-page templates would be automated. For readers, I reasoned that retaining the familiar look and feel of printed newspapers would simplify reading and navigating the electronic editions and thereby greatly reduce their learning curve. (Later, I abandoned this screen-replica idea although several companies would successfully adopt this model for services delivered to PCs and fax machines in the late nineties.)

While I could see publishers opting for this low-cost approach in the beginning, I believed they would migrate to more sophisticated concepts that took greater advantage of digital technologies as soon as they saw evidence of tablets diffusing into the general consumer market. I held no doubts that tablets ultimately would be rainmakers for content providers, especially those that delivered timely news and advertising in compelling mixed-media formats.

At this stage in my conceptualizing, I was more intrigued by how readers might consume content on tablets than by how newspaper front pages might be designed in the future. Based on the changes I had seen in newspaper typography and design since the beginning of the 1980s, I was certain that newspapers would continue modifying their formats to include more color, information graphics, and larger photos.

For my API essay, I created a scenario to describe how tablets might be used to access and read electronic newspapers in 2000, twelve years hence. My vision was still in a formative stage at that time, so I made a number of assumptions that I later regretted, such as conflating the display device with the newspaper and expecting publishers to give free tablets to readers with annual subscriptions. Nevertheless, my 1988 scenario did provide a reasonably accurate description of tablets and how they would be used for reading news ... in 2010. For example:

> "The newspaper [tablet] I am using is a new color model manufactured by Apple Computer. It's 9 inches wide by 11 inches deep and about a half-inch thick. The display is a high-resolution active-matrix. All of the functions are built into the computer chips. There are no moving parts and no programs to load, so they [tablets] are compact, lightweight and relatively trouble-free."

(I would revise and expand upon this scenario for several magazine and journal articles in subsequent years. I included the final version in my 1997 book, *Mediamorphosis: Understanding New Media*. In that version, the date I chose for the scenario was September 21, 2010.)

When I arrived at the API offices in Reston, Virginia, on September 11 (1988), enlarged copies of the front pages envisioned by the participants were displayed along the conference room walls that surrounded a large round table. In the bull's eye sat an Apple Mac II.

About half of the participants had imagined some version of an electronic newspaper. They ranged from facsimile editions and interactive databases to alternative news products produced with Apple Hypercard software. The other half chose to merely enhance traditional newspaper formats or proffer ideas for re-educating journalists and publishers. Bar codes for directing readers to additional information on personal computers and phone numbers for accessing audiotex services were their only concessions to electronic technologies.

I was hopeful that when my vision was presented and critiqued, it would be well received and stimulate a discussion about tablets. Instead, it was summarily dismissed. Roger Black's only comment before moving on to the next concept was "What can I say?" I was dumbfounded. I could accept that the front page I created was relatively plain, but so were some of the other ones used to illustrate electronic newspaper concepts. All I could imagine was that he might not have read my essay. (Later, several participants suggested to me in private that the rejection might have been influenced by my being an outsider and critic of the Society of Newspaper Design's northeastern-centric inner circle.)

The disappointment, however, did not discourage me from continuing to pursue my tablet vision. (When the API brought most of us back together again two months before the turn of the new century to revisit our 1988 predictions and look ahead to 2020, Black and the other participants had a very different opinion of my tablet newspaper concept.)

Author's notes

I cannot claim to be the first to envision reading electronic newspapers on portable, letter-sized tablets. More than a decade before my 1981 APME essay, Arthur C. Clarke introduced the idea in his science fiction novel, *2001: A Space Odyssey*, released in 1968 with Stanley Kubrick's film adaptation. The following passages from Clarke's book describe this vision, which unlike his vision of shuttles routinely ferrying people between Earth and the Moon, is now a reality.

> "There was plenty to occupy his time, even if he [Dr. Heywood Floyd] did nothing but sit and read. When he tired of official reports and memoranda and minutes, he would plug his foolscap-sized [8-inch x 13-inch] newspad into the ship's information circuit and scan the latest reports from Earth. One by one he would conjure up the world's major electronic newspapers....
> "Floyd sometimes wondered if the newspad, and the fantastic technology behind it, was the last word in man's quest for perfect communications. Here he was, far out in space, speeding away from Earth at thousands of miles an hour, yet in a few milliseconds he could see the headlines of any newspaper he pleased."

I read the book and watched the movie soon after they were released, but I have no recollection of Clarke's newspad making an impression on me at that time. Nevertheless, I cannot be certain that it did not subconsciously influence me when I was conjuring my tablet vision. While reading the book and watching the movie again in 1997 for an article I was writing about print media and life after 2001, I rediscovered Clarke's newspad.

———

In the spring of '91, Ada and I worked with Paul Hoyle, a Peruvian arranger living in Miami, to produce an album of romantic creole songs composed by Luis Abelardo Takahashi Núñez, who was well known in Peru as the "Composer of the People." Ada had sung with Abelardo, while he provided guitar accompaniment, at Lima's historic Municipal Theater and *peñas* (informal music halls) around the region for several years. They became close friends, and later he would play an important role in both of our lives. When I proposed producing a CD with Ada singing ten of his songs, he urged us to adapt the music for an international audience and to give free copies to people we met on our travels so they would have an opportunity to know Peruvian music. We agreed and have since given away several hundred copies around the world.

CHAPTER SEVEN

Advancing the Vision

With the onset of the nineties, the digital publishing revolution burst into the public consciousness. A plethora of commercialized electronic media suddenly began flooding the general consumer market. Among them were notebook computers and handheld game consoles, cell phones and personal digital assistants (PDAs), e-books and interactive laser discs. By then, my tablet vision no longer seemed like a sci-fi fantasy.

After considering a proposal from Raychem in 1990 to partner with Knight-Ridder on a tablet venture, I had to concede that hardware development was best left to the consumer electronics companies. That belief, however, didn't dissuade me from trying to influence the design of tablets or prodding companies to produce them. The following year, I accepted a fellowship to Columbia University to learn more about the new media technologies.

Tablets, as I envisioned them, would be used mostly for consuming and interacting with content. That meant their success would depend upon their ability to provide easy access to an abundance of content. While there were many possible sources, none in my view could match the quantity and quality of timely, relevant news and information provided by daily newspapers. I thought this would give newspaper chains considerable sway over the development of tablets. This was one of the arguments I used to convince Knight-Ridder to let me establish the Information Design Lab in Boulder, Colorado.

The emergence of liquid crystal displays

By 1990, the active matrix liquid crystal display (AM-LCD) technology Peter Brody invented in the seventies at the Westinghouse Laboratory was on the verge of spawning a multibillion-dollar global industry. But none of the AM-LCDs used in portable devices would be produced by Westinghouse or Panelvision, the company Brody founded in 1980. Nearly all would be fabricated in Japan and Korea by companies that saw the enormous potential of flat-panel displays and had been willing to invest huge sums, with their governments' support, in the development of complex manufacturing processes and facilities.

Apple released one of the first battery-operated personal computers with an AM-LCD — the Macintosh Portable — in the fall of 1989. The monochrome display got rave reviews from critics and users, but the computer's retail price — $7,300 (nearly $15,000 in today's dollars) — stifled sales. While AM-LCDs would become progressively cheaper in subsequent years, their high price would continue to hobble sales of portable computers and tablets throughout the nineties.

The liquid crystals were not the culprits. They are organic molecules that occur commonly in the natural world and are relatively inexpensive to isolate or synthesize. The types used for electronic displays have a unique characteristic that stems from their ability to realign in the presence of an electrical field. When electricity is applied, these normally opaque reflective materials can be made to appear transparent. In other words, their two states, which roughly correspond to "on and off," can be switched on demand.

What made the AM-LCDs so expensive was the complex electronic wizardry required to instantly switch each tiny liquid-crystal pixel (picture element). A typical computer display in the early nineties had more that 300,000 pixels that had to be precisely mapped and controlled. (Contemporary displays can have several million pixels.)

Less-expensive LCDs were developed in the eighties for use in watches, calculators, handheld devices, and some portable computers. However, the cheaper alternatives to the active-matrix drivers tended to be quite slow and could not be used for anything that required rapid switching, such as videos, animations, and fast-action games.

That didn't discourage a number of American companies from trying to enter the flat-panel display market. One of those early entrants was Raychem.

Raychem and The Newpanel video

Around the beginning of summer in 1990, I received a call from Steve Diaz, a Raychem engineer. He told me he had seen an article about my tablet vision and wondered if Knight-Ridder might be interested in a new LCD technology his company was developing. I was intrigued, so we arranged to meet at his corporate offices in Menlo Park, California. Before my visit, I didn't know Raychem was one of the world's largest suppliers of components to consumer electronics companies as well as to a variety of other major industries.

The small LCD prototype Diaz demonstrated used the company's patented NCAP liquid crystals. As engineers are wont to do, he proudly explained in technobabble that NCAPs are "Nematic Curvilinear Aligned Phase liquid crystals that have been encapsulated in a polymer matrix." According to my notes, NCAPs didn't require polarizers, so their on-state light transmission was significantly improved over the types of liquid crystals commonly used in displays. I honestly didn't understand any of this. My knowledge of display technologies in those days was confined to articles I read in *Scientific American*.

During that first meeting, Diaz hinted Raychem might be interested in working with Knight-Ridder to develop a "newspanel." (This is what I called the tablets back then.) He proposed creating a tablet mockup and a video, with my assistance, that could be shown to Knight-Ridder and Raychem executives. I agreed to present his proposal in Miami knowing that getting Knight-Ridder to participate in a partnership with Raychem was a long shot.

To my surprise, Jim Batten, who then was Knight-Ridder's chief executive and chairman, was more receptive to the proposal than I had expected. He instructed me to coordinate a Raychem meeting with Tony Ridder, who recently was promoted to corporate president, and advised me to apply for project funding from the Edge of Knight-Ridder program that he had initiated in 1989 to stimulate innovation and entrepreneurial ventures. The funding allowed me to hire John Mayo-Smith as a temporary project consultant.

On my next visit to Raychem, Diaz introduced me to the company's graphic artist who would create the animated video based on an updated version of my 1988 tablet scenario. The computer graphics software he used ran on Raychem's mainframes. He needed nearly a week to complete the visually realistic three-minute animation with a voice-over narration. It showed a businessman's view of waking up in a hotel suite at 4:30 in the morning, taking his newspanel from a nightstand, inserting it into a docking station to load several newspapers while preparing coffee, and then going to a table to read them.

While at Raychem, Diaz and I mulled over methods for efficiently delivering electronic newspapers to docking stations. By the time the animation was completed, Diaz had worked out a scheme for using satellite links, which he said the company might patent.

The *Newspanel* video would be shown at Knight-Ridder's Miami headquarters on September 10. In addition to Ridder, Diaz, Mayo-Smith, and myself, the meeting was joined by several Raychem executives. (Another commitment prevented Batten from attending.)

To provide an outside perspective, we invited Dr. Alan Kay, one of the pioneers in the development of mobile computing. At that time, Kay was an Apple Fellow with Apple's Advanced Technology Group (ATG). While working as a computer scientist at the Xerox Palo Alto Research Center (PARC) in the seventies, he developed the Dynabook concept that is credited with defining the conceptual basics for laptops and tablets.

After watching the video and listening to the Raychem presentation, which included a tablet mockup and the proto-type NCAP display I had seen in California, Kay inquired about the company's ability to develop or acquire essential components beyond the display. He was particularly concerned about the operating system and user interface. One of Raychem's executives suggested they might partner with a computer manufacturer. That prompted me to ask Kay if he thought Apple would be interested. He politely answered that he would discuss it with his ATG colleagues.

Throughout the meeting, I remember having the impression that Ridder was either perplexed or disinterested. He asked few questions. The only one I can recall was, "Could the newspanel be made to work just for Knight-Ridder newspapers?" I probably turned Ridder against me and my vision that day by telling him I thought exclusivity was a bad idea. (Ridder was known for not taking well to being contradicted.)

Even though I still narrowly envisioned the newspanel as an electronic newspaper platform, I firmly believed that readers would not want to carry around multiple newspanels to access newspapers delivered by different media companies. And that publishers would not want to deal with competing tablet and telecom technologies.

My concluding argument that a universal, standardized newspanel would be beneficial to the newspaper industry as well as to Knight-Ridder got Ridder's attention, but not in the way I had hoped. He responded by nixing the idea of investing in a newspanel that competitors could use.

While I was disappointed, I had to agree that development of a universal newspanel should involve a consortium of news organizations. But after witnessing all of the failed efforts to get competing publishers to work together on standards for electronic publishing systems, I doubted that a consortium could come together on a newspanel project. Also, after listening to Kay's comments, I was having reservations about Raychem's ability to produce a suitable newspanel. Apple seemed to be a more likely developer.

(Later, I would learn that in 1990 Apple's Advanced Technology Group was already secretly developing a small pen-based tablet it would call the Newton Message Pad. Raychem did not pursue the development of NCAP displays for tablets or other mobile media after the Knight-Ridder meeting.)

An unexpected return to my past

I didn't get much time to reflect on the meeting. That afternoon my mother called. She was sobbing as she told me her third husband had died suddenly from a heart attack, and she was all alone. The couple who managed the trailer park where she lived assured me they would look after her until we arrived. The following morning, Ada and I flew to Eugene.

We would spend several weeks in Oregon helping with the funeral, arranging for her move into a senior foster home, organizing her finances, winnowing her possessions, and hosting garage sales. This was the most time I had spent with my mother in the nearly quarter of a century since I left the Pacific Northwest to work in Japan and travel the world.

We had never had a close relationship. I grew up mostly on my own. For as long as I can remember, my mother was almost always away from home. In Oregon, she worked nights in a cannery and cleaned houses most weekends. When I was not in school or working, I devoted most of my free time to activities with Boy Scouts and the astronomy club, so we hardly saw each other. My dinners were usually alone at home with Chef Boyardee or at the Dairy Queen with friends. I had not known her second husband and had only met her third husband, a retired truck driver, once before he died.

Tattered suitcases and cardboard boxes stuffed with memorabilia consumed about half of her bedroom closets. Among our finds were my baby pictures and shoes, as well as a family photo album and genealogy compiled by my Mormon cousins. She also had saved all of my report cards from kindergarten through high school, my Boy Scout uniform, my science fair trophy, my slide rule, and a scrapbook with stories I had written.

Discovering so much of my past preserved among my mother's possessions surprised me. I had no memory of her showing emotions, other than occasionally crying, or of her ever hugging me. Now I could see that even if she couldn't overtly express her feelings, she obviously loved me in her own way. A wave of guilt washed over me as I recalled how I had never acknowledged her sacrifices and how immaturely embarrassed I had been of her obesity and limited intellect.

With help from the couple who managed the trailer park, we located a senior foster home on the outskirts of Eugene. It had four women and one man, all around her age (she was 75 at that time), who were cared for by an extended family that included two nurses. She seemed happy after we introduced her to everyone and showed her the bedroom she would have all to herself. The homemade desserts in the kitchen sweetened her transition. When we said goodbye, I hugged her and promised to visit and call her more frequently.

Time for a mid-career sabbatical

Soon after returning from Oregon in the fall of 1990, Dr. Everette Dennis invited me to speak at a technology conference that the Gannett Foundation's Center for Media Studies was hosting at Columbia University in New York City. Dennis was the founder and executive director of the Center. We had met while we were students at the University of Oregon and crossed paths on numerous occasions but had not maintained close contact.

During the conference, Dennis urged me to apply for a Gannett Center Fellowship. I felt honored that he would consider me as a worthy candidate. In the six years since its beginnings in 1985, this distinctive fellowship program had earned a reputation as one of the most prestigious and sought-after in the world. If appointed, he told me I would have an opportunity to pursue a project of my own design alongside other distinguished media professionals and scholars during the '91-'92 academic year at Columbia.

The Raychem experience had made me realize that I would need to acquire more knowledge about emerging new media technologies if I was going to continue advancing my tablet newspaper vision. Taking a sabbatical from Knight-Ridder to study and possibly write a book about the computer-ization of newspapers seemed like the right thing to do.

When I told some of my cohorts about the fellowship, all contended I would be making a big mistake to interrupt my career. In their minds, giving up my corporate responsibilities meant Knight-Ridder might not have a job for me to return to at the end of the academic year. That argument didn't dissuade me. I had confidence in my ability to persevere.

Batten had no objections; he even wrote a reference letter on my behalf. The signs that I was becoming restless must have been plainly obvious to him. In the nearly 12 years since he recruited me for the Viewtron development team, he always seemed to know when I needed a new challenge.

The following spring, I received an acceptance letter from Dennis along with a request to write an article for the fall 1991 issue of the Center's *Media Studies Journal*. That article would be the first in which I used "mediamorphosis" — a word I had coined to describe the metamorphosis of newspapers from print to digital media. Later I would apply that term more broadly to the transformations of human communication since the emergence of speech and spoken languages. This would become the basis for the book I would begin to write as a fellow — *Mediamorphosis: Understanding New Media.*

That summer, the Gannett Foundation, founded by Frank Gannett in 1935 to promote freedom of information, better journalism, and community projects, underwent a transformation of its own. Allen Neuharth, the retired chairman of the Gannett Company and founder of *USA Today*, had a different vision for the foundation. After taking control in 1991, he convinced the board to sell its name and assets back to the Gannett Company. He then used the money to form the Freedom Forum, independent from Gannett.

As its chairman, Neuharth dedicated the new foundation to promoting free press, free speech, and free spirit. He also apparently added "free spending" after moving its headquarters from Rochester, New York, to more luxurious accommodations in Rosslyn, Virginia, near his former Gannett corporate offices.

I learned about the change from a letter sent by Dennis on July 11 to all of the '91-'92 fellows. He explained: "From July 4 forward we are The Freedom Forum Media Studies Center, and henceforth fellows appointed here will be known as Freedom Forum Center Fellows." He reassured us that the new foundation remained committed to media studies and that the Center's programs would continue as they had at Columbia University.

After turning over PressLink to Rick Blair, Ada and I sublet our condo, sold our car, packed our essential personal possessions into a U-Haul van, and drove to New York City. We arrived in time to spend a sunny Labor Day holiday weekend walking the streets of the Big Apple and tasting the city's multicultural delights before beginning my fellowship.

The university had assigned us to the apartment of an art history professor who was taking a sabbatical. It was on the fifth floor of an early twentieth-century Riverside Drive edifice just a few blocks from Columbia's Broadway entrance in Morningside Heights. The most distinctive feature of her one-bedroom flat, aside from an unobstructed view of Riverside Park and the Hudson River, was an octagonal dining room painted passion red.

The Center occupied the entire first floor of the building that housed the Graduate School of Journalism. When Ada and I arrived, Dennis and associate directors Jane Coleman, Shirley Gazsi, and John Pavlik greeted us with sincere warmth and respect, as they would every day during that year and whenever we visited in the years that followed.

The resident fellows were ensconced in modest rooms clustered close together around a small journalism library and informal meeting space in a wing across from the administrative offices. Our proximity to the library and the comfortable chairs in the meeting space intentionally invited reading and casual conversations between fellows.

A large conference room provided the venue for weekly seminars that fellows took part in with media industry leaders and scholars. The technology lab in the basement introduced us to computer-assisted reporting, research databases, desktop publishing, and the internet, which then was limited to academic institutions and research facilities. Each of us would have the use of a graduate student assistant for 20 hours a week.

Among the other fellows I would get to know that year were: Bernard Kalb, formerly a network correspondent; M.S. Rukeyser Jr., formerly an NBC executive vice president; Jannette Dates, a Howard University professor and associate dean of the School of Communications; Alexei Izyumov, a Russian journalist; and Dr. Cleveland (Cleve) Wilhoit, an Indiana University journalism professor and associate director of the Institute for Advanced Studies. Kati Marton, an '87-'88 fellow, returned that year as a visiting scholar to research another book. Through her, I also got to know Peter Jennings, who then was her husband and the ABC World News Tonight anchor. All helped to make my year at the Center the most intellectually stimulating experience of my career.

Ada and I soon developed a close friendship with Cleve, whose room adjoined mine, and his wife Frances, a nationally renowned librarian on leave from Indiana's School of Journalism. He was recovering from a bicycle accident and still needed a cane for walking, but that didn't prevent him from going out on the town with us and other fellows.

While Cleve and I were confined to the Center on the weekdays, Frances and Ada were usually exploring museums and shopping together — when they weren't talking about life over coffee and pastries. In addition to making our time in New York more enjoyable, their coaching would influence my book as well as my career's future direction.

Before arriving at the Center, I believed nine months would be more than enough time to consummate a book. How naïve I was! By the end of the fellowship year, my book still was embryonic. I had not considered how much time would be consumed by the invaluable opportunities afforded by the Center to socialize with Columbia faculty, media leaders, and the other fellows; to participate in conferences and forums; to read books from its well-stocked library; to experiment with new technologies; and to partake in Manhattan's diverse cultural and culinary offerings.

Moreover, Dennis and his associates were masters at promoting us and our projects. Through their tireless efforts, all of us would be invited to give presentations to students, media professionals, and corporate executives, as well as to appear on radio talk shows and television news programs. Dozens of interviews and stories about us and our work would be published in newspapers and magazines around the world.

The media exposure I was receiving for my tablet newspaper project did not go unnoticed by Knight-Ridder executives. After I appeared on the MacNeil-Lehrer NewsHour, a popular primetime PBS news program, near the end of December, Batten sent me a brief congratulatory handwritten note, as he had done after reading my article in the *Media Studies Journal*. In his December note, he indicated that he was looking forward to meeting with me at Columbia.

During my first couple of months at the Center, I came to realize that talking and writing about my tablet concept were not enough to convince publishers and developers of its viability; they would need something more tangible. So, I shifted from researching and writing a book to creating a more realistic tablet mockup and an interactive demonstration of a format I had designed for reading newspapers on tablets. The plastic mockup that I showed on the NewsHour was relatively easy to make. The demo, however, was more challenging given the limited software tools available in 1991.

Fortunately, the database software I had mastered to create the information management and billing system for PressLink two years earlier, had everything I needed to build and demo my tablet newspaper prototype on a Macintosh computer. In February, Pavlik installed a portrait-oriented monitor on a Mac in the Center's tech lab that could be used for demos.

The corporate visit

Batten's secretary called in mid-April to arrange a meeting with me in New York that also would include Ridder and Bill Baker, the VP for news. I was excited by the prospect of discussing my future and showing them my demo in the Center's lab. But that was wishful thinking. Our meeting would be limited to about half an hour at the Algonquin Hotel.

Not only did they not visit the Center to see my demo; they didn't discuss my future. About all they told me was that Knight-Ridder was evaluating a number of new projects and that they were eagerly awaiting my return. I left the hotel puzzled about the purpose of the meeting. They hadn't asked any questions about my work or offered any hints about what my role might be when my fellowship concluded at the end of May.

After talking with Ada, I decided not to wait for corporate. I would go to Miami with a proposal to establish the Knight-Ridder futures lab that I had suggested to Batten just before I began my fellowship. An opportunity to present my proposal, however, would be delayed by speaking engagements in Europe and events at the Center, as well as by Batten's and Ridder's vacations. Dennis agreed to extend my fellowship through the end of the summer.

My tour of Switzerland, Spain, and Italy during the first three weeks of June was at the behest of newspaper publishers and associations. I was lucky to have Ada with me. Her fluency in Italian, French, and German, as well as her native Spanish, made the tour far more interesting. Her singing talent also opened doors for us, especially in Spain. One of our most memorable experiences was in Jerez de la Frontera, where we were invited to a flamenco dance performance and exquisite dinner at the palatial estate of Señor Juan Pedro Domecq, one of the heirs to the Domecq sherry dynasty. He was so charmed by Ada that after the dinner he played his guitar and sang several romantic duets with her.

Soon after our return to New York, I received a request from the organizer of my tour in Spain to host a seminar with about a dozen journalism students who would be arriving in early July. All, he told me, were the presumptive heirs of the publishers with whom I had met. The Center had no events scheduled for that time, so Dennis agreed to let me use the conference room and lab. They mostly wanted to see my tablet demo and to hear my views on the future of newspapers, which for most of them would be their future, too.

After the seminar, Ada and I hosted a casual dinner party for them in our flat. The especially hot summer evening was made even hotter by the intensely passionate sevillana and flamenco songs and dances they performed for us, appropriately in our passion red dining room, and by the untimely failure of our air conditioner. Luckily, none of the other tenants appeared to be home that evening, so we were able to open our windows to the slightly cooler night air and to the sounds of our revelries without incurring complaints.

The crying souls of the guitars, the emoting notes of the singers, the stamping rat-tat-tats of the dancers' heels on the hardwood floor resonated with our palpitating hearts and burned the memory of that night into our minds. This was life lived to its fullest — an apt ending for my sabbatical year and beginning for my life's next chapter.

The futures lab negotiations

On June 28, 1992, *The New York Times* had devoted a full page in its Sunday Business section to my tablet newspaper concept. The 6-column headline on the article by John Markoff, the *NYT's* technology writer, read "A Media Pioneer's Quest: Portable Electronic Newspapers."

If I ever needed proof of the power of the press, this was it. In the following weeks, I received scores of calls and letters from media and technology executives, as well as from prospective investors and more than a few people who believed the tablet mockup shown in one of the photos was real and wanted to know where they could buy one. Nothing like this had happened after my appearances on the PBS NewsHour and radio talk shows.

After a couple of weeks passed without a call or note from anyone at Knight-Ridder about the *NYT* article, I started to become antsy. I assumed Batten and Ridder must have read it, so not hearing from them seemed odd. Moreover, I had been told in May that someone would get back to me in July to schedule a meeting after they returned from their vacations. Finally, as the month's end was fast approaching, Ridder's secretary called. She informed me the meeting was set for 11 a.m. on July 28 in Miami.

I arrived early that morning with copies of my proposal and the memo I had written to Batten the previous August. In that memo, I suggested that Knight-Ridder should adopt the "skunk works" model that Lockheed Martin had successfully implemented to secretly develop spy planes and other advanced aircraft during the Cold War. (Skunk works was the name given to the moonshine factory in the popular "Li'l Abner" newspaper comic strip.) I wrote:

> "To succeed, a Knight-Ridder skunk works would have to be an autonomous entity that reported directly to you. [Someone from corporate] could provide oversight, but the leadership and support would have to come from you.
>
> "I would propose starting with a core team of three or four carefully chosen people.... The mission of this skunk works would be broad: To seek out new media opportunities and make them work."

My proposal included a budget request for $350,000 through the end of 1992. I also asked for a substantial raise plus relocation expenses. (My salary and travel expenses would continue to be paid out of the corporate budget.) The one item I thought might be a problem was my choice for the location — Boulder, Colorado.

I had three justifications for my choice: Boulder was less congested, more affordable, and more scenic than Silicon Valley, so attracting talented people would not be difficult (Boulder county already was becoming a popular high-tech alternative to Silicon Valley for those reasons); Knight-Ridder owned the local newspaper — the *Daily Camera* — which could provide content and serve as a test site; and it was centrally located in the country, about 2,000 miles away from the Knight-Ridder corporate headquarters in Miami. I must admit to having had another more personal reason for choosing Boulder. Ada and I had fallen in love with the region and wanted to put down roots there.

Just before 11 a.m., Ridder's secretary informed me the meeting would be delayed until after lunch. No time or explanation were given. While I waited, I thought about my career and realized this was the first time in my 18 years with Knight-Ridder that I was attempting to negotiate a pay raise and my personal relocation expenses. I had always accepted whatever was offered without question. Freedom to create and follow my interests had been more important to me than titles and money, but now I recognized that my value to the company justified greater compensation.

Around 4 p.m., the secretary finally ushered me into Ridder's office where he, Batten, and Baker were waiting for me. Their icy greeting instantly conveyed that I was in trouble, but I had no idea why. Almost as soon as I sat down, they let me know the reason: They were upset by a sentence in the *NYT* article that stated I had developed the tablet newspaper concept independent of Knight-Ridder. After a long moment to collect my thoughts, I explained that this was the result of a misunderstanding. I recalled telling the reporter that I had created the prototype I demonstrated for him at the Center as part of my fellowship project, which apparently led him to assume I had developed it independently. My explanation appeared to satisfy them, but I could still sense a lingering frostiness, particularly from Ridder. Nothing more was said about the article or my fellowship year.

When I presented my proposal for the skunk works, which I called the Information Design Laboratory (IDL), the only immediate point of contention, as I had anticipated, was the location. Baker argued that it should be based in Boca Raton, Florida, where he had overseen Knight-Ridder's initiative to "reinvent newspapers for the baby boom generation" called the "25-43 Project" using the *Boca Raton News* as a lab. Ridder argued for San Jose or Philadelphia where the chain owned metropolitan newspapers and already had online initiatives underway. After I gave my justifications for Boulder, Batten told me they needed time to review my proposal in private.

During the hour they took for their meeting, I felt as if I was in a space-time warp where minutes stretched to infinity. By the time I reentered Ridder's office, I was expecting a handshake and a thank you for your service followed by "you're fired." Instead, Batten was smiling when he told me they had agreed to fund my proposed lab in Boulder with only one modification — my salary. The amount I requested, he said, was more than they could justify at that time. His counteroffer, however, still amounted to a hefty raise, so I happily accepted. Before I left, he let me know that he was changing my title to corporate director of new media development.

The formal agreement to establish the lab was signed on July 31 — a fitting gift for Ada's birthday. A few days later, we were in Boulder scouting possible locations for the lab and house hunting. Within a couple of weeks, we put a down payment on a townhouse and signed a tentative agreement to lease office space in downtown Boulder. We then arranged for a mover to collect our furniture and remaining personal possessions from the Biscayne Bay condo we had been subletting.

Our move did not go as planned. On August 24, the day the movers were scheduled to arrive, Hurricane Andrew, which had accelerated and intensified to a Category 5, made landfall just south of Miami. So much for our move! A few days later, we learned that our condominium building had sustained only minor damage. But the devastation and disruptions caused by hurricane Andrew made retrieving our furniture and remaining possessions problematic. After talking with a friend at the *Miami Herald*, we decided to donate everything, including Ada's piano, to a shelter for women and children. We would start the next chapter in our lives in a new home with all new furnishings.

Photojournalism joins the digital revolution

In the early nineties, while I was a Freedom Forum Center Fellow at Columbia University and establishing the Information Design Lab in Boulder, Knight-Ridder was leading another major advance in the digital publishing revolution — the online distribution of digital photos for newspapers and other news media worldwide. While I had no direct involvement in that initiative, it arose from the two companies I founded and led in the eighties — Knight-Ridder Graphics and PressLink.

According to Tom Priddy, who had been a photo and graphics editor before I hired him to be PressLink's managing editor, the initiative began with a phone call in the fall of 1990 from Steve Schaffran, the president of an outfit called The Color Group. "I think we have found a way to make scanned photos small enough to be transmitted over a dial up," he told Priddy.

File size was a major concern at PressLink because clients were charged for the minutes they were connected to the network plus a fee per kilobyte (thousand characters) for downloading content. Efforts were always made to keep graphics files to less than 40 kilobytes. Uncompressed scanned photos could be more than 100 times that size.

Schaffran was working with Storm Technology on an Adobe Photoshop export module called PicturePress that would compress scanned images using the newly developed JPEG (Joint Photographic Experts Group) standards. He wanted to know if PressLink would be willing to assist in a test at Super Bowl XXV in Tampa, Florida, on January 27, 1991. Priddy didn't hesitate to accept his invitation.

Several sports photographers had agreed to share some of their game photos and post them on PressLink for participating papers to evaluate and use as they saw fit. The Color Group set up a trailer outside of the stadium where film could be processed, scanned, edited, compressed, and uploaded.

Storm's PicturePress software was able to compress the scanned color photos, which averaged 3.5 megabytes, down to about 175 kilobytes. It also simultaneously created 15 kilobyte thumbnails of the images that editors could download in less than a minute for evaluation. The 18 newspapers that took part in the test were given free Storm software for decompressing the images as well as PressLink for accessing the files.

In March, Priddy initiated a follow-up test at the Tournament Players Championship in Florida so he could understand and explain the process to clients. A selection of photos that he and another photographer took were posted on deadline and made available at no additional charge to all PressLink customers. That October, Knight-Ridder/Tribune Photos and the U.S. Army Public Affairs Office, which was distributing digital images from the Gulf War, began regularly posting their photos on PressLink.

Around the same time period, the Associated Press began installing digital photo desks developed by Leaf Technology in the newsrooms of AP members. Because the AP Leaf Desks required expensive satellite links and proprietary hardware that could be used from only one location, PressLink held obvious advantages. With PressLink, photos could be easily uploaded and accessed by any Macintosh computer almost anywhere for a relatively low cost using standard telephone lines. Additionally, many newspapers already were familiar with PressLink and routinely using the service on Macs to access news graphics and syndicated features.

A second Super Bowl test conducted by The Color Group in Minneapolis in January 1992 involved a much larger number of photographers and newspapers. For this test, Priddy made their photos available to all PressLink customers. The resulting publicity attracted attention around the world and established PressLink as the optimum photo service for newspapers of all sizes.

Most photo agencies quickly recognized the benefit afforded by PressLink of not having to install and maintain satellite dishes on members' roofs and setting up dedicated computers in their newsrooms. By the end of 1992, Reuters, Agence France-Presse (AFP), Allsport, NYT, and the Bettmann Archive had signed up with PressLink to deliver photos.

In April 1993, Knight-Ridder moved PressLink to larger offices in Reston, Virginia, where Priddy remained as managing editor of the rapidly growing service. A short while later, he worked with several "smart guys" to take satellite feeds directly from agencies and post their photos automatically to PressLink.

The addition of digital photo services accelerated the growth of PressLink worldwide. A corporate report from the beginning of 1995 indicated that PressLink had more than 1,500 newspaper customers with more than 3,000 individual accounts, and that its archives had more than 200,000 photos and graphics online with more than 4,000 being added monthly. Additionally, the report noted that 96 of the top 100 newspapers worldwide were using PressLink.

The final years of PressLink

In 1996, PressLink underwent a total makeover of its structure and business model. After 11 years of using GEISCO's proprietary dial-up network, the company began migrating its customers and content to a website it called PressLink Online. When the transition to the web was completed on January 30, 1997, the GEISCO contract was terminated.

The switch to PressLink Online greatly reduced costs and increased transmission speeds, which attracted more photo agencies and newspaper customers. That led Priddy to develop and manage the first global image bank for photos from agencies large and small. It allowed all to compete through the use of database software that responded quickly to search queries across all available agencies.

In the same period, Knight-Ridder consolidated all of its online and digital initiatives under KnightRidder.com and formed a new subsidiary called MediaStream that would encompass PressLink and the chain's two other online services — NewsLibrary, a searchable archive of newspapers (formerly known as Vu/Text) that had served the library and education markets since its founding 1982, and SAVE, an integrated text and image archiving system. The MediaStream headquarters would be located in Philadelphia.

In a March 20, 1997, press release about MediaStream, Bob Ingle, then president of KnightRidder.com, affirmed that "the breadth and depth of the PressLink Online offering is unmatched by any service in the publishing industry." He indicated that nearly 40 key sources, including KRT, Reuters, UPI, AFP, NYT, and the major TV networks, were offering photos, graphics, illustrations, and text. And that PressLink

Online provided sports content from the NBA, NFL, Major League Baseball, Bruce Bennett Hockey, and Allsport. Other offerings mentioned included Archive Photos, The Bettmann Archives, and Index Stock.

According to Priddy, PressLink Online already was seen by news organizations in that year as the "one-stop shopping site." He proudly recalls that "You could put out an entire newspaper with our content. There was really nothing that we could not supply."

In 1996, KRT Graphics, the other company I founded and directed in the eighties, began offering its graphics and illustrations on KRT Direct as well as PressLink OnLine. The KRT Direct website was created and managed by Tribune Media Services exclusively for subscribers to Knight-Ridder/Tribune content. Billing for content accessed through KRT Direct was handled by TMS. All KRT content, however, would continue to be accessible at the same time through PressLink Online, which handled its own customer billing.

By the end of the decade, competition from other services was increasing, but PressLink OnLine still had more than 1,000 customers in more than 30 countries downloading around 20,000 photos and graphics monthly from more than a dozen agencies. NewsLibrary and SAVE also were holding their own with more than 75 newspaper clients.

Nevertheless, in the spring of 2001, Ridder shuttered Media-Stream and laid off all of the staff. The NewsLibrary and SAVE archives and assets were sold to NewsBank, a Vermont-based news resources provider for libraries and education.

Ridder decided to merge PressLink with NewsCom, a Tribune Company. The only justification he gave in his formal announcement was, "Knight-Ridder needs to concentrate on its core business of newspapers." All of the PressLink archives and clients were turned over to NewsCom, which would manage the merged service from Los Angeles. According to a press release, profits were to be split 50/50 between the two chains.

After a five-month hiatus, Priddy accepted a job with the KRT News Agency as its assistant systems manager for KRT Direct. In 2005, he resigned and returned to South Carolina where he worked for the next 11 years as the assistant managing editor for digital at the *Spartanburg Herald-Journal*.

(KRT Graphics remained as a component of the KRT News Agency until McClatchy purchased Knight-Ridder in 2006. The name was then changed to McClatchy/Tribune Graphics. In May 2014, Tribune Publishing acquired McClatchy's 50 percent stake in the service. Tribune subsequently laid off the staff and shuttered the Washington office.)

Author's notes

In 1996, the Freedom Forum moved the Center for Media Studies from Columbia University to the top floor of the former IBM building in midtown Manhattan and incorporated it into an international consortium of universities. This marked the beginning of the end for the fellowship program.

By all measures, the Center's programs at Columbia were consummate successes under Dennis's leadership. Between the Center's founding in 1985 and move in 1996, 133 journalists, scholars, and media executives had produced more than 100 books, hundreds of articles, and dozens of other products. Many of its fellows went on to help shape the future of journalism and the news media.

Despite its many successes, the journalism-serving, New York-based Center had always been an outlier in Neuharth's more self-serving, Washington-based vision for the foundation. Early in 2000, the Forum closed the Center and disbanded the consortium. All of the foundation's highly praised international programs and most of its other journalistic initiatives met a similar fate around the same time.

(When the foundation closed the Center, Dennis resigned to become a Distinguished Professor at Fordham's Graduate School of Business. In 2011, he was appointed dean and chief executive officer of Northwestern University in Qatar.)

Financial reversals and a general economic downturn were given by Charles Overby, Neuharth's anointed heir, as the justification for the cutbacks, which was only partially true. Within the Freedom Forum, everyone understood that the underlying reason was to concentrate the foundation's resources on Neuharth's and Overby's pride and joy — the Newseum.

In 2002, the foundation acquired the last commercially undeveloped real estate in Washington, D.C., on Pennsylvania Avenue between the White House and Capitol to relocate and expand the Newseum. The original museum, which opened in 1997 in a modest facility adjacent to the Freedom Forum's headquarters in Arlington, Virginia, closed soon after the acquisition. The new 250,000-square-foot Newseum opened its doors six years later in April 2008.

Attendance and income from memberships and donations, however, never lived up to projections. By January 2019, it was evident to all that the Newseum was an albatross for the Freedom Forum, which had poured more than $600 million of its assets into the venture. The only viable option for the foundation was to sell the building to John Hopkins University for $372.5 million and relocate the Newseum in a smaller, less expensive facility.

CHAPTER EIGHT

The Information Design Lab

By the end of 1992, the golden decade of print had succumbed to a convergence of economic pressures. A deepening recession, growing competition from technology-driven alternatives to newspaper advertising, and increasing demands for higher profits were pushing owners deeper into the risky, uncharted territory riddled with "quicksand" that Jim Batten, Knight-Ridder's chief executive, had alluded to during the Viewtron trial.

Moreover, the notion of using online media to deliver newspaper content that many publishers thought had died with Viewtron in 1986 was now being revived by the America Online and Prodigy dial-up services for home computers. Of greater consequence to the future of newspapers, Senator and soon-to-be Vice-President Al Gore was actively pursuing government funding to build nationwide high-speed computer networks he called "information superhighways." His vision was to expand and commercialize the internet so all Americans could gain access to the advanced technology that the Defense Department had developed to tie together diverse computers at military bases and research facilities.

Emerging touchscreen tablets and Knight-Ridder's support for the Information Design Laboratory also served to make my vision of reading newspapers on tablets more credible in the eyes of publishers and journalists. My pursuit of that vision, however, would soon be interrupted by a tragedy that changed the course of Knight-Ridder and my career.

Building a network of collaborators

On the first day of September 1992, I took possession of the vacated rooms that would become the Information Design Lab. They were on the top floor of the Randolph Center — a two-story office building above a parking garage, conveniently located in downtown Boulder, just two blocks from the *Daily Camera*. The southwest-facing windows provided a panoramic view of the city's iconic Green Mountain Flatirons.

The IDL's initial mission, as I saw it, was to investigate emerging digital technologies and build a network of collaborators. While my goal was to promote and develop my tablet newspaper concept, I knew retaining corporate support would require exploring other new media opportunities that might benefit Knight-Ridder in the near term.

Barrie Hartman, the *Camera's* executive editor, recommended Mark Timpe to be my first hire. He was a dutiful, mild-mannered man in his late 20s who had been the paper's editorial systems manager and jack-of-all-trades for several years. Mark would prove to be invaluable as the IDL's operations manager.

My second hire was Yukari Miyamae to be the lab's office manager. Hartman and I interviewed a number of qualified applicants, but Yukari stood out, not just for her organizational skills and agreeable personality. It was her determination to join the lab and her convincing argument that she could help us connect with Japanese news organizations and consumer electronics companies.

The opening of the IDL immediately attracted the attention of technology and media enterprises. Even before the phones were installed, Shashi Raval, the general manager of the Hewlett-Packard Laboratory in Palo Alto, California, contacted me at the Marriott where Ada and I were temporarily residing. He reminded me that we had met at Columbia University in July. My tablet demo, he said, had so impressed him that he wanted me to visit with the HP Lab managers and engineers.

The agenda Raval put together for my visit to the HP lab on September 21 included meetings with teams working on the technologies that would be required to produce the tablets I had envisioned. Over dinner, Raval and a couple of other HP executives discussed the future of pen-based computing and ways in which a small development team might be able to work with the IDL. Other American and Japanese companies soon followed with similar overtures, which led me to believe my tablet newspaper vision might be realized within a few years — certainly before the end of the nineties.

Five days after my visit to the HP Lab, Ada and I boarded a flight to Barcelona, Spain, where I was invited to be a keynote speaker at the Catalonian Newspaper Publishers Conference. My vision captivated the publisher of the region's largest newspaper, *el Periódico*. A few years later, he would convince the European Union's R&D organization to fund a "NewsPad" project using his newspaper as the test site.

Upon my return to Boulder at the beginning of October, Mark and Yukari informed me that someone had quietly leased offices adjacent to the IDL. They didn't know who, but they had seen boxes of Macintosh computers and two men. One they recognized as Dennis DuBe, a Colorado native who was a well-known local journalist and entrepreneur.

Several weeks later, I finally had an opportunity to introduced myself to Dennis and his boss, Scott Converse, whose business card revealed he was a senior manager with Apple Online Services and founding director of the Apple Electronic Media Lab. Scott admitted that as soon as he heard Knight-Ridder was establishing the IDL in Boulder, and that I would be its director, he made the decision to locate his lab close to us. My tablet vision, he said, was something he believed Apple needed to get its head around.

The prospect of collaborating with Apple obviously excited me, but Scott was evasive about the lab's objectives. All he would tell me was their work involved Apple's Newton and online services. The specifics, he emphasized, were secret.

Before the end of 1992, I would be invited to give presentations to executives at *The New York Times* and *Washington Post*, the Rogers and Southam newspaper groups in Canada, and *El Clarin* in Argentina, as well as the American Press Institute (API) and Newspaper Association of America (NAA). In between my travels, representatives from several newspaper chains, associations, investment firms, electronics companies, and telecoms visited with me at the IDL. Their feedback convinced me that my tablet vision had struck a chord and that useful collaborations would be forthcoming.

Additionally, that October I hosted the first in a series of IDL brainstorming sessions with Knight-Ridder executives, editors, and advertising managers to gain a sense of their interests and priorities, as well as to acquaint them with the lab. The night before, I took advantage of a nearby Russian restaurant (with lots of vodka shots) and a new virtual-reality arcade to get everyone loosened up and touching the future.

Batten let me know in his November 9 response to my first report that he was encouraged by the progress I was making on the IDL startup and that: "All of us here are enthusiastic about the leadership you're providing." But even though he said he recognized that my interchanges with visitors to the IDL and my presentations at conferences would be invaluable to creating a network with collaborators, he expressed concerns.

> "I do wonder how we can be sure to build these important connections while at the same time side stepping any diminution of the proprietary nature of this fascinating work. In the final analysis, of course, we are building IDL's capacity for Knight-Ridder's benefit, rather than that of other interested parties and the electronic-information industry in general.
>
> "Sometime at your convenience I'd be interested in a note helping me understand how we do the indispensable networking/information-sharing while still protecting KRI's essential proprietary interests."

In Batten's usual gracious manner, he closed with:

> "All this is a long way from redesigning page ones in Fort Wayne or building Viewtron together, but each chapter leads to the next! I'm proud of what you're doing."

I attempted to assure him in my reply that I understood his concerns and that I was not revealing anything of a proprietary nature. My meetings with technology companies, I explained, dealt mainly with their relevant hardware and systems developments. As for my meetings with executives from other news organizations, my intent was to solicit their support for collaborating on industry-wide standards. In my view, the IDL's proprietary developments would most likely involve electronically delivered content and services. I also added that the lab would be evaluating business opportunities that could quickly exploit emerging technologies and products as I had done with PressLink and the graphics service.

So much of my time in those first months was consumed by meetings and presentations that I had no time for developing or evaluating anything. I obviously needed to hire an assistant post haste. My search ended in late November when I was introduced to Peggy Bair at the NAA headquarters in Reston, Virginia. She was the manager of computer applications and had been with the association for six years. Bair's extensive knowledge of newspaper publishing and background in computer programing combined with her friendly, professional demeanor made her an ideal candidate. She didn't need much convincing from me or Batten. In January 1993, she joined the IDL as our applications manager. (A year later, I changed her title to administration and technology director.)

The New Media KnowledgeBase project

The first two months of the new year were relatively quiet, so we were able to devote most of our time to identifying projects we thought might yield results within a year or two. Our first project proposal evolved from my efforts to manage the information I was gathering for my book at Columbia University.

Soon after moving into my fellow's office in the fall of '91, I had my assistant start making copies of articles we found that related to the future of news media. Within a few months, my desk was buried under stacks of paper. Even after winnowing the chaff, I still had formidable stacks that defied organization. A better method had to be found.

A solution emerged while I was creating the demo of my tablet newspaper concept. The software was the same one I had used to build the PressLink billing system, so I was able to quickly create a searchable digital repository.

Instead of keyboarding whole articles into a single database, I planned to enter distilled and updated nuggets of information into a set of topical databases about technologies, products, companies, and people. All were hyperlinked to each other and to a master database that contained references to the sources. By the end of my fellowship year, we had entered around a thousand items extracted from several hundred articles.

When I demonstrated the system to Peggy Bair, she agreed that it would be useful for the IDL and might interest Knight-Ridder. We assigned Yukari to start gathering relevant articles, which we would mark-up for distilling and entering. I also began adding graphics. Our working name for the project was "The New Media KnowledgeBase."

The pace of visits to the lab and my travels for meetings and conferences picked up again in March, so I hired Greg Stone, a recent Colorado Business School graduate to assist us. By the end of May, Peggy and Greg had drafted a proposal that I would present at a corporate meeting scheduled for the end of June. In the executive summary, we defined the New Media KnowledgeBase as an intelligent information management and reporting system focused on new media. In addition to supporting the IDL's mission, we explained:

"[It would] assist KRI in its strategic planning and
development of new products. ... While it contains
aspects of traditional clipping and abstract services,
online databases, and emerging agent-based software,
the KnowledgeBase represents a new approach ...
that blends human intelligence with machine
efficiency to build a dynamic repository of knowledge.
In the broadest sense, it is an encyclopedia that is
always current."

Our proposal called for initially developing and maintaining the system with a small dedicated staff at the IDL and
providing access to Knight-Ridder properties through an
online network. We suggested that once we were confident in
its stability and our ability to maintain it, the KnowledgeBase
could be marketed as a commercial product with revenue
coming from annual subscriptions and site licensing. We
estimated that the development phase could be completed in
about six months with a modest investment of $110,000.

Batten gave his tentative endorsement for the project along
with another proposal I had put together at the request of the
Journal of Commerce editor to prototype an electronic edition
of the paper. Funding, he said, would be decided by Tony
Ridder. (As corporate president, he was the money man who
handled budgets and business-side interests.)

In July, I learned that Ridder had declined to fund the
KnowledgeBase project because he could not see a clear path
to profitability in the near term. He was more receptive to the
Journal of Commerce proposal but would not allocate funding
for the project, arguing that the project should be included in
the *JoC* budget.

(Several years later, web-based versions of the Knowledge-
Base concept began emerging. They were generally referred to

as collaborative online encyclopedias. The most widely adopted version, called "wikis," led to the founding of Wikipedia in January 2001, which rapidly became one of the most popular websites globally. In fairness to Ridder, Wikipedia and most other Wikis are not profitable ventures. They are usually funded by businesses and associations or donations to foundations.)

Mercury Center ascending

I was not the only presenter at the June 1993 corporate meeting in Miami. Robert Ingle, the executive editor of the *San Jose Mercury News*, made a compelling case for an online publishing venture he called Mercury Center. With Ridder's support, Ingle had just launched the first phase on America Online. Even though Ingle had been planning the venture for more than two years, this was the first I had heard about it. His vision, as stated in his report, was...

> "...to create an experimental electronic service, integrated with the *San Jose Mercury News*, that would offer the public new paths to information, communication, advertising and entertainment, while extending the life and preserving the franchise of the printed newspaper."

To avoid the mistakes made with Viewtron, Ingle said he planned to take measured, low-budget steps that had potential to quickly generate revenue. His budget request for the first full year of operation was about $600,000. He expected significant revenue from a percentage of AOL's national subscriber fees and from direct local Bay Area subscriptions and access fees, as well as from advertising and fees charged to retrieve articles from the paper's archives. He set a first-year goal of having 16,000 subscribers.

(Later, I learned that the actual number of subscribers at the end of the first year was less than 6,000, and the amount Mercury Center received from AOL for its percentage of the national subscriber fees was far below what was projected. Mercury Center also was unable to attract advertising. The newspaper archives proved to be the only significant source of revenue. As with Viewtron, making money from online news media would prove to be problematic for the *Mercury News* and all other newspapers.)

The *Mercury News* was an ideal host for this venture. As the flagship of Ridder Publications, the newspaper, which circulated mostly in Santa Clara county south of San Francisco, was known more for its high profit margins than its editorial quality. After the merger with Knight Newspapers, steps were taken to significantly bolster its journalistic integrity and increase circulation. In 1977, Knight-Ridder transferred Larry Jinks from the *Miami Herald*, where he was the paper's highly respected executive editor in the Knight mold, to San Jose to assume the same role at the *Mercury News*, and promoted Tony Ridder, a great-grandson of the Ridder Publications founder, from general manager to publisher. Under their leadership, the paper increased its news staff, opened international bureaus, and even won awards while maintaining a more than 30-percent profit margin. (When Ridder was named president of Knight-Ridder in 1989, he moved to Miami. Jinks then returned to the *Mercury News* as its publisher, a position he held until his retirement in 1994. A year later, Jinks was appointed as a director with the McClatchy Company, the chain that would acquire Knight-Ridder in 2006.)

During the eighties, the city of San Jose and *Mercury News* benefited enormously from the transformation of Santa Clara from a sleepy rural, agricultural county into a major American technology hub and burgeoning Bay Area suburb with a youthful, affluent demographic. It would come to be known as the heart of Silicon Valley.

By the beginning of the nineties, the *Mercury News* had fully embraced the new hip identity of the region and rebranded itself as "The Newspaper of Silicon Valley." The paper, with its lucrative and steadily growing classified advertising sections, then contributed about 10 percent of Knight-Ridder's annual operating revenue. Its proximity to the headquarters of Apple, Adobe, Intel, HP and dozens of high-tech start-ups, as well as to Stanford University, positioned the paper in the nineties to provide extensive technology coverage for online national and international audiences.

Ingle had forged a close relationship with Ridder at the *Mercury News* in the years since 1981, when he was transferred from the *Miami Herald* to replace Jinks who moved to the Miami corporate offices to become the senior vice president for news. Like Jinks, he had worked his way up through the newsroom, but the similarities ended there. Whereas Jinks was pleasant and accessible, traits he shared with Batten and Lee Hills, Ingle was abrasive and diffident. He had a reputation for being very smart and making everyone he dealt with aware of it.

I had met Ingle at technology conferences and Knight-Ridder meetings during the latter half of the seventies but didn't get to know him until after I joined the Viewtron development team in Miami in 1979. The following year, I collaborated with him on the *Herald* redesign and the creation of the Business Monday section.

We worked reasonably well together on those projects, but, soon after Ingle became the *Mercury News* executive editor, the camaraderie we had shared devolved into a rivalry. Our first clashes came when I launched the KR Graphics service in 1984. He made it known to Jinks and Ridder that he did not see any value in the weekly mailed packets and would not encourage the *Mercury News* artists to share their graphics.

By the June 1993 Miami meeting, the animosity between us was evident to nearly everyone. Somewhat less evident was how our differences reflected the internal power struggle simmering between the Knight tribe of dedicated journalists led by Jim Batten and the Ridder tribe of bottom-liners led by Tony Ridder. None of us could have imagined then that four months hence the dynamics that had held their divergent visions for the future of the chain in check would be disrupted by a mysterious accident.

The beginning of the end

As the Miami meeting drew to a close, Batten invited me into his office for a private conversation. He wanted to know if I could see a way for the IDL and Mercury Center to work together. I wasn't sure what to make of his question, but I suspected it had something to do with the vice president for new ventures position announced at the beginning of the meeting. My first thought was that Ridder might be planning to merge the IDL and Mercury Center under the new VP.

When I asked Batten directly if that was being considered, his response was noncommittal. Returning to his original question, I remember replying that I would welcome sharing information and collaborating on projects that contributed to our individual missions, but that would depend on Ingle's willingness to work collegially with me and the IDL team. He seemed to understand what I meant.

I then asked Batten the question that had been running through my mind since the announcement: Should I apply for that position? After a short pause, he responded with another question: "Are you sure that's what you really want?" Before I could answer, he politely suggested that I should consider how my life would change.

Aside from having to leave Boulder, which he knew Ada and I loved, and returning to Miami, I recall him confiding, to the effect of:

> As a corporate officer, you would not have the creative freedom and independence that you have been accustomed for so many years. Vice presidents don't create or take risks. They motivate others to do the creating and risk taking. Most of their time is spent attending meetings, reviewing budgets, implementing policies, and managing people. In all the years I have known you, I never saw you in the role of a corporate officer; not for lack of qualifications. I believed putting you in that position would have been a waste of your rare combination of talents. You are doing more good for the company working independently than you could possibly do as a vice president.

While I appreciated Batten's honesty, I could not help feeling disappointed. But, as I thought about what he had said, I knew he was right. I could not imagine being happy in that role either. I already had the job and life that made me happier than I had ever been.

I have no record or memory of meeting with him again during that summer. However, when an associate of McKinsey & Co., the firm Ridder had hired to interview candidates for the new VP position, visited the lab in late July, she let me know that Batten had urged her to meet with me. After a full day at the lab, she intimated over dinner that she found our work exciting and encouraging for the future of Knight-Ridder.

My files reveal a blur of travels and meetings between July and October. In those months, we also began "playing" with a first-generation Apple Newton mini tablet and a beta release of the NCSA Mosaic web browser, as well as producing a video we would use to help people visualize the tablet newspaper concept. All of us were feeling optimistic and confident in corporate's continuing support for the lab.

That would change in a fateful instant on Sunday, October 17, 1993. When I arrived at the corporate offices the following morning for my scheduled meeting with Batten, I remember feeling, almost immediately, that something was amiss. There were none of the usual "good mornings" and handshakes. Everyone I passed appeared stunned.

At Batten's office, I was surprised to find the door closed and no one sitting at his assistant's desk. The door to Ridder's office also was closed, as were the doors to adjacent VP offices, so I assumed there must be a meeting. Wandering down the corridor, I encountered Frank Hawkins, the VP for corporate relations. He looked visibly shaken. When I asked him what was going on, he blurted out: "We almost lost Batten last night."

Hawkins was in a hurry to deliver his draft of a press release to Ridder, so all he had time to tell me was that Batten had been seriously injured in an automobile accident, and he was still in a coma on a ventilator after brain surgery. Later, I learned that he apparently had blacked out while driving home from the airport. His car then jumped a curb and hit a concrete light pole. Fortunately, a passerby who witnessed the accident used Batten's cell phone to call for help. Within minutes, Jackson Memorial Hospital dispatched a helicopter that airlifted him to its trauma center.

Batten would need a couple of months to recuperate. His doctors had no explanation for what had caused his blackout. Brain scans did not reveal any tumors or aneurysms. At the end of the year, he was declared recovered, but that would not be the end of his ordeal. Within a few more months, the excruciating headaches would begin.

The Apple disappointments

For more than two years, John Sculley, the Apple chief executive who deposed Steve Jobs in 1986, had been touting a revolutionary computing device that the company would finally launch in the summer of '93 — the Newton Message Pad. Sculley called this pen-based mini tablet a Personal Digital Assistant (PDA). What made the Newton revolutionary was its simplicity and touchscreen, but the feature Sculley hyped most was its "amazing" ability to convert ordinary handwriting to computer text.

While its screen was too small for my electronic newspaper concept, I could see several possible newspaper uses. More importantly, it gave me hope that Apple would soon launch a letter-size Newton, which it was rumored to have under development.

In the meantime, I thought the IDL might be able to collaborate with our neighbor — the Apple Electronic Media Lab — to create Newton apps for some types of newspaper content. But that idea proved to be a non-starter. The first-generation had a limited capacity to send and receive content through an online network.

By the end of the year, my hopes of seeing a larger Newton anytime soon were dashed by reports of Apple's internal strife and declining fortunes, exacerbated by the Newton's dismal sales numbers and embarrassing problems with the handwriting recognition feature. Its frequent misreading of characters was widely derided in the media.

Even the Boulder Apple lab quickly put the Newton aside and focused all of its attention on developing a new online service. While Converse and DuBe would occasionally visit the IDL and join us for beer at the nearby Walnut Brewery to chat about electronic newspapers and tablets, they never shared any information about their secret online initiative or reciprocated with an invitation for me or anyone from the IDL team to visit their lab.

Their secret finally would be revealed on January 5, 1994, when Apple announced at the MacWorld Conference & Expo that it was preparing to launch a new consumer online service called "eWorld." I immediately signed up the IDL to become a beta tester for the proprietary dial-up service, which went into full operation on June 20 of that year. The portal software was based around a town square metaphor where each content branch was represented by a building. The innovative graphical user interface with its cartoon-like drawings was unlike the typical Mac desktop.

One of the buildings was a newsstand that initially only provided stories about Apple products and related technologies. This seemed like an opportunity for Knight-Ridder to occupy the building as a news provider. However, when I explored that possibility, I was told the chain's contractual commitment to America Online for Mercury Center precluded our involvement with the competing eWorld service.

The Tablet Newspaper video

During an IDL brainstorming session in March of '93, several participants told us they didn't know anything about the lab or the tablet newspaper vision before they arrived. All agreed we needed to do a better job of disseminating information about our work and new media developments that might affect newspapers.

That spring, I got corporate approval to hire Teresa Martin as our communications manager. She had recently earned a master's degree from the Harvard University Graduate School of Education with an emphasis on interactive media and had a bachelor's degree in journalism from Boston University. By summer, she was producing a monthly newsletter that we distributed throughout the Knight-Ridder chain and managing the New Media KnowledgeBase. But it was another project that would consume most of her time for the remainder of 1993 and nearly all of 1994 — *The Tablet Newspaper* video.

The idea for producing the video evolved from making a simple recording of my interactive tablet newspaper demo into a major production that would go well beyond the newspanel video I produced in 1990 in collaboration with Raychem. The project entailed creating realistic tablet mockups, recruiting a skilled videography team, and hiring local actors. Teresa would script the video, coach the actors, and work with the videographer.

My original tablet concept in 1981 and the model I created ten years later as a Freedom Forum Center Fellow anticipated a thin, lightweight, letter-size, flat-panel color display with a finger-sensitive touchscreen and no physical keyboard or buttons. The defining features of my vision were simplicity and ease of use. Tablets, as I saw them, had to turn on and off instantly like a radio or TV set and would not require a user manual. That meant doing away with the typical computer "boot-up" and shutdown procedures, time-consuming routines for installing software and downloading content, cryptic error messages, and befuddling terminology.

Several letter-size tablets already were commercially available in 1993, but none was as simple and easy to use as I had envisioned. All of these first-generation tablets were essentially slate-type laptop computers that merely replaced the keyboard and mouse with a pen-based touchscreen.

The biggest obstacles to realizing my tablet vision by the end of the decade, beyond overcoming the mindsets of computer engineers and information technology managers, were the high costs for color flat-panel displays and alternatives to hard disc drives. The lack of broadband wireless services and Wi-Fi local area networks also was an impediment.

Despite being told by engineers not to bank on low-cost, letter-size, color flat-panel displays within our time frame, I rejected the idea of using a monochrome display for the video. Color, I argued, was essential to the concept.

The engineers also tried to convince me that an internal hard disc drive was the only device that would have the capacity and speed to handle the tablet operating system, application software, and content. This would have necessitated the usual computer "boot-up" and shutdown delays, which were unacceptable to me. No matter what, I was determined to have the tablet described in the video appear to turn on and off instantly.

The only way, they said, for a tablet to have that capability would be to store the operating system in the device's memory ready for immediate retrieval even when there was no power.

That was a tall order in 1993. The low-cost flash memory technology that would be widely adopted after the turn of the century for use in digital cameras, USB drives, and portable computers was still at an early stage in its development. However, a nascent form of removable, rewritable flash storage media the size and shape of a credit card had just begun to enter the market as we were planning for the video.

A rep from SanDisc assured us that memory cards would have a capacity to store upwards of 32 megabytes and would be relatively inexpensive within ten years. (None of us could imagine then that we would be able to buy tiny flash memory chips by the second decade of the new century with more than a thousand times that capacity for less than ten dollars.)

In my final design for the tablet mockup, I took for granted that flash memory or some other technology would store the operating system internally so that it could be turned on and off instantly. I also added two slots for removable memory cards. I assumed they would be used for storing electronic newspapers as well as personal documents.

To get around not having broadband wireless or local Wi-Fi access in the nineties, I envisioned papers delivering their electronic editions via satellite/cable television or optical-fiber networks to public kiosks and personal docking stations. With this concept, selected papers could be purchased and loaded onto memory cards.

We found a plastics molding company in Denver to produce the six tablet mockups that we would use for the video and presentations. The dimensions were slightly larger than the standard-size North American letter and about a half-inch thick. The plastic displays were 12-inches on the diagonal with a 3-by-4 ratio. Each weighed less than two pounds.

One of the design features that would distinguish my tablet concept from existing tablets was the rounded corners and edges. All tablets and laptops in the nineties had angular cases with square corners and edges. (Two decades later, the round-corner design would involve me in an acrimonious patent dispute between Apple and Samsung.)

To simulate the experience of reading an electronic newspaper on a tablet, the videography team captured my demo pages displayed on the Mac's portrait-oriented screen and then digitally merged them with the mockups used by the actors. The merging was done so well that nearly everyone who saw the video believed the tablet was real.

When the 13-minute video was completed in the summer of '94, we produced 250 VHS tapes. The first copies were distributed within Knight-Ridder. As soon as we began showing the video, we received numerous requests for copies from tech companies and other newspaper groups around the world.

While some people assumed from the video that Knight-Ridder was planning to manufacture tablets, that was never considered. Our intent was to spur the development of suitable tablets by established consumer electronics companies, as well as encourage news organizations to work with us on standards.

An invitation to speak at the Digital Media 2000 conference in Tokyo in mid-October provided an opportunity to meet with several of the largest Japanese electronics companies and newspaper publishers. Yukari Miyamae arranged the meetings and served as my interpreter. The videos and tablet mockups we brought with us had the intended effect. At the Toshiba headquarters, my presentation led to a request for a follow-up visit to the IDL by executives who had been evaluating the tablet concept. Executives we met with at the

Asahi Shimbun, Japan's second largest national newspaper, made the same request. Representatives from both organizations arrived in Boulder the following month.

The Journal of Commerce website

When we got onto the "information superhighways" at the IDL for the first time in the fall of '93, few newspaper publishers, or readers for that matter, were aware of the internet and even less of the World Wide Web. Our "on-ramp" was the just released free Mosaic software developed at the National Center for Supercomputing Applications (NCSA) at the University of Illinois. The progeny of this nascent web browser soon would rapidly accelerate the digital publishing revolution and unleash the disruptive power of online media globally, although that was not immediately apparent.

In 1993, there were only 130 websites worldwide. To locate them, you had to know their internet addresses or domain names. There were no directories or search engines then. Yahoo! would not launch its web portal until the middle of the next year; AltaVista followed in '95. Three more years would pass before Google launched its search engine.

The Mosaic software also provided relatively simple tools for creating and editing websites that presented images in line with text on computer screens. (All other online services displayed images and text in separate windows.) With these tools, anyone who had a basic understanding of computer programing could build hyperlinked websites and make their contents accessible to anyone who had internet access and a web browser. After "playing" with the software for several weeks, we put it aside. The video project, visitors to the lab, and travels consumed most of our time for the remainder of the year.

Early in '94, Scott Bosley, the *Journal of Commerce* editor, contacted me again. He had just formed a task force to investigate the idea of creating an electronic edition and now had funding for the project in his budget.

I had been waiting for this opportunity ever since the mid-eighties when I redesigned the paper. During the weeks I spent at the *JoC's* offices, I became convinced the paper was ideally suited to electronic delivery. Nearly every production process was state-of-the-art — already digitized and networked.

While reading about the *JoC's* storied past, I learned this was a newspaper born to be wired. Co-founded in New York City in 1827 by Samuel Morse, the paper quickly earned a reputation for employing innovative methods to get stories ahead of the competition, among them was America's first pony express to carry news to New York that had been gathered from the crews of merchant ships as they arrived in the Baltimore harbor.

In 1846, the *JoC* adopted a much faster method that touched the future of newspapers and journalism — Morse's electromagnetic telegraph. Four other New York City newspapers joined with the *JoC* that year to share the high cost of transmitting news of the Mexican-American War. Their organization led to the founding of the Associated Press and the first uses of newspaper "reporters" to submit stories from distant locations as events were unfolding.

My first assignment from Bosley was to meet with several of the paper's major subscribers and advertisers to assess their level of interest in an electronically delivered and displayed *JoC*. Most of the companies I visited were slow to adopt online technologies. Nevertheless, Bosley and I were encouraged by the younger managers who expressed a genuine interest in online access. By the beginning of summer, we were ready to begin creating mock ups. I had received approval to hire Curt Stevens as our lead software engineer and Bill Skeet as a designer. Curt had just earned a PhD in computer science from the University of Colorado. Bill had recently graduated with a master's degree from the University of Kansas. Our goal was to launch the electronic edition early in 1995.

Fate would again intercede that summer. Just as Knight-Ridder appeared to be getting back to relative normal after Batten's accident, we learned he had undergone brain surgery in Boston to remove a plum-size malignant tumor. His follow-up treatments and recuperation were expected to keep him away from the office for at least several months. During that time, we were told Tony Ridder would assume his responsibilities. While all of us who knew Batten hoped for the best, we feared the worst.

When Batten returned to his corporate office in the fall, the tolls taken by the surgery and treatments were visibly apparent. During a meeting with him and Ridder to review my 1995 budget proposal and the *JoC* project, he seemed distracted and tired; a couple of times he dozed off. As I walked by the open door of Batten's office later that day, he invited me in. He was alone and appeared happy to see me. He made no mention of the earlier meeting; his mind was elsewhere. A memory he related to me from his early childhood revealed he obviously was contemplating his future. He recalled that in 1941 "everyone wondered when the shooting war would begin."

A fate accompli

January 1995 began with optimism at the lab. We were feeling confident in our ability to launch the first phase of the *JoC* website by the end of the month. Then, a couple of weeks into the new year, Ridder called around 2 a.m. Without so much as a polite greeting, he ordered me to immediately stop working on the *JoC* website and not to discuss it outside of the lab. No explanation was given.

That sleepless night my mood oscillated between disappointment and anger as I tried to make sense out of Ridder's order. I knew Ingle was preparing to launch a Mercury Center website and wondered if he might have had something to do with it. When I attempted to call Bosley later that morning, I learned he had left the *JoC* to become publisher of the *Post-Tribune*, a KR newspaper in Gary, Indiana.

Early in the following month, I learned the reason for Ridder's order from a corporate conference call — Knight-Ridder had sold the *Journal of Commerce* to the *Economist*, an international business newsmagazine based in London. But that was not the only purpose for the call. Ridder also used it to announce that after an 18-month search he had selected Sharon Studer, a senior account manager for Peat Marwick who he met while in London, to be the corporate vice president for new ventures.

His next announcement caught me by complete surprise — he had named Ingle to be corporate vice president for new media. No one had alerted me prior to the call about this new VP position or informed me about how the IDL and my corporate reporting relationship would be affected by Ingle's promotion. Batten was uncharacteristically silent.

In March, Studer made a brief visit to the lab, during which she met with each member of my team privately. While she had seemed interested in the tablet newspaper vision and our collaborations, she said nothing about the future of the lab.

A short while later, she requested that I prepare a business plan for "TelePress," a new venture I had proposed during her visit. She then let me know that several members of the IDL team would be reassigned to Ingle's New Media Center (NMC) in San Jose. She did not tell me outright that the Boulder lab would be closed, but that's what I understood.

The reason for Batten's silence became clear in April when I learned his cancer had metastasized. The seizures and treatments were preventing him from performing his essential duties, so the board had elevated Ridder to chief executive and president. Batten retained his title as chairman, although it was apparent that his feared "shooting war" had begun, and he would soon be its casualty.

We continued to speak at conferences and receive visitors to the lab, but the wind had been taken out of our sails. In April, Curt, Bill, and Teresa left to take jobs at the NMC. Peggy, Mark, and Yukari stayed on with me to complete the TelePress business plan. It was an ambitious plan to build an online business around producing and globally distributing digital replicas of newspapers that could be read on personal computers as well as on future tablets and other portable display devices. Even though we thought the venture had potential, we knew it had little chance of getting Ridder's support.

When Studer called early in June, she only mentioned the plan in passing. Her reason for calling was to give me the news I had been expecting — the lab would be closed at the end of July. Peggy and Mark, she said, would be offered jobs at the NMC and I would be transferred to San Jose to work under Ingle.

She must have known that I would be unwilling to make that move because when I told her I had decided to resign, she did not seem surprised. With a frigid voice, she informed me that my severance contract would be mailed within a few days. (Peggy and Mark also chose to resign.)

The contract I received contained clauses that were dumbfounding. Among them was a provision that I could not use for monetary gain any skills, information, or ideas I had acquired during my 21 years with Knight-Ridder. I had naïvely assumed I would not need legal representation; now I realized I had no choice. The lawyer I hired acknowledged that the provisions of the contract were so broad that they would have effectively rendered me unemployable and poisoned any attempt to secure investors for a tablet-related start-up venture.

In my lawyer's letter to Studer, she took the facetious position that I would be willing to sign the contract if Knight-Ridder would agree to pay my full salary plus benefits and cost-of-living raises for the remainder of my life. Otherwise, she said, the restrictive provisions of the severance contract were a blatant violation of federal labor laws.

While awaiting Studer's response, the sad news I had been anticipating diverted my attention — Batten died on June 24; a week later I received word that my mother, whose health had been declining for several months, was on the verge of dying. Ada and I arrived in Eugene on July 2, just in time to hold her hand during the last hour of her life.

Shortly after we returned to Boulder, I received a call from Kathleen Yates. She was general manager for the *Mercury News* and director of new business development for the New Media Center. Studer and Ridder, she said, had asked her to resolve my contract issues and to handle the closing of the lab.

Yates met with me in Boulder a week before the closing. I found her to be honest and reasonable. While the final contract still included clauses that inhibited my ability to start or partner in a venture, she limited the restraint specifically to my TelePress plan for a period of five years. I also would have to sign a nondisclosure agreement that prevented me from saying or publishing anything negative about Knight-Ridder or its executives during that five-year period. The contract provided a generous severance package, so I accepted without reservations. Additionally, she approved my request to donate all of the lab's computers and software to the University of Colorado School of Journalism.

My last day with Knight-Ridder was July 31, which again happened to be Ada's birthday. That evening we celebrated at our favorite Indian restaurant. Whatever sadness we felt, we left behind and did not look back. We were looking forward to wherever our personal journey and my tablet newspaper vision might lead us. The digital future of newspapers that I and so many others touched, however, would have a far different outcome in the new century than we could have envisioned.

Author's notes

In 2010, a digital version of the lab's *Tablet Newspaper* video went viral on the web after Steve Jobs introduced the Apple iPad, which bore a striking resemblance to our tablet mockup. Some pundits have posited that Jobs stole my idea, but that's not a claim I have ever made. While I know Apple had copies of the video, I don't know if Jobs ever saw it. Even if the video did influence him, I would not begrudge his success. I never aspired to be the head of a large corporation or to become rich and famous. I'm happy that he had the wherewithal and determination to finally make the tablets I envisioned real.

As much as I had wanted to believe that I could convince computer companies to produce tablets as I had envisioned them before the end of the nineties, the essential technologies and manufacturing capabilities just weren't advanced enough in that decade. Moreover, it required the visionary power and tenacity of Jobs and the financial power and influence of Apple to break out of the notebook and tablet PC molds favored by Microsoft and other personal computer companies.

———

After the lab closed, Peggy Bair joined the @Home Network in California as content services product manager. When the company merged with Excite, she became the knowledgebase product manager. Mark Timpe joined StorageTek in Louisville, Colorado, as voice network manager. Yukari Miyamae went on to work as a translator/interpreter and consultant for media and technology organizations in the U.S. and Japan. In 1998, Curt Stevens left the New Media Center to join Apple Computer as a senior scientist/engineer. From 2010 until his retirement in 2017 he was the director of software engineering for Disney Interactive.

———

During my years at the lab, Ada and I travelled almost every-where together. Except for situations where I was a speaker at conferences that invited spouses and covered their airfare, I handled all of her travel expenses out of pocket. Doing so was well worth it. Had she not joined me, we would not have had much time together. Moreover, the experiences and adven-tures we shared enriched our lives and contributed to our mutual happiness. Her presence often opened doors and led to friendships that persisted long after our meetings.

CHAPTER NINE

Life After Knight-Ridder

The death of Jim Batten and ascendance of Tony Ridder to chairman, CEO, and president in the summer of ´95 marked the end of the delicate balance that Jack Knight had instituted between business-side and news-side interests. For the first time, there would not be an experienced journalist in Knight-Ridder's upper echelon to defend the editors and core values of the chain from the extreme bottom-liners. Nearly all of Ridder's career was in business administration; his forte was cost control.

While Ridder's decision to close the Information Design Lab was shortsighted and personally dismaying, his demands on KR newspapers to meet often unrealistic profit goals would have far more serious consequences for Knight-Ridder. Within a few years, several dozen publishers and top editors who shared Batten's commitment to quality journalism resigned.

In 1998, Ridder moved the corporate headquarters from Miami to San Jose and centralized control of digital and online news initiatives under KnightRidder.com. By 2001, he had sold off nearly all of the ancillary businesses that Batten had acquired or nurtured internally to diversify the chain's holdings.

During those years, I transitioned from corporate to the halls of academia where I remained actively involved with newspapers and continued to pursue my tablet vision. I also would finally complete my book and college degree, and then go on to become a tenured full professor.

A year of repairing and rewriting

In August 1995, two weeks after my "early retirement" from Knight-Ridder, my arthritic left hip joint gave way reluctantly to a stainless-steel surrogate at the Boulder Community Hospital. My range of motion and bouts of agony had been growing progressively worse for some time. Whenever Ada saw me limping or struggling to stand up after a fall, she would urge me to have the surgery, but I always found excuses to put it off. After so many years of living with arthritis, I had developed a high tolerance for pain, so I thought I could keep delaying the inevitable.

Now almost all movement caused paralyzing agony. And now, I no longer could use my work as an excuse. The surgeon had said the operation would take less than two hours; instead, a complication extended it to nearly four hours. Thankfully, Barrie Hartman, the *Camera* editor and our friend, insisted on staying with Ada at the hospital the entire time.

The six weeks of physical therapy and recuperation passed quickly. While my right hip still troubled me, I had more flexibility and less pain overall. Convalescing at home, I devoted most of my time to completing the book about the computerization of newspapers I began as a Freedom Forum Fellow in 1991. My working title was *The Mediamorphosis of Newspapers*.

Around the middle of September, a University of Colorado journalism professor introduced me to the editor and founder of Pine Forge Press, an academic imprint owned by Sage Publications. After reading my manuscript, he offered me a contract to publish the book as part of his "Communication and Journalism for a New Century" series. When I signed, I thought the manuscript was about ready to be published. How wrong I was.

Before sending my manuscript to his academic reviewers, the editor urged me to make "a few" changes. What the book needed, he said, was more about how newspapers had adapted to the emergence of new communication technologies since the invention of the telegraph, and how they might adapt to the web, which still was quite new in 1995.

With an assist from my New Media Knowledgebase, which I had saved and continued to maintain, I managed to send him a revised manuscript before I had to leave for three international speaking engagements at the end of October. They began with a new media symposium in Cuenca, Spain, followed a few days later by a keynote at the AdAsia Conference in Bali, Indonesia, and a University of Malaysia lecture in Kuching, Sarawak, on the island of Borneo. All of the running down long airport concourses gave my new hip joint a good workout.

Soon after Ada and I returned home in mid-November, the editor met with me to share the feedback he had received. The manuscript, he told me, is good as far as it goes. BUT... to be used as a supplemental textbook, it would need more work — a lot more work. Focusing on newspapers, the reviewers argued, was too narrow. They wanted me to apply my principles of mediamorphosis to broadcast media and provide a broader context for understanding how technological and social changes have transformed human communication.

After taking a deep breath, I nervously asked the editor when he would need the new revised manuscript. With a firm voice, he said, "By the middle of April at the latest." After another deep breath, I told him I would be consulting and conducting seminars in Southeast Asia in December and Europe in March, but I would do my best. Meeting his deadline required me to forego teaching a course at the Colorado School of Journalism during spring semester.

On April 11, 1996, I shipped the editor what amounted to an almost entirely new manuscript. At several points, I had been on the verge of giving up on the book, but each time Ada used her charms to keep me going. As we were leaving the FedEx office, Ada suggested that we visit a nearby pet store. As soon as we entered, two kittens — a Bengal and an Ocicat — tugged at our hearts with their affectionate meowing and playfulness. We hadn't planned on adopting pets, but it was mutual love at first sight. An hour later, we left with both kittens in travel carriers and a carload of supplies. We named our first "children" Media and Morphosis.

A few days later, two invitations from Kent State University in northeast Ohio would touch my future. One was from Dr. John West, director of the Liquid Crystal Institute, to participate in an electronic display seminar. The other was from Pam Creedon, director of the journalism school, to speak with students and faculty about my tablet newspaper vision.

They had scheduled my visit for May 4, a significant date for the university and the country. On that day in 1970, Ohio National Guard soldiers shot four students dead and wounded nine others during a mass protest on the Kent campus against the Vietnam War. Each year since then, a May 4 commemoration has been held on campus.

The Liquid Crystal Institute is world-renowned and recognized as the birthplace of liquid crystal displays. I felt out of my league among all of the scientists and engineers who were attending the seminar that morning, but my presentation appeared to hold their attention. As I was preparing to leave, West told me he hoped I would be willing to return in the fall to speak at another seminar and spend more time at the institute.

The School of Journalism and Mass Communication then was located in Taylor Hall. Ada and I arrived just after noon as the university's Victory Bell rang in memory of the students who had been shot in front of the building. Creedon greeted us warmly and guided us to a conference room where I would show *The Tablet Newspaper* video and have an informal discussion with students and faculty. I hadn't realized at the time that they also were interviewing me for a job. The following month, I received an offer to join the journalism faculty as a professional-in-residence for three years beginning with the fall semester. West would get his wish.

In mid-June, my right hip joint succumbed to the surgeon's tools and skilled hands. This time, Ada and I were less anxious and the surgery went smoothly without complications.

About a week before I entered the hospital, I received a package with the latest feedback from the reviewers, and the editor's assessment of my rewritten manuscript. My spirits were uplifted by the generally positive reviews and editor's encouraging comments. However, the book still was not ready to publish. I would spend most of my second recuperation time addressing their constructive criticisms.

During that period, Morphosis became my taskmaster and muse. Every morning at around 4 a.m. he would alert me with a couple of cries close to my ear that it was time to begin writing.

He would then lead me to my home office and perch on top of the computer monitor where he would watch me intently, with one paw hanging over the screen, until the electric warmth seduced him back to sleep. Media was more attached to the bed. He preferred to remain snuggled with Ada in a shared dream state until time for breakfast.

On the last day of July, exactly a year after my departure from Knight-Ridder and again on Ada's birthday, the editor signed off on my manuscript and sent it out to be prepared for printing. The expanded book, which we renamed *Mediamorphosis: Understanding New Media*, included a forward written by Alfred C. Sikes, a former FCC chairman and then president of Hearst New Media and Technology. A week later, Ada and I packed our suitcases and "children" into our Jeep Wrangler and headed east out of Colorado on Interstate 70 for Kent, Ohio, to begin the next chapter in our lives.

My reintroduction to academia

Exactly thirty years had passed since I dropped out of the University of Oregon. While the lack of a college degree had not hampered my career, the disappointment still lingered on my mind. I always told myself that someday I would return to complete my degree requirements. Now I thought I might have that opportunity.

We arrived a couple of weeks before the beginning of fall semester to locate and rent an apartment that allowed pets. We had decided not to sell our townhouse in Boulder or ship our furniture and household possessions to Kent until we were sure about staying for at least three years. So, for the first 12 months we bivouacked like college students with an air mattress for a bed and a small dining room set we purchased at a garage sale. My salary was a fraction of what I had earned at Knight-Ridder, but it was adequate to meet our modest living expenses.

My first office in Taylor Hall was a huge comedown from my modern, spacious IDL office in Boulder. The cramped, windowless former storeroom had an ancient metal desk and bankers chair like I had had in Detroit. I obviously was not going to be given VIP treatment.

Creedon assigned me to teach "Media, Power and Culture" three hours a week. She explained that it was one of the Kent Core lecture courses, so it usually attracted several hundred undergraduate students from across the campus who were not enrolled in the journalism program. All she gave me were a sample syllabus, a recommended textbook, and the university's faculty handbook. How I taught the course, she said, was my decision.

About 350 students casually straggled into the lecture hall on the first morning. Most had laptop computers they opened as soon as they sat down. I had spoken at hundreds of conferences and given presentations in auditoriums with several thousand participants during my career, so I thought speaking in front of this group would be easy. It wasn't.

The only teaching tools at my disposal that fall were low-tech projectors for slides, VHS video tapes, and overheads. They didn't seem to help much. From my vantage point on the podium, I had the impression no one was paying attention to me or any of the material I projected on the screen. More than a few students had their heads nestled in their folded arms on the desks, obviously sleeping. When I asked if anyone had questions about ten minutes before the end of the 50-minute class, nearly all of the students immediately started noisily filing out of the hall.

This was not how I remembered Roy Paul Nelson's lectures at the University of Oregon in 1964. Though, I couldn't be sure if that was because it was a different era in which students actually were more respectful of professors or my memory of the experience as a student had faded with age. Regardless, it was apparent that I had a lot to learn about engaging students. Fortunately for me and the students, the school had excellent teachers to learn from. All had professional experience and took pride in nurturing future journalists and media practitioners. Many of the students, like me in the sixties, were the first in their families to attend college.

In February 1997, the Pine Forge editor called to tell me my book was finally coming off the presses in Ann Arbor, Michigan. He said the printer would send me 10 free copies in a few weeks, but Ada and I were too impatient to wait. Early the next morning, we drove north to pick up the free copies along with 200 more copies that I had arranged to purchase.

Back in Kent, I gave copies to all of the faculty and mailed others to the people who had assisted me with the book. The remaining copies I planned to sell or give away at the meetings and conferences where I would be speaking. To my relief, and the delight of the editor, the reviews that appeared in journalism and academic publications were all positive.

With my book finally in print and Ada's encouragement, I approached Creedon that spring about fulfilling my requirements for a bachelor's degree and possibly going on to earn a master's degree at Kent State. She was supportive and suggested that my experiences and book might be sufficient to complete my bachelor's degree. She had earned her master's degree from the Oregon School of Journalism and said she would talk with Dean Duncan McDonald and Emeritus Dean Arnold

Ismach. Both knew me well. They had invited me to speak at a number of events as well as to meet with students and faculty whenever I was in Eugene.

Creedon was right. The deans arranged for the University of Oregon to recognize me as a Class of '66 graduate with a bachelor's degree in journalism. That fall, I enrolled in the Kent Media Management master's program. During the next two years, I would create and edit a "Future of Print Media" website, conduct several research projects, produce an e-book version of *Mediamorphosis*, redesign the school's website, and write an academic paper on the preservation of digital news content, in addition to speaking at conferences and teaching undergraduate courses while also completing the required graduate courses.

In May 1999, at the age of 56, I put on a master's cap and gown and proudly walked onto the auditorium stage to receive my diploma. Later, Ada and I attended a banquet where I was inducted into the Kappa Tau Alpha journalism honors society. After more than three decades, I had finally tied up my academic loose ends. Now, I had to figure out what to do next.

As much as I loved newspapers, I decided against trying to start over with another newspaper company. While several chains had created their own new media labs, nearly all of their new hires were recent college graduates who had mastered web programming. Senior management positions for men who were over the age of 50 from outside of the chains and had not worked at a paper or a tech company for several years were practically nonexistent.

Moreover, nearly all of the editors and executives I had known and respected within and outside of Knight-Ridder had moved on, often under pressure for failing to meet onerous cost-cutting demands and resisting layoffs. While a lucky few found jobs with privately held newspapers where profits didn't supersede everything else, most migrated to new roles within associations, foundations, academia, and other businesses.

I also had decided against joining a tech company or going the dotcom start-up route. At that point in my life, I was not willing to make the sacrifices required to build a new business. Ada and I were happy with our lives and financially secure.

As it turned out, I didn't need to spend much time thinking about my future. Soon after graduation, Creedon made me an offer in the form of a question: Would I consider staying at Kent State if she could convince the J-school faculty and university's faculty senate to let her appoint me as a tenured full professor?

Ada and I had held out hope of returning to Boulder, but that no longer seemed realistic, at least not in the near term. My discussions with the Colorado J-school about joining the faculty that fall ended with the dean's abrupt departure. I toyed with starting a consulting business, but relocating in Boulder without a reliable income would have been financial folly.

Even though the dismal, rural town of Kent was a far cry from Boulder, the university had much to offer. What made Creedon's proposal most appealing was the enthusiastic support I had found for my tablet newspaper vision within the J-school and Liquid Crystal Institute, as well as the schools of computer science, library science, and graphic design.

That summer, the faculty senate approved my appointment. As a tenured full professor with a master's degree, I would be able to teach graduate-level courses and establish a lab I called the Institute for Cyber Information (ICI). All I needed were grants to fund my projects.

My first electronic newspaper project

I held no illusions about the main reasons for my appointment. The Kent State School of Journalism had no endowed chairs or significant research grants. And, like many states with politically conservative legislatures, funding for public education in Ohio was atrophying. The university obviously hoped my international reputation would be a magnet for grants.

My first modest grant came from Crain Communications Inc., a privately held media company based in Chicago that published an array of business journals around the country. Brian Tucker, the publisher of *Crain's Cleveland Business*, had a long history with the school and had become intrigued with my tablet concept. During a campus visit in the fall of '99, he offered to fund the creation of a prototype electronic edition.

Tucker arranged several meetings with his editors and art director early in 2000 to discuss the project. Accessing all of the text files, art work, and advertisements in their native digital formats from a single weekly issue did not pose a problem. Creating a prototype with all of the typographic styles used by the journal and its advertisers, however, was another matter. While Crain's had purchased Adobe's extensive library of scalable fonts, the licensing agreement restricted its use to the company's production computers. A copy could not be legally installed on the school's computers. Purchasing the library was financially prohibitive.

I had just begun to play with a beta copy of InDesign, a new desktop publishing application developed by Adobe to replace its PageMaker software. At the time, Adobe was engaged in a life-or-death struggle with Quark, which then was the dominant desktop publishing software provider for magazines and newspapers as well as journalism schools, including Kent. One of InDesign's compelling features was its ability to quickly render pages in Adobe's Portable Document Format (PDF). With PDF, the pages could be compressed into relatively small file sizes and displayed on any computer with a PDF reader.

I wagered that a call to Dr. John Warnock, Adobe's co-founder and chief executive, might provide a solution. During the eighties and early nineties, I had met with him on numerous occasions. After updating him on my becoming a full professor and establishing a research lab at Kent State, I told him about the Crain's project and my font problem.

Warnock asked a number of questions about the project and my use of InDesign and then put me on a long hold. When he returned, he said "your problem is solved." About a week later, I received a package containing CDs with the entire Adobe font library licensed for use on J-school computers, as well as 10 copies of Adobe's publishing suite that bundled the released version of InDesign with PhotoShop, Illustrator, and Acrobat (software required for enhancing and editing PDF files).

By March, I had mastered the new software and was ready to create the prototype. Working alone, I needed a couple of weeks to produce a complete interactive version. It had about 200 pages and weighed-in at just over 10 megabytes. The funding provided by Tucker made it possible to conduct several focus group sessions. A finding that stuck with me was the subscribers' attachment to print for leisure reading. Nearly all indicated that they usually kept the printed issues on their desks or office tables for at least a week so they and others could read them whenever they had free time. What would be more useful, they opined, were personalized updates sent to their computers every weekday morning.

Based on the project's findings, Tucker decided to focus the company's immediate attention on developing topical e-mail newsletters and a more robust website. While he didn't rule out the possibility of publishing an electronic edition in the future, he surmised it probably would have to wait until tablets became widely available.

Microsoft's tablet PC and 9/11

In November 2000, Bill Gates, Microsoft's co-founder and CEO, demonstrated second-generation pen-based tablets at the annual Computer Dealers' Exhibition (COMDEX) that he called tablet PCs. While they overcame some of the problems that had stifled tablet sales in the nineties, they still were slate-type, pen-based laptops that weighed between three and six pounds.

The following year, Microsoft introduced a new Windows operating system for the tablet PCs that Toshiba, HP, Fujitsu, NEC, and several other companies were beginning to market. While they were readily adopted by some businesses and road warriors, they would be slow to catch on with general consumers.

Despite their shortcomings, Microsoft's tablet PCs served to reinvigorate interest in my tablet newspaper concept. Between March and July 2001, I was invited to speak at seven conferences and seminars across the country. The J-school had a minuscule travel budget for the faculty, so if the inviting organizations did not cover travel expenses, I had to rely on my grants, which by the beginning of summer were nearly exhausted.

My calls to senior newspaper executives finally resulted in invitations to give on-site presentations in September at *The New York Times, Wall Street Journal,* and *Los Angeles Times.* None of the companies offered to reimburse me, so I decided to put my accumulated United Airlines frequent flyer miles and Marriott Hotel points to use. Neil Budde, my contact at the *WSJ*, originally scheduled the presentation for Tuesday, September 11, but I later changed it to the preceding Friday morning so that I could dovetail it with an *NYT* meeting that afternoon and *LAT* presentation the following Wednesday.

My meetings in New York, especially with the *WSJ*, led me to believe funding for electronic newspaper projects might be forthcoming. Ada and I had scheduled our return home for Monday morning so we could enjoy a beautiful late-summer weekend revisiting our favorite haunts in lower Manhattan. On Saturday evening we had dinner at the Windows on the World restaurant located on the 107th floor of the World Trade Center's North Tower.

Back in Kent, I arrived at the ICI lab early on Tuesday to meet with my two grad student assistants. Ada was at home packing. We planned to leave around 10 a.m. so I could speak at a business luncheon downtown before catching an afternoon United flight from Cleveland to Los Angeles.

A few minutes before nine, Ada called to tell me she had just seen a video on CNN of a plane crashing into the Trade Center's North Tower. Moments after my grad students and I turned on a TV set, CNN announced that another plane had crashed into the South Tower. We stood in stunned silence as new videos showed flames engulfing several floors in each tower. No one knew what was happening or what might happen next, but we all realized the crashes were not accidents.

I immediately returned home to be with Ada. We sat together in front of our TV set petrified as we watched both towers collapse and learned that another plane had crashed into the Pentagon in Washington DC. Later we would learn that a fourth hijacked plane had flown directly over Kent around noon as it made a U-turn back toward Washington before crashing in a field near Shanksville, Pennsylvania. We also would learn that three of the planes — two American and one United — had been bound for Los Angeles.

Nearly all of the structures that surrounded the twin towers in the World Trade Center complex were either destroyed or severely damaged when the towers collapsed. Among them were the Marriott Hotel where we had stayed, the WTC Mall where we had shopped, and the *WSJ* office building where I had met with Budde and other executives. Fortunately, Budde and all of the staff were able to safely evacuate the building before the collapse. They would spend months regrouping at the company's New Jersey offices. Consequently, any hopes of grants from the *WSJ* in the near term were crushed beneath a mountain of rubble in Manhattan.

Contemplating how close we had come to being caught up in the 9/11 terrorist attack as we watched repetitive videos on cable news channels of the planes crashing into the twin towers, people jumping out of windows, and the towers collapsing overwhelmed our neurons. The surreal images brought to my mind George Orr's dreaded reality changing dreams in Ursula Le Guin's science fiction novel *The Lathe of Heaven*.

We would soon learn that a dream actually was responsible for changing reality on September 11, 2001 — a malevolent dream attributed to Osama bin Laden and his Qaeda cohorts. Suddenly and profoundly, fear replaced complacency, pessimism trumped optimism, and anger overpowered reason. In its aftermath, pharmaceutical companies reaped enormous windfalls from their skyrocketing sales of medications for treating anxiety and depression. For Ada, the new reality imposed by 9/11 lacerated the carefree happiness and sense of security she felt after our marriage and her move to the United States. The attack unlocked her suppressed memories of bombings and deaths in Peru during the time of the Shining Path rebellion. As a journalist covering shanty towns around Lima for the leading newspaper, she had been in constant danger from the military as well as from the terrorists. Since 9/11, the anxieties and fears she thought she had left behind have frequently returned to haunt her.

The Los Angeles Times projects

In the days immediately following the 9/11 attack, the Earth seemed to stand still. All civilian aircraft were grounded, meetings and events were cancelled, shopping malls were devoid of shoppers, and people were afraid to venture far from home. When flights resumed, heightened security checks at airports created endless lines and frequent delays, and all passengers would be treated as incognito terrorists. Travel by air became an ordeal rather than an adventure.

My meeting at the *Los Angeles Times* was put off until the next year, which was a relief. Ada and I were not eager to get back on an airplane. To support the ICI team, the university provided funding to create interactive PDF versions of its catalogs, manuals, and publications that could be downloaded from its website.

In March 2002, I finally sat down with John S. Carroll, the editor, and other senior executives at the *Times* to present my digital newspaper concept and discuss a possible grant. I had known Carroll in the eighties when he was the editor of the *Herald-Leader*, Knight-Ridder's paper in Lexington, Kentucky. The meeting was arranged by Sean Reily, who would become my main contact. He was the chief financial officer for the news department, which then had more than 1,200 reporters, editors, and staffers, as well as numerous foreign and domestic bureaus.

The timing could not have been better. Two years earlier, the Tribune Company had purchased Times Mirror, the newspaper's parent company. One of the cost-cutting measures proposed by the new owners involved killing the *Times's* East Coast edition. Understandably, the edition made no sense from a purely business perspective. The paper only printed about 10,000 copies of the truncated, repackaged edition five days a week. It had no advertising and was distributed free along the eastern seaboard corridor between the nation's capital and Boston, mainly to media organizations, government agencies, and elected officials, including the U.S. president. Obviously, the *Times* never intended the edition to be a profitable venture. Its purpose was to showcase the paper's reporting and opinion writing, and to be an influential West Coast counterpoint to *The New York Times, Washington Post,* and other northeastern-centric media outlets.

I was surprised by how quickly Carroll and Reily saw in my concept a way to save the East Coast edition as well as an opportunity to economically produce and distribute a subscription-based digital national edition. The *Times* had a basic website, but Carroll resisted making all of the paper's editorial content available free online, especially in Southern California, fearing it would undermine print circulation. By the end of that meeting, Carroll approved a generous grant to create prototypes and conduct focus group sessions at ICI. With the help of my grad student assistants, the prototypes were completed in April and evaluated by focus groups in May. The following month, I demonstrated them to the *Times* executives on a couple of the lab's tablet PCs.

By the beginning of summer, Carroll was sufficiently convinced of the digital editions' potential to take the next step with the ICI — funding me to create, in collaboration with Reily, a plan for launching the East Coast edition early in 2003 and a national edition later that year.

We delivered the completed plan in mid-August 2002. A few weeks later, Carroll pitched it to the Tribune Company. After his meeting in Chicago, I learned from Reily that saving the East Coast edition had been a lost cause; the corporate executives were determined to kill it. Despite the setback, Reily remained a strong supporter of my concept. Carroll, he said, had managed to keep the door open to producing a digital national edition in the future, so he suggested that we meet again in October to revisit the idea.

Fortuitously for me, tablets and e-readers were becoming hot topics. That fall, I received four invitations to speak about my vision at newspaper association gatherings. Among them was the "Beyond the Printed Word" conference in Barcelona, Spain, hosted by the World Association of Newspapers.

A fifth invitation afforded me an opportunity to reach people who had interests well beyond the printed word and newspapers in New York City in December. The event would be titled "The First Tablet PC Conference to Spotlight ePublishing." Microsoft, Adobe, and the Open eBook Forum were the main sponsors. The proposed subject of my presentation would be adapting newspapers to tablet PCs. My first thought was to show the *Times* prototypes.

When Ada and I arrived in Los Angeles at the beginning of October for my follow-up meeting with Reily, we happened to read a fascinating story in the *Times* that chronicled the journey of a boy who traveled alone from Honduras to the

United States as a teenager in search of his mother. The story by staff writer Sonia Nazario and photographer Don Bartletti was part of a series titled "Enrique's Journey." I wondered as we read it, how many *Times* readers were likely to read any or all of the six parts before discarding the issues. And, how many people would even know about the series outside of California.

When I met with Reily, I told him how much Ada and I had enjoyed reading the "Enrique's Journey" story and asked if he could get us copies of the complete series. He said he would. My next question was about demonstrating the *Times* prototypes at the New York conference. He was hesitant. Showing them at this point, he feared, might alienate Tribune executives toward pursuing my concept at the *Times*.

Even though my grant agreement with the *Times* contained no language that would have prevented me from showing the prototypes at conferences, I respected Reily's concern and did not want to risk jeopardizing my relationship with the paper. But that left me without a current newspaper centerpiece for my presentation in New York.

As Reily and I were mulling over a proposal we hoped would gain corporate support for creating a digital national edition, my mind leapt to a different idea — What if I packaged the complete "Enrique's Journey" series as an interactive e-book that the *Times* could sell online and maybe give to schools? In addition to helping move our proposal forward, I thought it would be an effective medium for exposing students to the paper's high-quality journalism. The *Times* was participating in the national "Newspapers in Education (NIE)" program, so I assumed it would be a natural fit. If approved by Carroll, it would provide me with something new I could show at the December Tablet PC conference.

Approval came quickly. The *Times* had decided to publish the entire series in English and Spanish on its website, so I had no difficulty gathering all of the text, photos, and graphics. Back in Kent, I modified my InDesign newspaper templates for an e-book structure. With Ada's help, I was able to produce visually rich English and Spanish PDF versions, with Nazario's audio clips embedded, in a couple of weeks. I called them "Digital Newsbooks." They would be the first *Times* e-books and, to my knowledge, the first produced by any American newspaper.

I proposed having the carriers deliver copies on CDs with instructions to the teachers who were receiving the *Times* as part of the NIE program, but the circulation director balked. He argued that it would add costs at a time when corporate was pressuring him to cut costs, and it would not increase the paper's circulation numbers. Our counterargument that exposing students and teachers to the *Times's* socially significant reporting in this manner might have long-term benefits for the paper's circulation fell on deaf ears. I have never forgotten the director's veracious response: "The Tribune Company is not interested in long-term benefits."

Our fallback proposition was to link the newsbooks to the series web pages so readers could download them to their computers. Reily later informed me that the paper's webmaster was not enthused about posting PDF files on the website, so he didn't promote them or make them easy to access. Nevertheless, Carroll gave me permission to present the newsbooks at conferences and to demonstrate my digital *Times* prototypes in private meetings. (In 2003, Nazario and Bartletti were awarded Pulitzer Prizes for the "Enrique's Journey" series.)

A boost from Adobe

The tablet PC conference on December 5, 2002, exceeded my expectations. By the time it concluded, I had received invitations to visit Microsoft and Adobe, and had been interviewed for articles that would appear in dozens of newspapers, magazines, and trade journals. I left New York on a high note, believing projects and grants were sure to follow.

In January, the *Times* funded the ICI to produce a second digital prototype. With this version, I pushed the InDesign and Acrobat software to their limits, adding more interactive elements, video clips, and additional layers of information to graphics and advertisements. Soon after it was completed, Microsoft and Adobe followed through with formal invitations to visit their corporate headquarters.

I spent several days at Microsoft's Seattle campus in late February meeting with two project teams. One was exploring software for creating and selling e-books, the other had its sights set on developing an online news service that would work with newspapers. Both teams seemed interested in my digital newspaper and newsbook concepts, but were dismissive of using PDF. We discussed having Microsoft fund the ICI to explore alternatives, but all I could get from them was: "We'll get back to you." They didn't; however, a short while later a rep met with Reily at the *Times* about participating in the proposed online news service. (The *Times* and to my knowledge none of the other papers Microsoft contacted agreed to participate.)

My visit to Adobe's San Jose offices in early March had an entirely different reception and outcome. On my first morning, the large auditorium where I demonstrated the prototypes and newsbook was filled to capacity. Later that day, some of the engineers privately admitted they had not anticipated all the ways I had found to use InDesign and Acrobat.

When I met the next day with Warnock, he congratulated me and asked if Adobe could use the prototypes in its demos to clients. Carroll had given me permission to show them publicly, so I told him the company could, so long as the *Times* and Kent State were credited. He then arranged for me to meet with a senior software engineer who revealed several new tools that Adobe was considering for the next version of InDesign.

My excitement must have been obvious as we discussed how the tools could be used to semi-automate layouts. I remember him smiling when I asked if I could play with a beta copy at the ICI. Just before leaving Adobe, he gave me a nondisclosure agreement for the university to sign along with a copy of a memo from Warnock authorizing his department to fund a research project at Kent State. I could not have been happier.

With the Adobe grant and ongoing financial support from the *Times*, the ICI had enough funding to support three grad student assistants and cover everything we needed to continue developing my tablet newspaper concept, which I then called the Kent Electronic Newspaper Tablet (KENT) Format, until the summer of 2004.

During that period, several other American and Canadian newspapers also funded the ICI to produce newsbooks and digital editions. Our most significant project, however, involved developing a technical application that would facilitate creating InDesign scripts for semi-automating layouts. All of the credit for developing the application and scripts belongs to Carrie Garzich, a brilliant journalism grad student who worked with me at the ICI for two years while completing her master's degree in information architecture and knowledge management.

In my view, she possessed the essential qualities that newspapers desperately needed to adapt and survive in the digital era.

(Immediately upon graduation, the Gannett Company hired Garzich as an assistant news editor for online at the *Cincinnati Enquirer*. Her efforts to apply her talents to its website, however, were thwarted by corporate directives to cut costs in order to meet unrealistic profit goals. After three-and-a-half frustrating years, she quit to take a job with the Marriott hotel chain as an information architect. She quickly rose to senior manager. Since 2012, she has been the director of experience design dealing with online reservations and customer loyalty programs.)

A second fellowship offer

In 2003, Ohio's Republican-dominated state legislature made steep cuts in funding for public universities. To make up for the shortfalls, Kent State had to raise tuitions and reduce teaching waivers for research projects, which served to increase semester course loads for professors.

My grants for the ICI projects had justified two course waivers, so I only had to teach one course each semester. Beginning with the 2004 spring semester, I had to teach an additional undergraduate course. Around the same time, newspapers began cutting budgets for discretionary spending, and Adobe underwent a reorganization that ended my prospects for future funding. Without a major new grant, I would lose my last waiver and would have to teach three courses in the fall. While I enjoyed working with graduate students on projects and theses, I found teaching undergraduate courses frustrating and unfulfilling. After eight years of disappointing efforts to engage students, I had to accept that I was not cut out to be a teacher.

Luckily, fate provided a solution in mid-March. The American Press Institute invited me to speak at an event it was hosting in Newport Beach, California, called the "Mediamorphosis Leadership Retreat." I assumed the title had been inspired by my book; however, the event organizers adamantly denied it. They were firmly convinced the term "mediamorphosis" had been coined by Marshall McLuhan, the Canadian philosopher best known for introducing the expression "the medium is the message" in 1964. Even though I believed they were wrong, I chose not to press the issue.

(Upon my return to Kent, a grad student and I did a thorough search. We found no uses of the term by McLuhan or anyone else prior to 1991 when it appeared for the first time in an article I wrote for the *Media Studies Journal*.)

As it turned out, fate overshadowed the organizers' slight as well as the event. The next chapter in my life would be revealed unexpectedly during a private lunch meeting arranged by Dr. William L. Winter, the former API president and executive director. I had been a frequent speaker at API and had known Winter in his earlier years as an editor with Knight-Ridder. After retiring from API the previous year, he told me he had been named as special assistant to the president of the Donald W. Reynolds Foundation based in Las Vegas.

Prior to the meeting, I didn't know anything about the foundation or the other participant — Dr. Dean Mills, the dean of the Missouri School of Journalism. While we waited for lunch to be served, Winter explained that the foundation had just awarded the J-school a $31-million grant to establish the Donald W. Reynolds Journalism Institute. (Reynolds was a Missouri J-school alum and the founder of Donrey Media Group, which owned more than 100 newspapers and other businesses in mostly small markets. When he died in 1993, he bequeathed the bulk of his fortune to the foundation.)

The Institute's goal, Winter said, would be to encourage innovation, collaboration, and research within media companies. The first phase included a fellowship program they hoped to launch in the fall. As a waiter filled our glasses with iced tea, the meeting's purpose became clear. It was to see if I would consider becoming the Institute's inaugural Reynolds Fellow.

Of course, I considered it. The opportunities to be involved in the founding of a new journalism institute and to continue pursuing my tablet newspaper vision at one of the most respected journalism schools in the country were powerful incentives. However, before I could commit, I told them I needed to discuss it with Ada and the director of the Kent J-school.

The fellowship offer brought back happy memories for Ada of our year at Columbia University, so I didn't need to spend any time convincing her. Besides, she knew I was restless and not looking forward to teaching full time in the fall. I also knew she had not been content living in Kent either. Moreover, the new J-school director, though friendly and supportive, was struggling to make the required budget cuts. So, the prospect of my taking an unpaid sabbatical during the '04-'05 academic year and not having to fund the ICI out of his diminished budget pleased him.

In April, we traveled to Columbia, Missouri, to learn more about the fellowship and future Institute as well as to scope out the city and campus. On the first morning after we arrived, Dean Dean Mills (his first name was Dean) took us to a conference room where I demonstrated the *Los Angeles Times* prototype and discussed my tablet newspaper vision with students and faculty, much as I had done on my first visit to the Kent J-school.

My presentation apparently convinced the dean and faculty of my qualifications for the fellowship. After hearing the dean's plans for the Institute and briefly touring the city, Ada and I also were convinced that the fellowship offer made sense. The stipend was less than my salary at Kent State, but money was not an issue for us. What mattered was finding a place where we would be happy. Even though the dean made no promises about hiring me after my fellowship year ended, we both sensed that Columbia would be our future home.

Author's notes

In the fall of 1999, the American Press Institute invited all of the 1988 seminar participants back to assess how well we had done at predicting what newspapers might be like at the beginning of the new millennium and to look further out to the year 2020. Seventeen returned. Roger Black would again analyze the pages. What a difference 11 years made. As soon as we were seated, in walked a participant dressed as Moses who declared in a booming voice, "Fidler was right" and presented me with two wooden tablets. Black acknowledged my vision in his opening remarks with, "And then there was [Fidler's] tablet, which I discounted because it wasn't portable [his mistaken assumption]. So, I'm as guilty as anybody else of getting it wrong. And now I wonder why it has taken so long to get there." The API again published all of the participants' essays along with the discussions in a book titled *2020: Visions of the newspaper of the future.*

CHAPTER TEN

Journey's End

The maiden years of the twenty-first century have not been kind to newspapers. This is the future newspaper executives and journalists most feared when they first touched electronic publishing systems and began experimenting with online news media back in the seventies and eighties. Their initial fears were alleviated somewhat when the first generation of online services failed to take hold and printed news continued to produce "rivers of gold" for publishers, as media magnate Rupert Murdoch once described the profits flowing from his global chain of newspapers. However, by 2000, the rivers were drying up.

In the years following the implosion of the dotcom bubble, a more formidable array of online competitors began diverting the flow of advertising gold away from newspapers. Knight-Ridder and most other newspaper chains responded by imposing draconian cost-cutting measures, which only served to accelerate their decline. While I was aware of Knight-Ridder's struggles, I never imagined they would lead to its precipitous demise.

Upon completing my year as the inaugural Reynolds Fellow at the Missouri School of Journalism, I forfeit my tenured professorship at Kent State to help establish the school's Reynolds Journalism Institute as a leader in digital/online publishing and mobile media research. When Apple launched the iPad in 2010, the tablet vision I had been pursuing for 30 years was finally realized, but by then few newspapers had the wherewithal to fully exploit it.

Westward into the sunset of my career

During our eight years in Kent, Ohio, our family had grown to include six "children" — a large mixed-breed dog that Ada and I had rescued and three chinchillas in addition to our cats, Media and Morphosis. Finding a rental in Columbia, Missouri, to our liking that would accept all of our pets seemed unlikely. What's more, we were not willing to "camp out" for a year as we had done when we moved to Kent. We had a good feeling about Columbia, so buying a house made sense to us. After two scouting trips, we found one that met our requirements. This time, we decided to ship our furniture and belongings to our new home. We would hold on to our house in Kent until we were confident about staying in Columbia.

Getting to Missouri with our pets during an especially hot summer posed a problem. Taking all of them in our Jeep was out of the question. Our solution was to buy a small used RV. In late July, Alfonso Morales, arrived from Peru for Ada's birthday. He was her colleague at *El Comercio*, who after his retirement became our close friend and frequent traveling companion. We were delighted when he offered to help us with the move. On August 9, 2004, we rolled out of Kent in the RV with Alfonso following close behind in the Jeep. Our journey would again follow Interstate 70, this time heading back west into the sunset of my career.

The ground had not yet been broken for the Reynolds Journalism Institute (RJI) building, so Dean Mills, the J-school's dean, assigned me to a temporary office in the basement of Lee Hills Hall. This relatively new building was named for the late chairman of Knight-Ridder who also was a distinguished Missouri alum. It was designed to house the *Columbia Missourian*, a daily community newspaper and teaching lab affiliated with the J-school. The paper had competed with the family-owned *Columbia Tribune* since 1908.

The Missourian eMprint editions

The project I proposed for my fellowship year involved conducting a public 10-week field test of my tablet format under deadline conditions using content from the Sunday *Missourian*. I would spend most of fall semester developing production methods and creating a prototype in the new version of my tablet format I now called Electronic Media Print or eMprint.

Educating the ad staff and getting a buy-in from prospective advertisers required me to actively participate in the sales calls. My demonstrations of the prototype on tablet PCs and laptops always wowed the owners and managers. They would often extend our "5-minute" sales calls to 30 minutes or more and invite other employees to see the demo.

All of the ads I created combined elements from the local enterprises' print ads and websites — if they had one. I included interactive features and video clips wherever I thought they added value. For businesses that had websites, I embedded hyperlinks to their relevant web pages. (In 2004 and 2005, only about a third of the Columbia businesses we contacted had websites; small businesses rarely had their own domain names and e-mail addresses.)

We would get the same two questions after nearly every demo: "Are these print ads or web ads?" and, "Who will create these ads?" I would explain that eMprint ads were hybrids that could provide hyperlinks to additional information and play video clips even when readers were not connected to the internet. As for creating the eMprint ads, that would be my task.

During the first two months of 2005, I created dozens of ads and trained two grad students — Brendan Watson and Wan Xu, a Chinese student — who had no previous experience working with the InDesign page-layout software. Both made up for their lack of experience with their enthusiasm and dedication.

Our goal was to have the editions uploaded to the web no later than 3 a.m. on Sunday mornings. That meant the grad students would have to sacrifice most of their weekend social activities and sleep. In early February, the *Missourian* and a J-school marketing class began promoting the eMprint field test, which would launch on March 6 and run through May 8.

Stories published by the Associated Press and *USA Today* gave a major boost to sign ups, which far exceeded our expectations. More than 5,000 people registered from across the nation and 12 countries. (Nearly 3,000 downloaded more than one issue; of those, around 600 downloaded all 10 issues. That year the *Missourian* had less than 8,000 print subscribers.)

While the eMprint editions were free to those who registered, advertisers had to pay for their ads. As an added incentive, the *Missourian* also published versions of their ads in the printed edition. To the surprise of nearly everyone, a majority of the enterprises that advertised in the eMprint edition were new to the *Missourian*, and the project more than paid for itself.

The success of the field test convinced Dan Potter, the *Missourian's* general manager, and Tom Warhover, the editor, to add regular twice-weekly eMprint editions beginning with the fall 2005 semester. It also convinced Dean Mills to offer me a full-time position with the RJI. We discussed the executive director role, but both of us agreed that serving as the digital publishing director would make the best use of my talents.

While that was my desired outcome, there was a hitch. I would have to give up my status as a tenured full professor. Under the terms of the Reynolds endowment, funds could not be used to pay faculty salaries. The only alternative would have been for the Missouri School of Journalism to create a new tenured professorship for me and cover my salary out of its budget, which, according to the dean, was not feasible in the '05-'06 academic year.

I was disappointed, but the opportunity to play a role in the creation of a new, well-funded journalism institute at an internationally respected J-school, and to continue my work on digital newspapers was too compelling to pass up. In June, I resigned from Kent State and assumed my new position as the RJI's first hire. By then, Ada and I had comfortably settled in Columbia and had no regrets about selling our Kent home and the RV.

Relaunching the eMprint editions after a three-month hiatus meant essentially starting over. Both of the students who worked with me on the field test graduated in May, and the *Missourian* features editor who assisted us had taken a job with another newspaper.

During the summer, I had to train the editor and advertising artist that the *Missourian* hired specifically for the paper's website and eMprint editions. I also had to rebuild my page masters, create new prototypes and marketing materials, and help sell ads.

Near the end of August, Rob Weir, who had been given the title of managing editor/digital, recruited four journalism grad students to produce the Wednesday and Sunday eMprint editions. All had some experience laying out newspaper pages using InDesign, but none was familiar with Acrobat's interactive and mixed-media features.

After an intense two weeks of training and dry runs, we launched the first regular edition on September 14, 2005. The *Missourian* and a J-school marketing class again promoted the eMprint editions with local radio and television spots and promo ads in the newspaper and its website. E-mail messages about the relaunch were sent to everyone who had participated in the field test. Several regional newspapers and journalism publications along with the university's alumni magazine ran stories about the eMprint project, but this time none of the national newspapers mentioned it. Consequently, a majority of the around 2,000 people who registered in September were alumni, relatives of students, and curious media professionals. Less than a quarter were Columbia residents.

I remained actively involved in the production process for a couple of months. By the end of fall semester, the eMprint team assured me they would no longer need my assistance. My only ongoing role would be to occasionally provide critiques and help solve problems.

The *Missourian* continued to produce eMprint editions for two academic years with supplemental funding from the RJI. However, well before the last issue on April 29, 2007, the editions had stagnated. After I moved on to other projects, the students assigned to the eMprint editions demonstrated no willingness to create interactive graphics or experiment on their own. I had hoped for more creativity, but I was not surprised by the lack of it. As I had learned at Kent State, students assigned to projects in which they have no vested interest or perceive no immediate benefits are unlikely to do more than the minimum required. Three other factors worked against continuing the eMprint project: the paper's decision to focus on its website, the economic downturn that reduced advertising revenue, and the end of RJI's project support.

My return to the Los Angeles Times

Early in 2006, Sean Reily, my *LAT* contact, called to ask if I could create another prototype using the eMprint format. He said he had participated in the *Missourian* field test and urged Dean Baquet, the paper's new editor, to revisit the national digital edition idea.

The stately art deco lobby of the *Times* building in the historic central district of Los Angeles where Reily greeted me in mid-February belied the hard times that had befallen the paper in the three years since my last visit. After 2000, when the Tribune Company acquired Times Mirror, the paper's former parent company, the new corporate masters began relentlessly slashing editorial budgets and staffing. Resistance to the cuts had proven futile. Baquet was the third editor in less than six years. As Reily guided me to his office, he told me, that under orders from the Tribune, the editorial staff had shrunk from around 1,200 to less than 900. Most other departments had experienced similar reductions. Discarded desks and computers filled a vacated floor that we visited.

Like John Carroll, the editor I met with during my first visits to the *Times*, Baquet was a respected journalist and inspiring leader. Despite the daunting challenges he faced trying to maintain the paper's reputation for quality journalism with a greatly reduced budget and staff, he managed to project an optimistic outlook. With Reily's encouragement, Baquet agreed to fund another prototype and a study to assess the potential market for a national digital edition.

In May, Reily and I presented the new prototype and results of our study to Baquet and several other *Times* executives. They all gave their nod of approval. Baquet then instructed Reily to create a business plan he could include in his proposed 2007 budget that September.

This time, the odds on launching the digital edition within a year seemed favorable. Even the regional representatives for CCI, the paper's editorial systems vendor, were enthused by the project. They had just installed a content management upgrade that allowed text, photos, and graphics to easily flow between print and digital editions, as well as the websites.

Once again, the Tribune's corporate bosses had no interest in funding new projects. Between March and September, circulation had fallen by 8 percent to 776,000, and revenue had declined even more steeply as advertisers accelerated their migration to the internet. As a result, the paper's profit margin, which still exceeded 20 percent, failed to meet corporate's goal. In October, they fired the publisher for refusing to make their ordered cuts. The following month, Baquet suffered the same fate when he, too, baulked at eliminating between 50 and 75 newsroom jobs. (Baquet went on to become the executive editor of *The New York Times*.)

With Baquet's departure, the national digital edition proposal died on the vine; however, that would not be the end of my involvement with the *LAT*. Fortunately, Reily held onto his job and continued to share my belief in the digital future of newspapers.

Founding the Digital Publishing Alliance

While I obviously was saddened by the *LAT's* inability to proceed with a digital edition, several other projects in 2006 kept me busy. In June, Chris Peck, the editor of the *Commercial Appeal* in Memphis, Tennessee, and Jeffrey Kanige, the editor of the *Daily Deal*, a business journal based in New York City, contracted with me to create digital prototypes.

The growing number of requests I was receiving for information about tablets, the eMprint model, and digital newsbooks (newspaper stories on a single topic repackaged as e-books) led me to propose hosting an RJI digital publishing forum. Pam Johnson, the Institute's newly hired executive director, enthusiastically approved the idea and urged me to arrange it with the J-school as soon as possible. (The RJI would not have its own building until 2008.)

Toward the end of July, just as I was making plans for the forum, Jeff Paleczny, the North American representative for iRex Technologies, called. He explained that iRex had recently spun off from Royal Phillips Electronics to focus on developing electronic screens for digital reading. Its Iliad e-reader, he said, was one of the first to use a new paper-like display technology called E Ink that, unlike backlit liquid crystal displays, reflects light and can be read comfortably in bright sunlight. (Amazon would use the same display technology for its Kindle e-readers in 2007.)

A few days later, Paleczny personally delivered an Iliad e-reader to my Lee Hills office. To test it, I loaded one of the digital newsbooks I had created. Even though the device only had a six-inch, gray-scale display, I was surprised by its readability, and how easy it was to hold and use. I knew this was something that would interest newspapers, so I invited him to speak about the Iliad at the forum I was planning.

The forum on August 22-24, 2006, attracted 21 participants, in addition to Reily, Peck, and Kanige, from 12 organizations around the country. After an update on the *Missourian* eMprint project and a demonstration of the Iliad, I presented the group with a proposal for its consideration to form a cooperative I called the Digital Publishing Alliance (DPA). Its purpose would be to jointly pursue digital publishing strategies, products, and research. The discussions and survey taken on the last morning encouraged us to host another forum in October.

In September, I purchased several NEC Versa LitePads for use in my focus group research and presentations. The LitePad was the first tablet PC to match the dimensions and weight of the tablet mockup I had created for *The Tablet Newspaper* video.

Even though the thin, two-pound LitePad was comfortable to hold and suitable for reading eMprint editions in portrait orientation, it did not fulfill my vision of a consumer tablet that was more like a radio or TV set than a PC. The LitePad was just another slate-type, pen-based PC with a Windows operating system and all of the legacy complexities that tended to frustrate nontechnical users. Among the missing attributes were instant on-off switching, a finger-sensitive touchscreen, and a simplified unobtrusive operating system.

Despite having more familiarity with personal computers than most older adults, a majority of the university students who participated in my research said they found the LitePad confusing and cumbersome to use. Albeit, their difficulty with the Windows operating system was understandable given that nearly all Missouri students were using Macintosh computers in those days. Their frustrations, however, served to reinforce my argument that, to be widely adopted, consumer tablets would need to function more like simple radios and TV sets.

The Iliad e-readers purchased later for my research were more "user friendly" than the LitePads and provided a more paper-like reading experience, but their Linux operating system, which was simpler and less obtrusive than Windows, still required a PC-like boot-up and shutdown that took a couple of minutes and occasionally displayed cryptic error messages. The Iliad also lacked a finger-sensitive touchscreen.

What intrigued me most during the focus group sessions with students was their strong preference for printed textbooks over the digital versions available online. For several years, publishers had been promoting e-textbooks with supplemental hypermedia elements believing students who were born after the emergence of personal computers and were exposed to online media in their teens would rapidly abandon printed text-books. They didn't, at least not in large numbers.

Unsurprisingly, their attachment to printed textbooks did not carry over to printed newspapers and newsmagazines, even among journalism majors. In 2006, they were already getting almost all of their news from the web, television, and friends.

Representatives from six more organizations attended the second digital publishing forum at the J-school on October 19. I devoted most of the day to defining the benefits of joining my proposed alliance, the types of research and projects that could be undertaken at the RJI, the obligations of member organizations, and the annual dues. The forum concluded with a consensus in support of forming the DPA under my leadership.

Stories about the founding of the DPA that appeared in several newspapers and trade journals more than doubled the turn out for the meeting on February 26, 2007. The main attraction was a conversation with Michael Rogers, the recently named futurist-in-residence at *The New York Times*. After the meeting, Rogers convinced the *NYT* to become an active DPA member and to participate in my digital newsbook project. Of the 28 other organizations represented at the meeting, 18 agreed to join.

Among the incentives for becoming dues-paying members were my offers to consult on their digital publishing initiatives and to produce their digital newsbooks at the RJI free of charge. (During the next six years, I consulted on about a dozen projects and created more than 50 digital newsbooks, in addition to producing digital editions of the *Global Journalist* magazine.)

The introductions of the Apple iPhone in June and Amazon Kindle e-reader in November helped to grow membership in the DPA. By the end of 2007, the Alliance had nearly 30 dues-paying members. That year, newspaper executives were feeling slightly more optimistic that steadily increasing revenues from their websites would soon offset a significant portion of their papers' losses from declining print advertising and circulation. Their optimism, however, would be dampened in the following two years by a perfect storm.

The Great Disruption

By the end of the nineties, newspaper publishers had nearly exhausted their cost savings from adopting digital production technologies and were facing increasing competition from dotcom entrepreneurs for the advertising dollars that provided about 80 percent of their revenue. Most vulnerable to online competition were the highly profitable classified ads, which for daily newspapers provided between 40 and 70 percent of their advertising income. Their slowness to innovate and confront the threats posed by Craigslist and other free online classified services cost newspapers more than $5 billion between 2000 and 2007, according to the Newspaper Association of America.

In those years, publicly held newspaper companies came under relentless pressure from Wall Street analysts and major shareholders to maintain the year-over-year profit growth they had come to expect, despite their steadily declining circulation numbers and shrinking advertising revenues. Nearly all owners responded by making steep cuts in their work forces and news content, and by raising prices. But, for many newspapers, even that would not be enough.

To achieve more growth, some media conglomerates saw the opportunity to acquire struggling newspaper companies as a winning proposition, even if it meant incurring huge debts. They reasoned that consolidation of operations and central-ization of purchasing would result in greater efficiency and higher profits. Historically, newspaper companies had done well during economic rebounds, so future growth could be expected to easily pay off their debts.

What they had failed to see were the unprecedented, epic storm clouds building on the digital horizon. Practically all established enterprises and institutions, not just newspapers, were on the verge of being massively disrupted.

Then in 2008, an apocalyptic El Niño-like event precip-itated by an imploding American housing bubble and a global financial meltdown — The Great Recession — brought devasta-ting floods of red ink. Daily newspaper publishers in the United States saw their circulation and advertising revenues suddenly plummet by as much as 50 percent. Visions of producing new rivers of gold from their websites had not materialized.

Between 2000 and 2010, when the Great Recession officially ended, more than 100 daily newspapers were shuttered and nearly 20,000 newsroom employees were laid off. Also, in that decade, several once prominent newspaper chains faded into history. Knight-Ridder was one of those chains.

Commercialization of the internet had just begun when Tony Ridder became Knight-Ridder's chairman and chief executive in 1995. He recognized the threats from emerging dotcom competitors and took a number of early steps in an attempt to head them off. Among them was his decision to fund the *San Jose Mercury News* to launch MercuryCenter.com, the first website to put the entire contents of a mainstream newspaper online.

In 1998, Ridder moved the corporate headquarters from Miami to San Jose, ostensibly to immerse the company in Silicon Valley's high-tech culture, and a year later he created a new subsidiary called KnightRidder.com (renamed Knight Ridder Digital in 2001) to centrally control all of the chain's websites and digital initiatives.

Making money from news websites, however, proved to be problematic. As Knight-Ridder and other newspaper companies would discover, meeting the demands of readers for continuously updated news online 24 hours a day, 7 days a week was an expensive proposition in the nineties. More troubling was their resistance to paying for news online.

Mercury Center's early attempt to charge a subscription fee stifled growth and soon was replaced by a registration system that offered free access in exchange for completing a personal profile. But, even this approach had to be abandoned after it met with angry protests from internet denizens who regarded it as an invasion of their privacy.

Without an ability to provide demographic information about users, advertisers were reluctant to pay more than token amounts for placing ads on newspaper web pages, which did little more than provide hyperlinked buttons to the advertisers' web pages. As Knight-Ridder found with its Viewtron venture in the early eighties, the traditional newspaper business model did not work well in the online world.

Moreover, by not charging readers for access, news provided on newspaper websites quickly came to be regarded as a free commodity, which devalued the printed editions and accelerated circulation declines. Online content aggregators, such as Yahoo! and Google, were quick to exploit the freely available newspaper content for their own gain.

Consequently, Knight-Ridder's costly, albeit necessary, investments in online news media put greater pressure on the chain's newspapers to offset the mounting losses. To meet Ridder's onerous profit goals, publishers had to make even deeper cuts in staffing and costs, which had an obvious debilitating effect on the extent and quality of their editorial content.

While nearly every publicly held newspaper company was cutting staff and costs at the dawning of the new century to deal with the economic downturn and increasing competition from online media, Knight-Ridder stood out for its aggressiveness. Rick Edmonds, the Poynter Institute's media business analyst, found that Knight-Ridder's stated goal of reducing its news staff by 10 percent was more than twice that of all other public newspaper companies.

By 2005, Ridder had sold nearly all of the chain's ancillary businesses and several under-performing newspapers to purchase additional newspapers that he hoped would be more profitable. All of his efforts to save the company his family and the Knights had built, however, failed to satisfy the major institutional shareholders. After 10 years of effectively erasing the Knight legacy, Ridder would be forced to put the company on the auction block. When the McClatchy Company agreed to buy Knight-Ridder in March 2006, it still was one of the largest chains in the country with an overall profit margin greater than many Fortune 500 companies.

A month later, McClatchy sold off several of the former Knight-Ridder properties, including the *San Jose Mercury News*, which had been the Ridder Publications flagship newspaper, and the *Miami Herald* building on the shore of Biscayne Bay, which had been Knight-Ridder's corporate home, to help meet its debt obligations. McClatchy would sell more KR properties in the following year as the economy steadily worsened. But that would not be enough to shore up the company for what was to come.

When the U.S. economy nosedived at the beginning of the Great Recession, McClatchy almost was pushed into bankruptcy by the crushing weight of its debt. Before the Knight-Ridder purchase, McClatchy's share price was above $75. In late 2008, it dropped to below $1.50. McClatchy wasn't alone. Several other major newspaper chains, including the Tribune Company, filed to reorganize under chapter 11 bankruptcy protection in the same time period.

While I was saddened by the demise of Knight-Ridder and the plight of daily newspapers before and during the Great Recession, this was the great disruption and reckoning I had foreseen and had been writing and speaking about since the beginning of the eighties. During the nineties, I often was viewed as a Cassandra, and, like her, my warnings were ignored.

My Viewtron experience had convinced me that the only way for newspapers to avoid being disintermediated by the digital publishing revolution and its voracious online progeny was to embrace an electronic alternative to pigmented ink printed on pulp paper. I argued that paper and printing presses were not essential to newspapers and print journalism; that their role and form could be replicated and even enhanced on mobile, handheld flat-panel displays optimized for reading text. That was the message I intended to convey in the 1994 *Tablet Newspaper* video.

Despite the dismal financial outlook for newspapers in 2008 and '09, the growing popularity of e-readers and smartphones infused the industry with a ray of hope. During those years, the DPA would grow to include nearly all of the nation's largest papers and establish the RJI as a global leader in mobile media research.

The worst of the Great Recession's economic disruptions gratefully bypassed Columbia. Residents benefitted from the city's good fortune of being home to multiple large employers that were relatively recession proof — three universities, two regional medical centers, and two major national insurance companies — in addition to being the retail, entertainment, and cultural hub for central Missouri.

On September 10, 2008, the Reynolds Journalism Institute formally dedicated its new headquarters building in conjunction with the Missouri School of Journalism's centennial celebration. The RJI used the occasion to introduce the six '08-'09 Reynolds Fellows who would make up the first class since the '04-'05 academic year when I was the lone inaugural fellow. One of the main events in the RJI building that weekend was an E-Reader Symposium that I had organized in conjunction with a Digital Publishing Alliance meeting.

The following year, Sean Reily, who was a founding member of the DPA, took leave from the *Los Angeles Times* to work with me on mobile-media publishing strategies and business models as a Reynolds Fellow in the class of '09-'10. Initially, we focused on how newspapers might profit from producing content for e-readers; however, our attention soon shifted to opportunities afforded by another, more promising mobile display device.

Realizing my tablet newspaper vision

On January 27, 2010, Reily and I joined a clutch of staffers and students in the RJI Futures Lab to watch the much anticipated online announcement of a new Apple product. Rumors about an Apple tablet had been circulating for weeks.

Waiting for Steve Jobs to appear, we speculated about what he might call a tablet. Most proposed iTablet or iTab. I opted for iPanel. None of us considered iPad. Some of the students made fun of the name when Jobs announced it, but that didn't matter to me. I was jubilant when I saw him sitting in a black-leather lounge chair on the stage holding an iPad like a magazine as he described features and glanced at a digital edition of *The New York Times* displayed on its screen in portrait orientation. I had no doubt then that this was the tablet that would finally realize the vision I had been pursuing for 30 years.

As soon as Apple began taking advance orders for iPads, I went online and ordered one. A courier service delivered it to my home on April 3, the first day it went on sale. As described in Chapter Six, I was not disappointed, nor were a million other consumers who bought iPads that month. While it resembled my 1994 tablet mockup, Apple had taken my concept to another level. The incredible lightness of its being made holding and carrying it even more comfortable. And, its brilliant, high-resolution, full-color, finger-sensitive touch-screen made browsing and reading even more pleasurable.

One of the first things I did after it arrived was sit with the iPad in my white-leather lounge chair at home and read *The New York Times*. I was happy to see that it had adopted a page-based structure for its iPad app similar to my eMprint format.

Not everyone was happy with the iPad, however. Web and iPad app developers were incensed by Jobs' decision not to support Adobe's Flash Player, which was widely used for displaying video clips, animations, and interactive graphics. Jobs argued that Flash was a dead-end platform and that better alternatives existed. Developers were caught by surprise. Early adopters of iPads saw empty rectangles wherever Flash elements had been embedded.

Samsung and other consumer electronics companies used the conflict to aggressively promote their own tablets that supported Flash. That didn't deter Jobs. In keeping with his reputation, he tenaciously refused to give in to the pressures from developers and competitors.

By the end of 2010, the empty rectangles finally disappeared and the loss of Flash no longer mattered. But, as I would discover, there were other problems with the iPad related to my use of Adobe Acrobat and Adobe's PDF Reader that were even more frustrating to resolve. When I loaded an eMprint *Missourian* edition and the *Los Angeles Times* prototype on my iPad, I found that, even though I had embedded Apple's QuickTime Player instead of Flash, I could not make the videos play. Nor could I make the navigational buttons and show/hide layers work with any of the PDF reader apps for the iPad, including Adobe's.

I learned later that Jobs also had decreed that the iPad should not support most of the enhanced PDF features built into Acrobat. My Adobe contact told me the company had no intention of modifying Acrobat for the iPad and suggested that I consider rebuilding the files using Apple iBooks or some other application.

Soon dozens of newspapers and newsmagazines, including *USA Today, Washington Post, and Time,* launched iPad editions. Most adopted typical magazine or web formats. A few merely displayed screen replicas of their printed pages or repurposed their websites.

Jobs made it known that he was disappointed with the periodicals being produced for the iPad and called on publishers and designers to break out of their print-era straightjackets. His call would be answered by a notorious print-era media magnate — Rupert Murdoch, the 79-year-old chief executive of News Corp, one of the world's largest media conglomerates. Jobs and Murdoch apparently had a meeting of the minds and agreed to collaborate on the creation of the first digital-only newspaper designed specifically for the iPad. Murdoch had wanted to call it the *Daily Planet* after the fictional paper where Clark Kent, aka Superman, worked as a reporter, but he was unable to secure the rights from DC Comics, so he settled on *The Daily*.

Murdoch quickly assembled a team drawn from across the New York media landscape to secretly create *The Daily* in News Corp's Manhattan headquarters building. Unlike the *NYT, The Daily* had no print counterpart, so the staff was free to innovate and try out new ideas. Simultaneously, Apple began developing a new payment model that would allow recurrent paid subscriptions to be initiated from within iPad apps. *The Daily* would be the first to deploy it.

When News Corp launched *The Daily* on February 2, 2011, I immediately signed up for a two-week free trial. After that, I had the option of subscribing for 99 cents a week or purchasing an annual subscription for $39.99. I browsed it almost every day during the free trial. *The Daily's* around 100 pages of original content consisted mostly of soft news, sports, and entertainment stories, although it did occasionally publish investigative news stories that scooped other national newspapers. I don't know if my tablet newspaper vision influenced any of the designers, but some aspects of *The Daily's* presentation bore a resemblance to my eMprint format. The main difference was its adoption of a magazine-style sequential-reading structure rather than the newspaper-style nonsequential-browsing structure I had developed.

After the free trial, I purchased an annual subscription and read issues at least once a week to follow its evolution. While I was impressed with the overall quality of its stories and presentations, as well as some of its innovative features, *The Daily* did not revolutionize news presentation and delivery or attract readers and advertisers as much as Murdoch had hoped.

In the last quarter of 2012, *The Daily* reportedly had around 100,000 subscribers, which was far less than had been projected. Even Murdoch, with News Corp's deep pockets, could not justify to shareholders losing more than $80 million on a venture that had little hope of turning a profit anytime soon, especially while the conglomerate was in the midst of a turbulent period. On December 15, after just 21 months, Murdoch announced that he was pulling the plug on the pioneering tablet newspaper experiment he had championed.

When I saw the announcement, I felt a touch of déjà vu. Jim Batten had made a similar announcement back in 1986 when Knight-Ridder shuttered Viewtron, the pioneering online newspaper experiment he had championed, after 29 months and losing more than $50 million. Both were examples of visions that touched the future but had the misfortune of being realized at the wrong times. Viewtron was born too soon — before the technologies and consumers were ready to support it. *The Daily* was born too late — after the technologies and consumers had already moved on to support a different vision.

Newspapers in the age of mobile media

By the iPad's third anniversary, newspapers had all but given up on having editors and designers curate and package fixed-format digital editions specifically for tablets. The growing popularity of smartphones and less-expensive tablets with different operating systems and screens in a variety of sizes and proportions put pressure on newspaper publishers to deliver their digital content in adaptive, dynamic formats.

Additionally, owners of mobile devices were steadily gravitating toward news stories aggregated by customizable, algorithm-driven news apps or recommended by social media users and bots (agents). Getting what you want, when you want it, and how you want it obviated the need for traditional newspaper design and typography.

All of this was the result of advances in high-speed wireless telephony that made mobile internet access affordable and popular much sooner in the new century than had been believed possible in the nineties. The widespread deployment of third-generation cellular and optical-fiber cable services, combined with low-cost Wi-Fi local area networks (LANs), ushered in the age of mobile online media and a radical transformation of human communication. The dream of continuous connectivity and pervasive computing — anywhere, anytime — now was a reality.

All mainstream newspaper companies that had survived the disruptions of the Great Recession, including *The New York Times, Washington Post,* and McClatchy, were still struggling against the riptide of declining circulation and advertising when Apple introduced the iPad. In the years that followed, the high cost of trying to keep up with rapidly changing technologies and mobile devices, content aggregators, and social media compounded their problems. For many family-owned newspapers, the only viable option was to find a buyer.

Even the venerable *Washington Post,* which had gained international fame for doggedly investigating the Watergate scandal that brought down President Nixon and bravely publishing the Pentagon Papers that exposed government lying about the Vietnam War, could not escape the maelstrom. In the fall of 2013, the Graham family who had owned the paper for 80 years sold it to Jeffrey Bezos, the billionaire founder and chief executive of Amazon.com. He has since used his internet expertise and wealth to reinvigorate the paper.

Other distressed newspapers were not so lucky. The chains and investment firms that bought them typically gutted the news staffs, savagely cut budgets, and sold off their real estate assets in order to squeeze as much profit out of the companies as they could before selling the carcasses to other chains and investment firms or shutting them down.

Consequently, few newspapers had the wherewithal to experiment with new publishing models for mobile media, much less to invest in R&D projects or even to send members of their staffs to meetings and conferences. At the RJI, hopes of securing large grants for research and lucrative contracts for consulting gigs from newspaper companies evaporated. Many of the managers and journalists who had participated in the founding of the DPA no longer worked for news organizations, so membership steadily dwindled from its peak of 42 organizations in 2009. Newspaper associations also experienced precipitous membership and revenue declines.

While I continued to produce digital newsbooks at no cost for the remaining DPA members, most of my attention focused on conducting and analyzing results of annual national phone surveys. They were mostly funded by DPA dues and used to assess who was using tablets, e-readers, and smartphones, and how they were using them. After giving DPA members advance access to my reports, the RJI published them on its website.

Each survey found that accessing news was one of the most popular uses for tablets and smartphones, but that was of little consolation to newspapers. Even though the respondents who owned mobile media devices consistently ranked *The New York Times, Wall Street Journal,* and *Washington Post* among their top ten news sources just behind CNN, each year around 10 percent said they had recently cancelled their print newspaper subscriptions, and another 15 percent indicated they were contemplating cancelling them within the following 12 months.

After 2010, the surveys found that smartphone and tablet users in all age groups were progressively more likely to get news from mobile apps and social media than newspaper websites. While the national newspaper apps were among the most often cited, respondents indicated a strong preference for news apps that aggregated content from multiple sources and had tools for personalizing selections.

In the fall of 2012, Apple released the iPad Mini with a 7.9-inch display to compete with the Amazon Kindle Fire and growing number of less expensive tablets with 7-inch displays. The Mini became my preferred iPad when I was away from home because it was lighter and could fit into my coat pocket. Like most iPad owners, I opted for the Wi-Fi only versions because I had a Wi-Fi LAN in my home and access was freely available on campus as well as in most other locations I frequented. For continuous connectivity, I relied on my iPhone.

By then, Apple's biggest competitor, Samsung Electronics, was finding a strong demand for its new smartphones with 5-inch and larger tablet-like displays that came to be known as "phablets." Apple initially scoffed at the notion of producing larger iPhones, arguing that the size and weight would make them too large to be used comfortably as phones and too small to be of much use as tablets. The real reason according to some business analysts was Apple's worry that larger iPhones would cut into their sales of iPads. Two years later, Apple finally gave in and released the iPhone 6 with a 4.7-inch display and the 6 Plus with a 5.5-inch display. They became Apple's bestselling and most popular models. I bought a 6 Plus as soon as AT&T offered it to replace my iPhone 4. As Apple may have feared, I quickly found that I no longer needed my iPad Mini; my standard-size iPad and iPhone 6 Plus sufficed.

By the end of 2014, smartphones already were much more prevalent than landline phones in most regions of the country, which played havoc with phone surveys. Because smartphone owners tended to keep their phone numbers when they moved, area codes no longer could reliably identify their locations. And because owners tended to be mobile, they were less likely to accept calls from phone numbers they didn't recognize or, if they did accept them, to participate in 15-minute surveys. Consequently, the increasing number of calls that had to be made to achieve the goal of around 1,000 completed surveys drove up the cost.

The RJI's understandable decisions to discontinue the mobile media phone surveys and disband the Digital Publishing Alliance convinced me the time had come to retire … again. I had no regrets. After more than 40 years of actively participating in the computerization of print, the luxury of unhurried time afforded by my retirement on January 1, 2015, allowed me to reflect on all that has been gained and lost in the past 50 years — the *incunabula* of digital printing and online media. My thoughts about this and how the digital publishing revolution might transform the news media and society in the decades ahead follow in the epilogue.

Author's notes

While Tony Ridder often is disparaged for agreeing to sell Knight-Ridder in 2006, the chain's demise mostly was due to a decision made at its birth. When the merged company went public in 1974, the Knight and Ridder families opted to maintain only one class of stock. Most other family-owned companies, including *The New York Times, Washington Post,* and McClatchy, set up two tiers of stock — one with voting privileges for the families and senior executives; the other for everyone else. With only one class of stock that gave voting privileges to all, control of the company steadily shifted from the Knight-Ridder families and senior executives, as their percentage of shares declined, into the hands of outside shareholders more interested in profit growth than quality journalism and public service.

Had Batten lived, he might have been able to resist for a while longer the pressures to increase shareholder value at the expense of the newsrooms, but that probably would not have made any difference in the long run. He already had planned to retire around the beginning of the new century. Without a change in the succession plan, Ridder still would have taken full control of the helm and undoubtedly succumbed to demands to sell the company from major institutional investors, who by then controlled a majority of the stock.

Additionally, I am often asked if I thought Batten would have continued to support the Information Design Lab after 1995. I would like to think so, but without a suitable tablet on the immediate horizon, the IDL would have had to focus on developing products and tools specifically for the internet and web. While I would not have objected, Ridder probably would have pressured Batten to merge the IDL with Bob Ingle's New Media Center in San Jose.

The internet and its progeny often are blamed for the precipitous decline of daily newspapers since the beginning of the twenty-first century, but the ways in which they have either directly or indirectly contributed are far more complex. Among the most significant factors are: The rapid shift by consumers to online shopping, which has decimated the department stores and bricks-and-mortar businesses that newspapers have historically relied upon for display advertising revenue; the emergence of Craigslist and other online classified services that suddenly and substantially diminished newspapers' high-profit classifieds revenue; the increasing amount of time people are devoting to online diversions on mobile media devices; internal corporate struggles exacerbated by shrinking revenues and investor demands for sustained profit gains; the devaluation and commoditization of general news; a growing distrust of mainstream news media; and extreme political and cultural polarization fueled in large part by the rise of online social media. None of these factors is likely to go away anytime soon, so prospects for printed newspapers after 2020 will continue to be precarious at best.

For readers who are interested, an excellent firsthand account of the internal struggles that led to Knight-Ridder's demise can be found in W. Davis (Buzz) Merritt's book, *Knightfall*, published in 2005 by AMACOM (American Management Association). Merritt was the editor of the *Wichita Eagle*, a Knight-Ridder newspaper, from 1975 through 1998, and was a close associate of Batten. He is considered one of the fathers of public journalism.

The second edition of Philip Meyer's book, *The Vanishing Newspaper: Saving Journalism in the Information Age*, published in 2009 by University of Missouri Press, also provides valuable insights into the causes for the decline of Knight-Ridder and American newspapers in general. Before becoming a journalism professor at the University of North Carolina in 1981, Meyer was a journalist and researcher with Knight Newspapers. From 1976 to 1981, he served as corporate director of news research for Knight-Ridder and led the Viewtron research effort during the online service's field test.

Epilogue

'Time has neither memory nor voice.
It's also deaf. It doesn't listen
to pleas or utter words, but it conveys
majesty and condemnation.'

Luis Abelardo Takahashi Núñez
Japanese-Peruvian composer, poet, and writer
1927-2005

'History doesn't repeat itself,
but it often rhymes.'

Mark Twain
American writer, humorist, entrepreneur, publisher, and lecturer
1835-1910

Nearly fifty years have elapsed since I first touched the digital
future of newspapers. In the quarter of a century that followed
my departure from Knight-Ridder in 1995, the digital publishing
revolution that I once embraced as the savior of newspapers
relentlessly deviated into their nemesis. Now the stately *Detroit
Free Press* building where I began my digital-age odyssey stands

as a forlorn and mute testament to the industrial past of printed news. The Knight-Ridder office overlooking Biscayne Bay and the Venetian Isles where Jim Batten recruited me for the Viewtron venture now occupies empty airspace above a posh art gallery. Different masters publish the downsized *Free Press* and *Miami Herald*. Knight-Ridder and Batten are no longer.

So, too, is the newspaper world I entered as a boy in the 1950s. All has changed. The pungent smells of hot molten lead, oil-based ink, and tobacco smoke now only permeate my aging memories. The digital 24/7 imperative has transcended "The Daily Miracle."

For retired print journalists like myself, nostalgia for the years when nearly every adult read at least one newspaper every day, and the stories that appeared on their pages had value and influence is difficult to mollify. While many may wish for a return to that bygone era, the erstwhile power of the (printed) press will not be restored. The electronically mediated world in which we now live is at a vastly different place in time.

Today, the Viewtron promise of "what you want, when you want it," unrealized in the early eighties, has come to be taken for granted and expanded to include "where you want it, how you want it, on whichever device you want it." Stories written by newspaper journalists are much more likely to be read on smartphone and tablet screens than on newsprint. Online media has effectively reduced general news stories to a low-value, ubiquitous commodity. And, the established newspaper editorial and design principles that I once espoused have been rendered superfluous.

By the time tablets as I envisioned them in the eighties and nineties finally emerged with the Apple iPad in 2010, electronic newspapers were already morphing into "personalized news apps" that replaced edition-delayed delivery, human curating, page layout, and distinctive typography with nearly immediate 24/7 access, data-driven algorithms, dynamic templates, and generic fonts. Even the newspaper websites have been subsumed by these mobile media apps.

Some comfort can be taken in knowing that the awesome roars of rolling newspaper presses, though greatly diminished, have not yet been silenced. Nor have the crucial voices of dedicated newspaper journalists who continue to inform with written words. Ada and I still haven't given up our habit of reading home-delivered editions of *The New York Times* and *Columbia Missourian* each morning. But, we are now among the few, not the many.

During brief pauses in our daily lives, we also read news stories on our iPad and iPhone. They have become useful not just for news. Among other things, I have written this book on the iPad, and we use both devices to make online purchases and to stay in touch with friends and former colleagues. Unlike many younger people, however, we still prefer to watch news programs and movies on our large flat-screen digital TV.

While mobile display devices, as I predicted, have become commonplace, I did not foresee billions of people around the world glued to their screens. Nor did I anticipate that these technologies would become powerful cultural and political forces with the ability to alter the course of global events.

The search for truth that is held as a sacred tenet of professional journalists and was a core value of Knight-Ridder and other reputable newspaper companies in the latter half of the past century has been overwhelmed in the first two decades of this century by a tsunami of Orwellian doublespeak, fact-free assertions, and fake news stories spread by partisan cable news channels — notably by Fox and to a much lesser extent by MSNBC and CNN — and by an array of internet-enabled social media platforms currently dominated by Facebook and Twitter.

The startling outcome of the 2016 U.S. presidential election provided clear evidence of online social media's ascendency, as well as ominous hints of a reformational period that might be arising from the *incunabula* (first stage) of digital printing and online media. The prospect of resurrecting in the remainder of this century the violent religious, political, economic, and social ferment that followed the *incunabula* of mechanized printing and print media in the sixteenth and seventeenth centuries is not beyond the realm of possibilities. Though this premise is worthy of scholarly exploration, it is beyond the scope of this book.

Nevertheless, some insights into the future of newspapers and communication media might be gleaned from a rudimentary comparison of these two revolutionary epochs. At the risk of over simplifying a complex era and offending my friends in the Gutenberg Society, I have attempted to compress the first seventy-five years of the mechanized publishing revolution into a few hundred words. My synopsis focuses mainly on salient occurrences that might have relevance for understanding the locus of our current revolution, so please bear with me.

———

When Johann Gutenberg initiated his "Work of the Books" in Mainz around the beginning of the 1450s, the Roman Catholic Church was the dominant gatekeeper of knowledge in Europe. For nearly a thousand years, its monastic workshops, called *scriptoria*, had been tediously copying and preserving selected texts that had survived the fall of the Western Roman Empire and destruction of ancient libraries. The Church's power over information emanated from its guardianship of the exemplars — certified perfect masters of collected manuscripts, which were the only guarantees of authenticity for copies.

The flowering of the European Renaissance in the fourteenth and fifteenth centuries created a burgeoning demand for copies of exemplars that overwhelmed the capacity of the *scriptoria*, as well as the adjunct regal and private scribal workshops. To manually copy and authenticate a single book could require anywhere from a few weeks to several years. Books were so rare and expensive that libraries chained them to desks and bookshelves.

Gutenberg's ingenious "artificial writing" system (as it was known) would do much more than solve this medieval production problem. Its widespread adoption and prodigious output would transform the world in ways that neither he nor any of his contemporaries could have envisioned. With his system, hundreds of exact copies of a book could be printed, without any sacrifices in quality, in the time it would take skilled scribes to manually make just a few authenticated copies. Gutenberg's perfectionism and sense of aesthetics are clearly evident today in the surviving copies of the great 42-line Bible that he printed between 1452 and 1455.

(As with so many visionary entrepreneurs, Gutenberg lost control of his start-up venture to investors and died in 1468 without fame or fortune. He was nearly forgotten until being rediscovered and recognized in the nineteenth century as the inventor of mechanized printing.)

For the Catholic Church, the ability of Gutenberg's system to mass produce flawless copies of exemplars at a greatly reduced cost per copy was initially seen as a blessing that would advance its mission. But, within a generation, mechanized printing would begin to disrupt its role as the gatekeeper of knowledge and its power over the flow of information.

As the expanding mercantile classes became increasingly committed to education and learning, a lucrative market for Bibles and books printed in languages other than Latin developed. Consequently, the art of printing diffused rapidly throughout Europe. Within the *incunabula's* first two decades, print shops blossomed in nearly 100 cities. By the year 1500 (the arbitrary end of the *incunabula*), historians have estimated that more than 1,100 shops in 200 cities had collectively produced some 12,000,000 books in 35,000 editions. This was vastly more than all of the manuscripts produced in the thousand years that preceded Gutenberg. Also, by then the prices of printed books had fallen to less than one fifth that of manually copied books.

Printed books steadily devalued the Church's collection of exemplars and contributed to the demise of nearly all monastic *scriptoria* and private scribal shops early in the 1500s. A few survived for a while longer by creating custom illuminated manuscripts and illustrating copies of printed books for wealthy families. Some of the displaced scribes became typeface and book designers as well as printers. (Scholars and university students would carry on the practice of manually copying books and documents for their own use well into the twentieth century.)

While classical literature, philosophy, and religious texts accounted for a majority of the editions printed in this period, books containing new knowledge and ideas also began to flow freely across borders. The educated laity's ability to read and interpret the contents of printed editions, including Bibles, without involving members of the clergy, stimulated indepen-dent, heterodox thinking that soon challenged the authority of the Church and State, and ultimately disrupted the whole social and economic structure of the Middle Ages.

Two decades into the 1500s, the mechanized publishing revolution facilitated a major schism within the Catholic Church that would later define the modern age. It began as a dispute between a German priest — Martin Luther — and Pope Leo X over the printing and selling of plenary indulgences — documents sanctioned by the pope that would rescind the owners' temporal punishments for sins.

According to the legend, Luther nailed his criticisms, known as the Ninety-five Theses, to the door of the All-Saints Church in Wittenberg on October 31, 1517. Within a few months, copies translated from Latin to local languages were printed and circulated throughout Europe. Luther's refusal to renounce all of his writings resulted in his condemnation as a heretic and excommunication by the pope in 1521. To protect Luther from arrest, his followers secluded him at Wartburg castle where he completed his translation of the New Testament into the German vernacular the following year.

These events are credited with launching the Protestant Reformation. Printing presses would be used extensively to rapidly spread his translation and teachings within Germany and neighboring countries. Other reformers with differing backgrounds and causes, such as Calvin and Zwingli in Switzerland, arose independently to found diverse Protestant denominations. They, too, made extensive use of printing presses.

This period gave rise to the printing and widespread distribution of pamphlets, often referred to as newsbooks, that chronicled current events and articulated the conflicting dogmas of Protestants and Catholics. The monarchies also would use them to spread propaganda and justify their campaigns against other countries and the Muslim Turks who were making incursions into Eastern Europe and the Western Mediterranean. (Newsbooks are generally regarded as the progenitors of newspapers that would emerge early in the next century.)

What followed the schism were centuries of bloody, chaotic, and costly religious wars that fragmented Europe and drove large-scale migrations of Europeans to the newly discovered and conquered Americas in search of new lands where they could practice their religious beliefs in relative freedom, as well as have more opportunities to acquire wealth and higher status.

While Gutenberg's artificial writing system played an integral role in these tectonic disruptions through its ability to rapidly replicate and disseminate printed material that agitated and empowered opposing groups, it also promoted the spread of standardized languages, modern political and economic concepts, scientific inquiries and discoveries, technological innovations, globalization, and new forms of literature and art that brought about the industrial and information ages, and led to the world we know today.

———————

Now, here we are some five centuries later trying to fathom where this latest epic publishing revolution might be leading us. Even though the occurrences I've just recounted won't be repeated in a literal sense, there already have been and will continue to be occurrences in this epoch that rhyme with the past epoch, just as the aphorism attributed to Mark Twain attests.

For this comparison, I have chosen to bracket the first stage of the digital publishing revolution between 1970, when digital-age computerized typesetting began to displace Gutenberg-age industrialized typecasting, and the end of the second millennium in 2000, which marks the ascendance of the commercial internet as a global communication medium. (The year 2000 also intriguingly follows the second coming of Steve Jobs at Apple and the beginning of the iProfit mobile media era that he would launch with the iPod music player in 2001.)

So, what might a comparison of these two world-changing epochs reveal? Four significant rhyming aspects stand out.

Both publishing revolutions began with the invention of radically new technologies that were exponentially more efficient and cost-effective for reproducing, disseminating, and storing written information.

Both revolutions spread like wildfire throughout the world by utilizing innovative publishing tools and methods that in their nascency were relatively inexpensive, uncomplicated to replicate, and easy to master.

Both greatly multiplied the amount of information available to literate people, which ignited an explosion of new knowledge and ideas that profoundly influenced the ways people think, interact, and communicate.

Both were eagerly embraced in their first stages as godsends by the established gatekeepers and authorities of the time, but as the new technologies spread and began to disrupt the status quo, they became fearful of being disintermediated and struggled to control or at least contain them.

———

I realize comparing the internet to the medieval Roman Catholic Church might seem to be a stretch. But, if we look past the antipodal organizational structures of the Church and internet, to the way in which both have functioned as unifying communication and information systems, several rhyming characteristics become apparent. Whereas the Church served as the dominant medium for conveying information throughout most of Europe well into the first decades of the sixteenth century, the internet has assumed that role throughout most of the world in the maiden decades of this century.

Both systems were developed to function as decentralized global networks of interconnected nodes (dioceses within the Catholic system; computer networks within the internet) linked by standardized protocols. While governing bodies define and enforce the protocols, each system was designed to continue functioning even when one or multiple nodes failed. In the case of the Catholic Church, the system still functioned during times when Rome (where the governing body resided) was being sacked and while European countries were engaging in major wars. Each system also globally imposed on its inter-locutors the language of its origin — ecclesiastical Latin for the Church; American English for the internet.

Today, the Catholic Church's system connects nearly 3,000 dioceses representing some 1.3-billion members worldwide. By comparison, the internet has grown since 1994 from a connec-tive network of mainly academic computer networks with only a few thousand users in North America and Europe into the lifeblood of today's world with more than four-billion active users spanning the globe. A majority of those users now rely mostly on mobile media devices to access internet-enabled online media. In this brief period, the internet has become so tightly woven into the fabric of modern civilization that even brief interruptions have caused serious problems. For most countries, an extended shutdown would have devastating consequences.

———

Comparing newspapers to the medieval Catholic Church's *scriptoria* also might seem to be a stretch, but here, too, are a couple of rhyming elements worth considering. Both evolved over centuries from simple copying shops into complex enterprises. Their influential power derived from their ownership and mastery of a singular means of production. The dependence of *scriptoria* on legions of scribes skilled with quill pens and newspapers on expensive, labor-intensive printing technologies would ultimately prove to be their greatest vulnerability. When a new, more efficient and cost-effective means of replicating documents suddenly emerged, both enterprises were quickly disrupted. The resulting decline of daily newspapers today closely rhymes with the pace and trajectory of the *scriptoria's* decline five centuries earlier.

In a 2017 CNBC interview, Warren Buffett, the multi-billionaire investor who happens to own 31 mostly small-town papers, said he believes the only newspapers "assured" of a long life are probably *The New York Times*, *Wall Street Journal*, and possibly *Washington Post*. "If you look, there are 1,300 daily newspapers left," Buffett said. "There were 1,700 or 1,800 not too long ago. Now, you've got the internet. Aside from the ones I mentioned, [most of them] haven't figured out a way to make the digital model complement the print model."

The three "assured" papers Buffett named are by no means typical. They are major national newspapers known for their journalistic excellence that have had the leadership and financial resources to experiment and find ways to make their digital models work effectively with their print models. (The future of the *Washington Post* appears to have become more assured since its purchase in 2013 by Jeff Bezos, the multibillionaire founder and chief executive of Amazon.)

Like the manual copying shops that survived for a while longer, these hybrid print/online national newspapers have adapted their business models to serve mostly elite readers.

By consistently providing high-quality, high-value content produced by dedicated teams of professional journalists, they have been able to convince people to pay a premium for their printed editions and online products. Well over half of their revenue today comes from their readers. In the heyday of print, up to eighty percent came from their advertisers.

Even though Ada and I are not among the elite, we now willingly pay more than $90-a-month for daily home delivery of the *NYT's* national edition and online access to the paper's digital content. This is about the same amount we currently pay monthly for our cellular phone service and about half of what we pay monthly for our cable television and internet services. By comparison, we only pay about $80 annually for our subscription to the *Columbia Missourian*.

Unfortunately, few other American daily newspapers are in a position today to adopt this elite model. The majority are not valued highly enough by their print and online readers to sustain significant increases in their subscription and single-copy prices. Many of the new profit-hungry owners have gutted (euphemistically "downsized") their papers' newsrooms to the point where they can no longer adequately cover their communities and are filling their emaciated editions with mostly wire service stories and press releases. Among the exceptions might be the *Los Angeles Times*, which was spun-off from Tribune Publishing and purchased by a multibillionaire investor in 2018, and possibly the *Chicago Tribune* if it, too, can be spun-off and acquired by a benevolent multibillionaire.

Money alone, however, won't restore their former glory days. Several recent high-profile failures have shown that relying on the largesse of wealthy patrons to save newspapers is not a sure bet. An alternative survival strategy that owners of some daily newspapers are now evaluating is to turn their operations into nonprofit entities. The *Philadelphia Inquirer* and *Tampa Bay Times* already are owned by nonprofit corporations.

Another category of hybrid print/online newspapers that might also have a long life is the non-dailies that serve small, cohesive communities. A dedicated staff using digital publishing technologies can now economically produce several thousand copies in a few hours. Most probably will need to become nonprofit entities that rely on supplemental funding from philanthropic organizations, donations, or journalism schools, as the *Columbia Missourian* has done.

An obviously controversial option might be for local governments to subsidize local newspapers as community resources. Clearly, owners and journalists will not get rich publishing non-daily small-town newspapers, so their personal rewards will have to come from the satisfaction of providing an important public service.

Back in the last century, I argued that paper was not essential to newspapers — it was just a wrapper that, as with the paper that wraps fast-food, is quickly discarded after the contents are consumed. I was wrong. While online news products obviously are more immediate, paper does afford newspapers with several inherent strengths unmatched by computer screens; notably, the ability to directly read saved copies in the future without having to rely on transitory digital technologies. For many people, having their names and photos, or those of relatives and acquaintances, printed in a newspaper still is a big deal. Copies are often proudly shared and saved as treasured keepsakes. Screens and printouts don't provide the same intrinsic value, at least for those of us who grew up with printed newspapers and magazines.

My personal treasures include pages from a book printed in 1491, several letter-size newspapers from the early 1700s, and dozens of newspapers that featured historic events in my lifetime, such as the first Moon landing and President Nixon's resignation, as well as newspapers and magazines with stories that I have written or were written about me. All are still readable and probably will be far into the future. I cannot say the same for all of the items that I have saved on disks, most of which cannot be displayed on my current computer.

————

Among the casualties of downsizing are the enterprise reporters and visual journalists — photographers and news artists — who have produced the investigative and explanatory projects that once were newspapers' most important and valued content. That vital work is now being left mostly to the major national and metropolitan papers and a few nonprofit organizations, such as ProPublica, the Center for Public Integrity, and International Consortium of Investigative Journalists. While their efforts have been commendable, they are unable to make up for all that has been lost during the past several decades.

The watchdog and investigative work performed by print journalists is all the more important now that online social media have become such formidable vehicles for spreading false stories and extremist content. The honest efforts of journalists, however, are frequently disparaged as fake news and met with hostile threats on social media. Politicians, including President Trump, have even called them the "enemies of the people." These online threats and accusations are not only inciting physical attacks against reporters, newspapers, and other news outlets, they also are serving to undermine the foundation of our democracy.

Countering false and misleading information has been made even more difficult by the swarms of automated social bots (agents) that distribute dubious and often mendacious messages mostly autonomously on Twitter, Facebook, and other social media platforms. They have effectively become today's digital equivalent of the confrontational printed pamphlets and flyers that circulated for centuries after Gutenberg to the chagrin of the establishment.

While internet-enabled social media and bots are useful tools for connecting and informing people, their abilities to affect the course of discussions and encourage hostility have played a significant role in nurturing political and societal dissension, and promoting distrust of mainstream news media and governments. Their use by international and domestic adversaries to influence elections and policies, as well as incite violence, has put intense pressure on social media enterprises to monitor and delete suspicious accounts and malicious content.

That is no small task. Continuously scanning billions of accounts, tens of millions of files, and an untold number of social bots in real time is beyond the ability of humans, so these enterprises are now developing and integrating complex algorithms that employ artificial intelligence. But, even with the combination of human and computer intelligence, they still cannot cull all of the "bad stuff" to everyone's satisfaction. They never will.

Five centuries ago, the Church and State struggled with the same problem, albeit on a much smaller scale, after printing shops began spreading across Europe and into the Americas. They, too, failed in their efforts to suppress what they considered the "bad stuff." The problem stems from the inability of regulators and censors to clearly define what constitutes "bad stuff."

Distinctions between acceptable and unacceptable content are subjective and variable. What is considered unacceptable in one place, time, or context, might not be in another.

For social media enterprises, culling requires making a Hobson's choice between erring on the side of deleting some "good stuff" along with the "bad stuff" or not deleting enough "bad stuff." Either way, they will be criticized for not doing enough to eliminate dangerous and toxic content or chastised for censoring legitimate controversial and critical content.

For journalists, increasing government censorship, legal challenges, and excessive culling by social media are already impeding their search for truth and ability to have their stories accessed everywhere. Even with constitutional protections, American journalists still face censorship or imprisonment in the U.S. and other countries for stories published online.

———

I must humbly admit to having far less than 20/20 clarity when it comes to envisioning what might follow 2020 in the next stage of the digital publishing revolution. The occasional glimpses I've had of the distant future are now much gauzier and more difficult to interpret than they were back in the final decades of the last century. That probably can be attributed to the aging of my mind's eye, though I suspect it also has something to do with the interconnectedness and increasing complexities of our stressed-out world. So, I hope I might be forgiven if my current visions of the future disappoint.

Employing the somewhat clearer optics of hindsight, we can see that since the first application of electricity to communication in the 1840s, with the invention of the electromagnetic telegraph, three major electronic forms of communication media emerged in roughly fifty-year intervals — radio beginning in the 1890s, television in the 1940s, and internet-enabled online media in the 1990s. Each new electronic medium initially was seen as a newspaper killer, but most publishers who innovated and adapted managed to survive.

If this pattern persists, today's surviving publishers might be dealing with yet another major electronic form in the 2040s. While I have no idea what new form might emerge twenty to thirty years hence, we can be sure there are visionaries today who have touched the future and are already pursuing concepts that might define the next new electronic medium.

There is, however, a distinct possibility that this pattern won't persist. Internet-enabled online media could be the apex of the digital publishing revolution. Since the 1970s, nearly all technologically mediated forms of communication have been literally blown to bits by digital technologies. As computer scientists oft remind us: In the digital world, bits are bits. There are no distinctions between written and spoken words, still and moving images, voices and music; everything consists of zeros and ones that can be readily manipulated. It doesn't matter if the content is intended for printing on paper or displaying on screens.

For this reason, I am inclined to believe that we won't see another major electronic form of communication emerge independently from the internet in this century. Nor are we likely to see new devices replace smartphones and tablets anytime soon. Consumer electronics companies will probably keep making them sleeker and more powerful for a while longer, but ultimately, they will be compelled to make them less costly and give them longer lives.

While e-readers, such as the Amazon Kindle, have been overshadowed by smartphones and tablets, they, too, are likely to stay around for quite a while. Their simplicity, lower-cost, and easy-to-read paper-like displays give them a competitive advantage, especially with the world's aging populations. As the manufacturing costs for electronic paper displays decline and the costs of pulp paper increase in the coming decade, I would expect environmentally friendly, inexpensive e-paper devices suitable for displaying, annotating, and exchanging ephemeral documents, as well as for note-taking, sketching, and doodling, to finally catch on.

Even if our world is not violently torn asunder in the next stage, as it was soon after the *incunabula* of mechanized printing and print media, we can be certain that international online disputes and confrontations will intensify. While some future occurrences are still likely to rhyme with past events, new variables and cross-impacts resulting from climate change, discoveries, pandemics, wars, and hundreds of other events beyond our ken, will affect outcomes in far different ways than any of us might expect or hope for.

We should not assume, for example, that our contemporary notion of progress, which has been a cornerstone of the modern era, will prevail in the future. The 10,000-year history of civilization has been a rollercoaster with many ascents and long descents. Moreover, we also need to acknowledge that the future is fluid and therefore cannot be judged as either better or worse from the perspective of the present. Like water, the shapes of the future as well as the past are defined by their perceptual containers in space and time.

Imagine for a moment that we are Catholic priests in 1455 who have just watched Gutenberg print the great 42-line Bibles. From our perspective in this location and period of time, his artificial writing system would appear as a miraculous gift from God that would serve the Church and ensure a better world to come. But, if we were instantly transported one hundred years into the future, our perspective in that period would be radically different. Upon seeing how our former world had been violently transformed by the disruptive powers of the printing presses, we undoubtedly would declare Gutenberg's system a work of the devil and try to suppress it.

We are in a similar, rhyming situation today. When the commercial internet emerged in the mid-nineties, it was enthusiastically perceived as a new medium for publishing and communication that would serve humanity by miraculously accelerating global access to vast amounts of information, promoting international collaborations to solve difficult problems, and bringing people together to ensure a better world to come.

Among newspaper publishers, the internet was perceived more narrowly as an esoteric medium with potential for reducing costs and increasing revenue, and as a conduit reporters could use for researching stories and connecting with technologically savvy readers. I saw it as an environmentally friendly medium that could reduce the dependence of newspapers on paper and physical delivery vehicles, and make newspaper content more accessible in distant locations.

Those perceptions now seem naïve. In just twenty-five years, the internet and its progeny have massively disrupted nearly every enterprise, institution, and polity; disintermediated the former gatekeepers, including newspapers; stoked sociopolitical ferment; and facilitated the spread of militant ideologies and hate speech. They also have imposed on users a Faustian bargain — convenience in exchange for their personal data. The resulting loss of privacy and abuses of that data by online enterprises and governments have become hotly contested issues globally.

What's more, what began as a democratized breeding pool that spawned schools of relatively small, entrepreneurial start-ups quickly grew into a huge green ocean dominated mainly by three voracious American-born online whales — Amazon (e-commerce), Google (search engine), and Facebook (social media); none of which existed prior to the internet. They have amassed colossal fortunes by feeding on the mostly free content and data provided by the medium's users and to a large extent by newspapers and other news media. (While Apple and Microsoft preceded the internet, both were revitalized by it and also have become rich whales as providers of mobile media and cloud computing technologies.)

———

The internet now appears to be at a critical juncture similar to that of the medieval Catholic Church just prior to the schism that begot the Protestant Reformation. Confrontations between global rivals are already tearing apart the original construct of the internet as a virtual Pangaea where people and countries would come together freely and peacefully to share knowledge. I am not alone in my belief that the global internet could soon split into two or more walled-off, competing environments, with each evolving along different paths and relying on different technologies. The conditions for such a reformational schism are already evident.

Through the internet's empowerment of the three American whales — Amazon, Google, and Facebook — the system quickly became this epoch's dominant gatekeeper of knowledge in most of the world. The source of their power over information has been their jealous control over the vast troves of commercially and politically invaluable data generated by the internet's users.

That dominance and power are now being aggressively challenged by China, which has empowered its own triad of whales — Alibaba (e-commerce), Baidu (search engine), and Tencent (social media). Today, they reign supreme in the Eastern realm of the internet.

Additionally, China and a number of other Asian and Middle-Eastern countries are routinely blocking access within their territories to foreign internet sites, social media, and news sources that they consider adverse to their values and threatening to their political, economic, and social stability. They also are employing armies of censors to thwart individuals and dissident groups from posting heterodox content online.

Among the most troubling concerns for the future are the increasingly sophisticated, malicious attacks on the internet-connected servers of adversaries by rogue hackers and spies. The hacking of e-mail and user files, installing of malware, and planting of fake and incendiary content on social media platforms and websites are now routinely being instigated by governments and organizations to disrupt elections, sow societal discord, gain advantages, and sabotage competing initiatives. The prospects for cyberattacks escalating into actual shooting wars in the not-too-distant future are now regarded as real possibilities.

Governments might justify a Brexit-like separation from the global internet under the guise of defending against terrorism, interference in elections, and the spreading of disinformation and "dangerous" content. Under autocratic or protectionist leadership, separate closed systems would be likely to severely impede free speech and the free flow of news and information, even in a system controlled by the United States. Conceivably, the governing bodies in a "multinet" world might go so far as to require something equivalent to digital visas for gaining access. They also might require journalists to be licensed and regulated in order to operate within their physical and virtual territories, just as nearly all countries inflicted on printing shops and publishers for several centuries after Gutenberg.

Another major concern, regardless of what might happen to the internet, is the growing use of pervasive surveillance. Several countries, including China and England, as well as corporations already are using the internet and advanced software tools, such as facial recognition and artificial intelligence, to monitor what people say and do, not just when they are connected to their computers and mobile media devices, but nearly everywhere they go in public and even in private buildings.

The adoption of "smart home" technologies that connect nearly every appliance and personal security system to the internet raises potential for even more intrusive government and corporate surveillance. Exploring the dystopian implications for the future is best left to science-fiction writers; however, given the accelerating pace of social, political, and technological changes, we might not have to wait a hundred, or fifty, or even ten years for a fictional dystopian future to become our present reality.

Like the medieval priests and many who are in my age bracket today, I now find myself wondering if we are losing much more than we are gaining. This of course has been the common lament of all generations in their waning years. But, this time, the world as we have known it does seem to be entering a destructive stage that could push civilization into retrograde. I cannot help but worry that the internet and particularly social media are becoming so infected by mendacious content and misguided echo chambers that informed rational thinking and discourse will no longer be possible.

Nevertheless, despite my concerns for the future of newspapers and journalism, as well as for our world, the determination and activism exhibited by some members of the current online social media generation have given me hope that the disruptions wrought by the digital publishing revolution might ultimately have positive outcomes. This epoch undoubtedly will be a compelling subject for historians to ruminate about in subsequent centuries … provided that humans can manage to avoid destroying themselves and the Earth's capacity to support life.

'Memories and visions have neither time nor voice. They wander freely and silently in our minds, but they are able to convey hope and inspiration.'

Roger Fidler
Irish-Bohemian-American journalist, designer, scholar, and pragmatic media futurist
1943

The quote by Abelardo at the beginning of the epilogue inspired me to create this corollary. During the three years I devoted to writing this book, I could not help but marvel at how our memories are disconnected from time.

Unlike our physical being, which is trapped in the space-time continuum where events are measured in fixed amounts of time that flow inexorably one after the other, memories are free to flow nonsequentially, in any order we may conjure in our minds. Moreover, distances in time between events have no relevance for memories. Many of the events I have recalled for this book appeared in my mind as clearly as if they had occurred yesterday.

While recalling the highlights of my digital-age odyssey, I also came to appreciate more fully how time was absent from my visions of the future. When I first conceived of reading electronic newspapers on portable displays at the beginning of the 1980s, I remember how easily I could visualize tablets. That deceived me into believing the realization of my vision was close — not more than 10 or 15 years. Instead, it took 30 years. Most of the other visions I pursued took far less time to be realized, although even they were typically conceived at least five years ahead of their time.

Contemplating the entirety of my life's journey, which now has spanned more than three-quarters of a century, I wonder about the ephemerality of it all. One of the revelations that comes with age is that whatever successes and disappointments we may experience only exist for brief moments in time. They, along with visions of the future, are ultimately relegated to memories of the past … or are forgotten.

Even though my visions and accomplishments accorded me with a small measure of worldwide recognition within the newspaper industry during its transition from print to online publishing, I have little doubt that I will not long be remembered. But, that doesn't matter. I can only hope that something I have said, written, or done has inspired others, as Batten and Abelardo inspired me, to risk doing more than just touching the future.

As for my personal life, the memories that give me the most gratification and happiness are of the love and adventures that Ada and I have shared for more than 30 years.

About the Author

Roger Fidler is an internationally recognized new media pioneer and visionary who has been on the leading edge of digital and online publishing development since the mid-1970s. He worked in the newspaper industry for 34 years and academia for 20 years. He is best known for conceiving and pursuing his vision of digital newspapers delivered online and displayed on mobile devices, which anticipated today's tablets and smartphones. He is the author of *Mediamorphosis: Understanding New Media* (Pine Forge Press/Sage, 1997).

Fidler was a 1991-'92 Freedom Forum Fellow at Columbia University in New York City. In 1999, the Newseum honored him as an electronic news pioneer and one of history's most intriguing newspeople in *Crusaders, Scoundrels, Journalists* (Eric Newton, ed., Times Books/Random House). In 2003, he was inducted as a Media Fellow in the World Technology Network. The following year, the Donald W. Reynolds Journalism Institute at the Missouri School of Journalism in Columbia selected him as its inaugural fellow, and the University of Oregon's School of Journalism and Mass Communication inducted him into its Hall of Achievement. In 2011, the Beijing DeTao Masters Academy in China designated him as a DeTao Master of New Media Development. Also, in that year, the Society of News Design presented Fidler with its Lifetime Achievement Award. (He was a founding member of the SND.) He currently lives in Columbia, Missouri, with his wife, Ada.

Made in the USA
Middletown, DE
19 February 2020